WRITERS ON COMICS SCRIPTWRITING 2

Tom Root & Andrew Kardon

TITAN BOOKS

WRITERS ON COMICS SCRIPTWRITING 2

ISBN 1 84023 808 9

Published by
Titan Books
A division of Titan Publishing Group Ltd.
144 Southwark St
London SE1 0UP

First edition: August 2004
10 9 8 7 6 5 4 3 2 1

A CIP catalogue record for this title is available from the British Library

Printed and bound in Great Britain by MPG Books Ltd, Victoria Square, Bodmin, Cornwall.

What did you think of this book? We love to hear from our readers. Please email us at:
readerfeedback@titanemail.com, or write to us at the above address. You can also visit us
at www.titanbooks.com

DEDICATION

To my extremely better half Allison, whose
unbelievable patience, support and countless
sleepless nights made this book possible
—Andrew Kardon

To Dad, for the writing gene — and all those
trips to Curious Book Shop
—Tom Root

Acknowledgements

While writing this book, I was amazed at how freely the interview subjects gave of their precious time. Hours of phone calls, numerous follow-ups and endless emails were involved in each and every chapter, not to mention the creators' sketches, scripts and notes, and we depended on their generosity for all of it. I would like to thank each and every creator I had the sincere pleasure of interviewing for this book: Geoff Johns, Brian K. Vaughan, Bruce Jones, Ed Brubaker, Bill Willingham, Dave Sim, Brian Michael Bendis and Brian Azzarello. Thanks also to my cohort in crime, Tom, who kept me sane throughout this tumultuous writing spree of ours. A special note of thanks to Jeff Grossman for... well, putting up with me. And to Mom, Dad and Beth for supporting my crazy comic book habits and always believing in me. And last but certainly not least, to my hero-in-training, Jason, whose every smile melts my heart.
—**Andrew Kardon**

Thanks to those creators who answered everything I threw at them, across time zones and entire oceans: Mike Carey, Andy Diggle, Greg Rucka, Paul Dini, Jill Thompson, Mark Millar, Mike Mignola, Kevin Smith and Peter Milligan — each was charitable and kind beyond the call of duty. Thanks to Nick Jones and Simon Furman at Titan for the opportunity, and for failing to kill me when deadlines became distant memories. Thanks to Andrew for his friendship and enthusiasm for bad Chinese buffets. Thanks to Pat McCallum for being the world's greatest sounding board and for that one panel where Green Arrow wins Employee of the Month. Thanks to Joe Yanarella and Scott Beatty for taking a chance on me when I needed it most. Thanks finally to Mom and Dad and Sue and Doug for all their love and support. Also: Hi, Zola!
—**Tom Root**

CONTENTS

Introduction 6

Brian Azzarello 8

Brian Michael Bendis 20

Ed Brubaker 32

Mike Carey 46

Andy Diggle 62

Paul Dini 78

Geoff Johns 94

Bruce Jones 108

Mike Mignola 124

Mark Millar 140

Peter Milligan 156

Greg Rucka 170

Dave Sim 184

Kevin Smith 198

Jill Thompson 210

Brian K. Vaughan 224

Bill Willingham 238

INTRODUCTION

The writer is back on top, and it's about time.

In the 1980s, comics grew up. Seminal works such as Alan Moore's *Watchmen* and Frank Miller's *Batman: The Dark Knight Returns* re-introduced comic books to adults and raised the bar for the entire art form. Complex themes, rich characterisation, masterful plotting — comics were suddenly on the map again with an entire generation of readers who revelled in this re-energized medium.

All of which made the 1990s such a bitter disappointment. Naturally, it's neither fair — nor accurate — to write off an entire decade, but the shallow glitz of chromium covers, variants, comics-as-investments and superstar artists filling whole books with pin-up art that bore little resemblance to actual storytelling cast a foul light on the entire industry.

Now, however, in the 21st Century, all that has changed. The true superstars of the comics industry are, once more, the writers. And comics' long nightmare appears to finally be over. While the circulation of mainstream comic books might never return to the million-selling days of the early 1990s, a trip to the comic store has never been so rewarding. An influx of new blood into the comic writers' ranks has made the medium vibrant and exciting once again, and veterans who weathered the previous decade are finally getting their due.

As in Mark Salisbury's first volume of *Writers on Comics Scriptwriting* (still absolutely relevant and an excellent read — and available through major booksellers everywhere, hint hint!), we've profiled the current cream of the writers' crop: their beginnings, their learning curves, their major breakthroughs, their highs and lows. But most importantly, we've asked each of them how they construct their amazing tales from the ground floor up; from the very germ of an idea to a fully finished volume of sequential artwork.

In the future, will the first decade of the new millennium top even the 1980s as comics' gilded age? We'd like to think so. And in this book, we believe we've captured the new millennium's masters at the height of their creative powers. Hopefully you'll find the experience as thrilling as we did.

Because, like we said, the writer is back on top.

And it's about time.

Tom Root and Andrew Kardon
Garnerville, New York
2004

BRIAN AZZARELLO

In just a few short years, Brian Azzarello has shot to the top of the comics heap. The Chicago-based writer first staked his claim on the industry with Vertigo's *100 Bullets*, the tale of Agent Graves and his mysterious suitcase filled with 100 untraceable bullets, a series which continually poses the question: if you could absolutely get away with murder, would you? Azzarello's streetwise dialogue and underlying layers of conspiracy and deceit have quickly propelled the title to cult status. Having got everyone's attention with *100 Bullets*, Azzarello embarked on a controversial tenure on *Hellblazer* — the first American scribe to tackle that comic — in the process toning down the magic and bringing back out the bastard in John Constantine. More recently, the writer has ventured into slightly unexpected territory. His six-issue arc on *Batman* with *100 Bullets* artist Eduardo Risso showcased a sexier, more ruthless Dark Knight. But most shocking of all is his involvement in a year-long stint on *Superman*, with an even more surprising collaborator: fan-favourite artist Jim Lee. At a time when crime seems to be ruling the comics industry, Azzarello's one writer who certainly gets to pick his shots.

How big a comics fan were you growing up?

I read comics. I still have a bunch of old comics. I guess like any kid, you think they're gonna be worth something so you don't throw them away. I liked the war books but not so much the superhero stuff.

Are there any specific titles or creators that influenced your work?

Yeah, but mostly out of comics I'd say. In comics, who doesn't like *Watchmen*? Who doesn't like *Dark Knight*? That stuff's influential. I also read *The Spirit* archives. I like those a lot.

You have an artistic background, but did you ever think you'd be a writer?

No, but I wanted to be an artist. Y'know, when you're a kid you want to be everything. Going to art school, they kicked being a comic artist out of me pretty damn fast. I wasn't going to a commercial art school at the time; it was fine art. And comics was not fine art.

So how exactly did you make the transition from painting to writing?

Have you ever tried to get a job with a painting degree? Yeah, five fucking years of school and I got a painting degree. Here's a roller, there's a wall. Get to work. I always wrote stories, and my paintings were very narrative anyway so it wasn't that much of a jump. I was doing graphic design work for a while. I started with some ads in *Previews* that were comic-based, and I got into comics that way. I asked Northstar, one of the companies I was doing ads for, 'Can I write a story?' And they said, 'I don't care, go ahead.' And they liked it. Then I met editor Lou Stathis. Which is funny, because I knew of Lou from a magazine called *Reflex*, which was sort of an alternative music lifestyle thing. And he'd also been an editor at *High Times*. At this point he was working at Vertigo and we got to talking and he said, 'Pitch me some ideas.' And it went from there. Lou was my connection, at least to what I'm doing now. We never got to work together though, because he got cancer. But once I was there, his assistant Axel Alonso took over and he and I really hit it off.

What was your first book for Vertigo?

The first thing that got published or rejected? [*Laughs*] It's funny, I think there are a lot of writers that have had a *Phantom Stranger* pitch rejected. Maybe everybody has. I don't know what it is. I made it up to the eleventh hour with this thing. We were almost approved and then boom. I was an unknown commodity at the time and to put a regular series in my hands was just not gonna happen. It was at a time when it was very, very difficult for anybody new to break into Vertigo.

Place of birth:
 Cleveland, Ohio, USA
Date of birth:
 11 August
Home base:
 Chicago, Illinois, USA
First published work:
 Weird War Tales #1
Education:
 "A good one."
Career highlights:
 Batman, Cage, Hellblazer,
 100 Bullets, Startling Stories:
 Banner, Superman

My Phantom Stranger had every element of a story that Lou hated. He told me that, but it worked. Tons of guest stars. Swamp Thing was in it. Death. There was a bunch of new characters that were created too. But it didn't work out. Nobody seems to be able to get him right. Maybe the Phantom Stranger is just some character that they tell you to try to develop and they have no intention of using. It's not even a test. It's a 'Get off my back and come up with something which we have no interest in doing anyway, but it should take you a long time so you won't be calling me.' I think 'Pitch me Phantom Stranger' means 'Get lost.' The first thing that did get published at Vertigo was a short story in *Weird War Tales* #1. Then I was in all those *Winter's Edge* anthology titles, and then *Jonny Double*.

What's your fascination with all the crime stories you write for comics?

They don't have happy endings. I'm not a fan of happy endings. And isn't every comic a crime story basically? Like a supervillain is a criminal; a superhero is a cop. I don't know if I even write crime. I write about character flaws, and I think I'll always write about character flaws. It's tough to do that with superheroes.

Yet you've just finished up a six-issue stint on *Batman*, and now you're writing the most iconic of all superheroes, Superman. How did that come about?

Jim Lee asked me. We had talked about working together on something. I never would have thought I'd be writing *Superman*. Ever. And I'd been offered *Superman* before and I'd always turned it down. I'd already been involved with Jim doing the 'SuperStorm' stuff that's coming out [creators from Lee's WildStorm imprint tackling characters associated with Superman], *The Man of Steel: Lex Luthor* book. I think he just decided that why should we hedge around Superman, let's just *do* Superman. And when he explained it to me that way, I was like, all right.

Now that you're on it, how has it been writing the Man of Steel? Are you enjoying it?

Yeah, I am. It's my Superman. But just because I'm enjoying it doesn't mean anybody else is. I hear a lot of, 'Eh, Superman. He's dull, he's boring.' And that's the kind of response that makes me want to do it more. Superman's supposed to be inspirational. Arguably there would be no other superheroes without the creation of him. He's the big one. And he's not relevant anymore.

After handling DC's top two icons, are there any other superheroes in your future?

I don't think so. I'm going back to Vertigo. I think I'm better suited for those types of stories.

Is it easier writing for Vertigo than something like *Superman*?

No, my approach doesn't change. Not at all. I just want to do more creator-owned stuff. There's more freedom.

You're roughly at the halfway point of your 100-issue run on *100 Bullets*. Any surprises so far?

No. It's my story, it shouldn't surprise me. The point is to surprise all of you. I started out with an outline but it was fairly loose. There's a lot of room for improvisation. But there's certain points in the story that have to be reached by what I consider a certain issue number. Like this has to be revealed by that particular issue.

Where did the initial idea for *100 Bullets* come from?

It came from a lot of different places. There were tons of different sources for this one. It came from talking with friends, talking with editors. It didn't come from just one place. It's not just one story.

There are certainly a number of different layers to the story, but the central idea of someone giving you 100 untraceable bullets and a photograph of someone who wronged you is what really hooked DC on the series, right?

The high concept? Oh God, yes. You think they would go for this far-reaching criminal conspiracy? That's a big yawn. Now, they might say yeah, but at the time they would have yawned. It wasn't easy. It was a tough sell. I mean, you've gotta understand, at the time there was nothing like it. At least not in mainstream comics. [DC President] Paul Levitz has called it the most successful non-powered mainstream book out there.

So what would you do if Agent Graves showed up at *your* door with the suitcase full of bullets?

What would I do? Would I use it? It depends on whose picture is in it. Now, your follow-up question would be: 'Well, whose picture is in it?' And I would say, 'She knows who she is.' [*Laughs*]

You've never really given it any thought, have you?

No. Not at all. Would I use it? More than likely.

Has DC or Vertigo ever stopped you from telling a particular story?

I've never been told no for *100 Bullets* on anything. But there's been a few instances on other books where things have been like, 'No, you're not gonna do that.' Which is perfectly fine. Those are their characters. On the flip side of that, they've actually let me take a lot of liberties. I think we got away with some stuff in *Batman* that was pretty strong for that book and for that character. They let us add something to that character. That is not a superhero story by any stretch of the imagination. There have been some arguments, but again they're their characters. If I were told from editorial that John Constantine suddenly has the ability to fly and I said, 'Well he's not flying in my book,' they have every right to say, 'You're not gonna write it anymore.'

Speaking of Constantine, ever think you'll return to writing *Hellblazer*?

There's a few more stories in me but I don't think I'll do it. He's just another superhero. I enjoyed writing that book. It was fun. But I don't like him. A lot of people like him. A lot of hardcore fans love him; they just think he's the cat's pyjamas. But you shouldn't like that character. You can enjoy his appearances, but you shouldn't like that guy. I didn't want you to like him. Same with Lono in *100 Bullets*. I don't want anybody liking him either but he's one of the most popular characters. The guy's a fucking rapist and people still like him.

How many books can you handle on a monthly basis?

About two and a half. I'm not one of those guys who can just throw up an issue in an afternoon. There's not a lot to edit on my scripts once they're in, because I don't use a lot of words. But the words I choose are *very* important in the story.

What sort of work schedule do you keep?

I work just about every day. I'm not one of the night owls. I get up pretty early, usually between 6 and 7am. I treat it like a job, and if you have a job you get up between 6 and 7. And I usually work till about 4. I don't drink when I write, unless

100 Bullets

It's a simple enough question. If you could get away with it completely, would you kill someone for revenge? That's the starting premise of Vertigo's *100 Bullets* series by Brian Azzarello and Eduardo Risso, which stars the mysterious Agent Graves, who always seems to show up at the right time at the door of some crime victim's house. With him is a suitcase full of 100 untraceable bullets, a gun and a photograph of the person responsible for the crime. This great high-concept definitely helps hook in new readers, as Agent Graves travels from door to door. But each self-contained story arc is also part of a much-bigger, grander theme. Agent Graves and his Minutemen are involved in one heck of a conspiracy that's slowly been revealed over time. And while the concept may be the same for each new arc, the outcomes are anything but predictable, with seemingly minor characters and events often reappearing and impacting down the line. That said, don't get attached to too many characters: you never know if they're heading for a grisly end. Just about the only solid fact fans can latch onto is that Azzarello has a definite end in mind for the series — quite appropriately, with the 100th issue.

it's getting late and I blow that 4 o'clock deadline. I do smoke when I write, which makes quitting smoking really hard. [*Laughs*] They seem to go hand in hand.

Are you currently trying to quit?

Well, that's why so many books are so late right now. [*Laughs*] As for my office, there's really nothing on the walls. There's piles of shit everywhere — reference material that I haven't even catalogued yet. It's like this fire hazard.

Walk us through the making of an issue. What do you do when you've got that blank slate?

I'm lucky. I don't ever have a blank slate. If I'm working on a story arc, I'm usually formulating the one that's two arcs down the road. But I do something unusual these days. I read the fucking newspaper. That's the first thing I do every day. Drink coffee and read the newspaper. That's a great place to find story endings. Most articles, they're all about endings. They really don't flush out how these people got into the situation. So I start with something to say. That's good advice. Have something to say or don't bother. There's always got to be a point to every story. It's good to have the point in mind when you start it. I work pretty loose in my head. I'm working backwards, so I have an ending but how do we get there?

Do you write a short one or two page plot to sort of pull it all together?

For myself, yeah I do. It's nice to have a map. Especially when you're working on periodicals. Once I've got the plot, then I'll break it down. I break down every issue per page. Usually when it's time to start scripting, I'll sit down with a legal pad and just write numbers 1 to 22 down the margin and then put in what's gonna happen on every page because I think every page has to mean something. I just write a line. Just so if something's supposed to be revealed earlier, I want to reveal it. You never want to run into the end of a book and you're just forced to espouse on all the things you didn't squeeze in.

And then I start dialoguing. I guess I do drink when I write, because sometimes I'll go out to a bar and start writing some dialogue and stuff. And just listening. When I actually do a script, I write all the dialogue first without any panel breakdown, action, nothing. I write the dialogue. I figure I gotta tell the story by what's being said before I can go down and put the action in.

Would you say the characters drive the plot then, rather than the plot driving the characters?

I think so. In my work, yeah, as much as that can be because I'm still driving *them*. Plot's driven by what's said or what's thought of. I'm not saying that's the best way to go, but it's the most interesting for me.

How closely do you work with your artists?

I tend to trust my artists. Coming from that background myself, this is a collaborative medium and if I'm so particular about what I want drawn, I should fucking draw it myself. I rarely put camera angles in a script. I hate doing art direction. I hate it. Absolutely hate it. I'll set the scene and then let the dialogue take it from there. If the dialogue's good, it's telling the story and the artist is gonna get it. I work with some talented guys that I give a lot of freedom to. I think that's important. You have to have the ability to bring their sensibilities to the story.

I've talked to other writers who are just such control freaks. They're just bitching and moaning about artists changing their scripts and that kind of stuff. I think if an artist changes your script, they're changing it because they're changing it to something they're more comfortable drawing and you'll get a better product that way. You'll get a better end result. If I call for a Mercedes and I get a Porsche, who fucking cares? It's a car. If I had a page with four panels on it and I end up getting six, it's because the artist is actually doing something with the action. Ultimately, he's the one who's staging it and he's gotta be comfortable doing that. Trust is key. Have confidence in their ability and just don't sweat the little stuff either. I can't treat an artist like a pair of hands. I have to leave room for an artist to interpret stuff. And as long as the dialogue is getting the story across, nine times out of ten, if the artist understands the point, you're gonna get what you want anyway. At the end of the day, a writer is only as good as his artist. I've yet to really be disappointed.

How do you figure out how many issues a story arc should be?

That's intuitive on my part. I know how long it's gonna take to tell a story. What the beats are. And if you miscount, just add an issue on.

More specifically, what about knowing how many words to use per page or panel? It has to be difficult not to overwrite.

I think that's a hard thing for a lot of writers. Goddamn. I find myself opening up a comic and you can't follow the action because there's all these fucking word balloons in the way. You look at it and you're just like, 'Ugh. I'm just not interested in wading through this.' So I tend not to be very verbose. Get to the point. Say what has to be said and get out. There can never be too little dialogue. If you're working with a good artist who can tell the story, you don't need the dialogue. In *100 Bullets*, I find myself cutting things. When we do the final edits, I rarely add anything. 'The Counterfifth Detective' [*100 Bullets* #31–36] was a lot of writing. But that was supposed to be a lot of writing. You're in this guy's head.

There's a lot of stuff in *100 Bullets* actually that's not so much about moving the main plot along. There's a lot of bits in there that are about telling a secondary story. The best example of what I'm trying to say — and I'm not saying that I'm getting anywhere near or as into it as much as Neil Gaiman was — is *Sandman*, which was always about other stories. He's commenting on Shakespeare at some point. That's probably where it's been used most effectively. That was a story about stories. Yeah, it was about this character Dream, but it was also about the whole history of fiction.

On average, how long does it take you to write an issue?

It depends on which book I'm working on. Some of them are a lot quicker than others. *100 Bullets* takes maybe a week and a half, two weeks. *Superman*'s like going to the dentist. [*Laughs*]

In other words, it's something you want to get over with quickly?

Yeah. I'm in there for more than an hour, something's wrong. No, *Superman*'s actually writing itself fairly quickly. But then the story's not as dense. There's gotta be some room for big operatic action. When *Superman*'s all said and done, I think people will look at it as a character study moreso than a straight adventure comic. Rather than the visual adventure, it's gonna be an adventure into this particular character's psyche. Every time I sit down to do Superman, I'm getting to like him better.

I don't think this works for anyone else, but Superman to me is like Sean Connery as James Bond. He's got that cocksureness about him. No matter how dire the situation, he's never out of control. For a long time now, Batman's been portrayed as the character with most control of himself. And I don't think that's true. Superman's the one most in control. He would have to be. He'd break your hand when he went to shake it. And Batman is absolutely not in control. An interesting thing for me about Batman is when I finally finished writing the 'Broken City' story arc [*Batman* #620–625], I realised it brought me to a place

Jim Lee

Jim Lee must have the Midas touch. After blowing fans away with his artwork on *X-Men*, helping to form Image Comics and then pulling the ultimate deal and selling his WildStorm Comics company to DC Comics, Lee seemed unstoppable. But then business demands saw his pencilling take a back seat to managing, with only the occasional piece of art appearing here and there. Recently, however, Lee has become DC's go-to guy for injecting much-needed energy into lagging titles. His twelve-issue story arc 'Hush' with writer Jeph Loeb in the pages of *Batman* set the industry abuzz and shot the Dark Knight back to the top of the sales chart. Loeb's character-driven mystery may have helped string fans along, but it's Lee's fresh takes on Batman and his whole Rogue's Gallery (everyone from a mutated Killer Croc to a seductive Poison Ivy) that really pulled them in. Following his *Batman* run, Lee set his sights even higher up DC's iconic ladder: The Man of Steel. Teaming up with *100 Bullets* scribe Brian Azzarello, Lee took the somewhat aged and tired-looking Superman and gave him a much-needed facelift. And once again, fans ate it up, propelling *Superman* to number one in the sales chart. Like we said, everything Jim Lee touches is gold these days.

where that character has never allowed himself to leave that alley or the death of his parents. He lives in the same house, he took over his father's company, he has never allowed himself to move on. And that's kind of sick. He makes sure he can never forget. By going out to fight crime every night, he's reminding himself that his parents were victims of crime.

What is it about your writing that draws readers in?

I don't know. I'm the wrong person to ask. I'm just the writer. I write for one guy: my editor. He signs the vouchers. He's the only person I have to worry about. [*Laughs*] I don't know what draws people into my work. People really seem to respond to my dialogue and that draws them in. And I think some of the intricacies of the actual story.

How involved does your editor get with your writing?

We talk story ideas but I don't leave him a lot of room to play around with my scripts. And it's not because I don't enjoy working with editors; I do. I've had really great relationships with them. I think they're very valuable in this whole process. I think his role is different for the different kinds of jobs he's doing. At one point he should be a good pair of ears to listen to the direction of the story. And once the story's direction is decided on, then he's got to steer the ship — pretty much make sure that's the direction I'm staying in. If you treat an editor like an ally instead of an adversary, you'll just have a better relationship.

On average, how many drafts of a script do you do?

I do one. That's all I do. My scripts are so tight that there's not a lot of editing involved. When I send it off, it's done. I've sweated it.

Do you ever have problems hitting your deadlines?

Who doesn't? I like to think that everyone does. No, it's not really a problem. Nobody's ever waiting for work from me, that's for sure. I've never left an artist without work. Never. That'd be so fucking irresponsible, you know what I mean? They have to eat too. So I have to have work for them. God, having an artist idle would be almost criminal. If I don't have pages in front of them, I'm taking food out of their mouths.

Do you have any special tricks or tips for how you physically write each issue?

I work in Microsoft Word. I've used [the screenplay software] Final Draft for some things. But Word's the most comfortable for me because that's what I started in. But that's just a tool. Some guys like to use a hammer; other guys like to use a nail gun.

What advice would you offer to any aspiring comics writers out there?

Don't do it. It's hard. It's *really* hard. [*Laughs*] I would say just write. Period. Be thick headed enough not to take no for an answer. Talking to a lot of new writers, the one thing about comics which is different from a lot of other types of media is that it's an industry where anybody who reads it thinks they can do your job better than you can. There's a lot of people in comics, a lot of professionals, who were fans. Every fan wants to be a pro. I go to the movies; I don't want to make movies. If you just want to write comics, you're doomed. You're not a writer. That's another thing. Just write, every damn day. Even if it's a diary. When I ask people what they want to write they say, 'Well, I want to write about the Flash.' That's all you want to do is write about the Flash? Really? Okay, go ahead, write about the Flash but I don't think you'll ever do it professionally.

Do you ever struggle with writer's block?

No. Never. You can't. You gotta work through that crap. You just keep going, keep writing. It's like prospecting, there's a lot of dirt and you gotta find the gold. And once you find the gold, you keep mining that vein. I love writing. When I'm finished, I usually get a little depressed. In 'The Counterfifth Detective', I didn't want to kill Milo. When I was done writing it, I was just like, 'Goddamnit it.' I enjoy writing these characters and when I'm stopping, it's like leaving a friend you're never gonna see anymore.

Where would you like to see your career go in the future?

I'm going to do more creator-owned stuff. I'm done with superheroes for a while, or maybe forever. We'll see how the industry goes and how I'm allowed to do my stuff. There's other opportunities out there. There's novels, video games.

You were actively involved with the *100 Bullets* video game. What was that like?

Coming at it from someone who doesn't play games, it was interesting. I wrote the story. But two guys sitting in a bar talking about who they're gonna kill next doesn't make a good game. You want to get right to the killing. So it's a third-person shooter. It'll be out in October and I think it looks great. The conspiracy is touched upon but it's an adaptation of the comic. There's gonna be elements that are changed that hopefully won't have comic readers screaming bloody murder.

It's ridiculous to me the way people are up in arms about Keanu Reeves being John Constantine in the *Hellblazer* movie. It's just a totally different world. That book sells, what, 20,000 copies a month maybe? There's 20,000 people living on one city block that'll go see a movie with Keanu Reeves in it even if it's a cameo! The stakes are a lot higher. Who cares about the movie? It doesn't affect the book at all. It's still the same book. Enjoy the book. You don't like it, don't go see the movie.

You're currently exclusive with DC. Are you going to stay with them or do you think you'll write for Marvel again?

As long as I'm able to do the types of stories I want to do with DC, sure. If Marvel starts doing creator-owned books again on a regular basis and doesn't just pay lip service to them, sure. But I don't think that that's something that's gonna happen. That's not their policy and there's nothing wrong with that. I did two Marvel stories, both with Richard Corben, and at the end of both of them a casual reader who wasn't familiar with the characters could say, 'Luke Cage just got killed and Bruce Banner just died.' I mean, Batman had a happy ending compared to them. [*Laughs*] It's fun to play with those things once in a while, I just don't want to make a career out of it.

What other projects do you have coming up?

There will be a western but it won't be out for a while. If it's by the end of the year, we're lucky. It's an ongoing creator-owned book through Vertigo that currently has the working title *Loveless*. I haven't been able to distill the high concept yet but it's not really a typical western as far as what immediately springs to mind. It's going to take place mostly during Reconstruction in the South, when the South was basically an occupied state. That kind of story has a lot of resonance with what's currently going on in the world.

Anything else coming up beyond the western?

In comics, no. Outside of comics, yes. I'm not thinking Hollywood. Though that doesn't mean Hollywood's not thinking about me. I've had discussions with

Richard Corben

Since his first self-published underground comic, *Fantagor*, in 1970, Richard Corben has been horrifying comic fans everywhere. Recently, however, he's brought his unique art style to a more mainstream audience with a number of projects in conjunction with Brian Azzarello. He helped Azzarello kick off his run on magic man John Constantine's *Hellblazer* with the controversial prison-based story arc 'Hard Times'. Following that tale, Corben teamed up again with the writer on two projects for Marvel. First up was *Startling Stories: Banner*, a four-issue series for Marvel's more mature MAX line that saw Doc Samson trying to bring the Hulk down hard — and actually succeeding in the end (kind of). Corben's eerie-yet-realistic style helped breathe new life into the Green Goliath, while also showing the absolute frailty and helplessness of the human being in Bruce Banner. Next up was another MAX miniseries, *Cage*. Based on the famed Hero for Hire originally created in the '70s in response to the wave of Blaxploitation movies, this Luke Cage is all about the streets. Gangbangers, mobsters, strippers and corrupt cops are just the surface of his seedy world. And when a woman comes to Cage after her daughter's killed by a stray bullet, he finally agrees to help her.

people. More likely, novels. With a novel, you write it and if it gets optioned, they change it. You have no say. But you wrote your story. Enjoy the book. I think it was Raymond Chandler who was being interviewed once and he was asked how he felt about Hollywood and what they had done to his books. He turned around, looked at his bookshelf and said, 'They didn't do anything. They're right there. They're fine.' And that's a good approach to have. It's funny but comic fans react completely differently to people who read books.

When you're finished with a script, how do you know when you've really nailed it?

You know when you do and you know when you don't. At least I do. When you hit your marks, you know it. *El Diablo*. Oh fuck man, I nailed that. I did. I knew it. When I was done with that it was just like, BAM, this is just tight. This works. Though nobody read the fucking thing; I think it sold eight copies. And I did a story in *Spider-Man: Tangled Web*. It was just a single issue story about Crusher Hogan, the wrestler who was in two panels of the first Spider-Man book. So I wrote a story about how he got to be on those two panels, and I thought I nailed that too.

What would you say is your favourite part of writing?

Doing the dialogue is my favourite. Telling the story through dialogue. Y'know, I find myself drawn more to plays than movies. The thing about plays is that the dialogue is so crucial. That's what drives the action. That's something I respond to. There's a lot more emotional weight in what's said in a play than there is in a film. Special effects are in the words, in what they mean.

It's funny, this lawyer told me once: novels are about what people think; plays are about what people say; and film is about what people do. And comics is about all of that, or has the potential to be about all of that. I guess it meant something to me because I didn't forget it.

*   *   *

BRIAN MICHAEL BENDIS

Brian Michael Bendis isn't a man of few words. The fan-favourite writer may have taken a decade and a half to become comics' latest 'overnight sensation', but he's certainly earned his place. Originally gaining praise on the independent scene with his crime-based creator-owned books *Goldfish* and *Jinx*, Bendis really started turning heads with *Torso*, his take on a 1935 crime in Cleveland that saw Eliot Ness try to solve a rash of brutal murders. He eventually made his way to the mainstream, helping to give *Daredevil* a shot in the arm, as well as kick off the entire 'Ultimate' Marvel Universe with *Ultimate Spider-Man*, a title he's still writing today. Toss in his creator-owned *Powers*, a whole-new direction for *The Avengers* and a new Marvel Universe series called *The Pulse*, and Bendis is certainly a busy bee. Even more astonishing, however, is that besides writing so many monthly books and staying on a title for long runs at a time, Bendis can fill just one issue with more dialogue than some titles have in a year. Wordy? Yes. But Bendis' dialogue invariably rings so true that you can't help but get instantly sucked into the world of his characters.

Okay, before we even get into anything else, how the heck do you write so many titles each month?

First of all, I'd be doing it whether I got paid or not. I'm not saying that facetiously; I was working this hard in comics when no one was paying me for years and years. My personal goal, in as much as I feel like I've accomplished something in life, is to write one really good comic book per week. And it's not that much. I'm really a big believer in what one man can do, another man can do. And if Aaron Sorkin can write *The West Wing* every week — which is, like, eighty-eight pages of geo-politics, economics and a thousand talking people — I can write one twenty-two-page Spider-Man comic book. I really do believe that. If the book isn't happening, I put it away. If the book isn't good, I don't hand it in. I don't just hand it in because the week is up and I have to hand it in.

Can you describe what your typical work day is like?

I get up at one or two in the afternoon and get all my business done. Then I get out of here and get on my bike — usually with my kid now — and we take off and do a bunch of stuff. Bike riding is a big part of my writing now. I know it is because the minute I took up bike riding as a daily activity, there was a response from people to my writing. It's just something about cardiovascular activity and the brain: the scenes start happening in my head and the characters start talking and I can't get home fast enough. So whatever my writing problem for the day is, it's been solved and I just have to transcribe it for the night. Then I do the family stuff, put everyone to bed and then write sometimes for fifteen minutes and sometimes for eight straight hours. I'm down there working on something, doing something work-related all night long. And then I go to bed about 7am.

You're not just a fan-favourite writer, you're a writer's writer as well. Other pros are constantly pointing out how realistic your dialogue is. How do you it?

I don't overly analyse how I do it because I don't want to ruin it. I do think about it almost all day. I've kind of trained my ear to listen to people. It's really annoying — if you're friends with me you can tell the difference between whether I'm actually listening to what you're saying or *how* you're saying it. It's like a glazed look I get on my face. I'm in a trance or something. I'm just a big fan of that style of writing in other mediums. David Mamet. Sorkin I mentioned. Woody Allen. It's all these playwrights who write naturalistic dialogue that isn't characters talking at each other to move the plot along for the reader; they're talking to each other and actually listening to each other. And I really, really, really, really believe there's not enough of that going on in comics, to an unbelievable degree. So I just made it a conscious decision to apply that thing I love so much about playwriting to comics. Having said that, there are other

Place of birth:
  Portland, Oregon, USA
Date of birth:
  18 August 1957
Home base:
  USA
First published work:
  Parts of a Hole
Education:
  Cleveland Institute of Art
Career highlights:
  Alias, Avengers, Daredevil, Jinx,
  Secret War, Powers, The Pulse,
  Torso, Ultimate Fantastic Four,
  Ultimate Spider-Man

people who have done it before me. Howard Chaykin [*American Flagg!*] was a big influence. He's done it.

The cool thing is, on some books where you have a lengthy stay, you really have an opportunity to let the characters dictate the story a little more than you would if you just had a mini-series or a one-shot. So it's really given me the chance to let the characters take over a scene if they need to. Sometimes they take over the plot and I pride myself in being open to it. There's an organic experience that happens.

You always kind of know where you're going with a story. You have to know where your end is, but sometimes the characters dictate a different ending once you get there and you kind of have to be honest about it. I know a lot of writers enjoy that about my work. You can always tell when another writer just went nuts. It's what I love about Warren Ellis' work. You can tell when he had an idea and the idea took over. And that's just fantastic. On the other hand, a lot of guys also have their little set way and they're gonna do it their set way and they're gonna cram a character into a story that doesn't belong there, and it never works. You have to be organic. You have to be open to it. Yet you have to have a plan. It's all about instinct, but that's very scary for some people. It's scary for me too because I've not always made the right decisions.

Over on *Ultimate Spider-Man*, you really nail the teenage feel. How do you get the overall tone and dialogue to be so believable?

There's two things. Number one is that teenage dialogue as it is today isn't that different than it was when I was a kid. And I haven't matured that much over the course of the years, so it's very easy for me to get into that mindset. The other cool thing is that the teenage characters in *Ultimate Spider-Man* — the lead ones, like Peter, MJ and Gwen — are intelligent, they're not dumb mall kids. I don't write them stupid just because they're kids. And I think people generally appreciate that. You know what? Dumb mall kids don't see themselves as dumb mall kids, so they're not really interested in reading about dumb mall kids. There's a couple of things about the dialogue that I don't do. There's certain colloquialisms that are very much of the moment and in two years will seem dated, so I try to avoid them. Also, kids swear like marines. They swear every other word. And I can't use swear words in *Ultimate Spider-Man*. If I was being truly honest, it would be called *Ultimate* Fucking *Spider-Man*. I have to come up with more clever ways to cover the dialogue that isn't a swear word. So I'm actually adding things into it that are nonsense words or that don't really exist in the English language that are my buzzwords for swear words.

Besides the swearing issue in *Ultimate Spider-Man*, are there any other times you feel handcuffed by Marvel when you're writing?

I don't feel handcuffed by the non-swearing. Actually, there's this quote by Ridley Scott that's been freaking me out lately. He says that nothing makes him more creative than a budget. He says, 'You give me a limitation and I will definitely get off my ass and think of something much better than I would've thought of if I was just given free rein.' So I don't consider the swearing or the format a limitation. The format's a bigger pain in the ass than the swearing. You gotta get those stories into twenty-two pages and that's hard. I see all those things as an excuse to try harder to be interesting. I also created a situation for myself where, with *Powers* and *Alias* and even with *Daredevil*, I've created certain series for myself where I can write as an adult for adults. I get to blow off that steam. I get to go to *Powers* and drop an F bomb and I feel good as an adult. The two outlets feed off each other really nicely.

How does working on a Marvel book like *Daredevil* compare to a creator-owned title like *Powers*?

I think more guys in my situation should do both. First of all, there's a very specific, unique, parent-like experience with creator-owned work. I think that situation lets me enjoy work-for-hire a lot more. I also have a tendency to treat *Ultimate Spider-Man* as if I own it because I'm used to that feeling. On the other hand, I'll always have *Powers* where I can go and do something off-the-wall insane. In *Powers*, I can kill [lead character] Christian Walker if I want to. I'll never be able to do that in *Daredevil*. Even though I've come close. [*Laughs*] To be a satisfied creator in comics, I think you need to do both at the same time.

I know some people that absolutely can't do work-for-hire. And those people absolutely should *not* do work-for-hire. If you think you're sucking on the corporate tit or you're just cowtowing to some audience, you absolutely should not be writing those books. I feel this is an honour and a privilege to be in charge of these icons for any amount of time. That's how you should feel. And if you don't feel that way, don't do it. This isn't a waste of time. This is like the greatest honour of my adult life.

You're definitely passionate about comics. But how did you first break in?

I had to make my own way. I was trying desperately to get Marvel and DC's attention with art samples since I was nine years old. Then I went and made a bunch of comics myself when I was a teenager, and then I got into art school. The whole time I was sending pencil submissions into people. It just wasn't happening. I wasn't drawing superheroes the way anyone wanted to see them drawn. So I got a job at a comics store and discovered the world of independent comics. Most of my tastes ran towards crime fiction, and the styles of art and photography that I enjoyed were more in line with independent comics anyhow. So I went and started making my own independent comics as part of my college thesis.

I was really lucky, because Caliber Comics starting publishing some of my stuff. There's where I met [*Kabuki* creator] David Mack, [*Powers* artist] Michael Oeming, [*Green Arrow* artist] Phil Hester and Ed Brubaker. I started making the graphic novels — *Goldfish* and *Jinx*. I started getting nice reviews and won an Eisner. Things started clicking, and all the time I would send my stuff to Marvel and DC because I really did want to work on their characters. Eventually, Todd McFarlane read one of my books and offered me one of my first mainstream colour series, *Sam & Twitch*.

That was a good deal of fun. It also spoiled me because he totally left us alone and let us do whatever we wanted. Literally a month later, David Mack had gotten a job writing *Daredevil* and I was like, 'Dude, you gotta show my stuff!' because I so want to be part of Marvel Knights in the worst way. Eventually Joe Quesada did read one of my graphic novels. He called me up and was like, 'Hey, what are you doing now?' And I said, 'I don't know, what do you need an artist for?' And he went, 'Artist? Your art sucks!' And it occurred to me that everyone did like my writing more than my drawing. Even the graphic novels that I was writing and drawing, people would rarely comment on the art. It was always talking about the writing.

So Quesada called to offer you *Daredevil?*

Well, initially I had pitched him to do Nick Fury. I was going to do Nick Fury with Bill Sienkiewicz, but that didn't work out in the end. So I thought I was going back to the end of the line. And then he called me up and said, 'We really need help getting *Daredevil* back on track. Would you and David like to do an arc just to get it together?' I was like, 'Yeah, that's like me working with my best friend on my favourite character at Marvel. That's awesome!' So I did that. And after I wrote the first issue, I got the call saying this guy Bill Jemas [Marvel's then Publisher] is gonna call and offer you this ground zero look at Spider-Man. Are you gonna want it?

Bill had been working on *Ultimate Spider-Man* — at the time it was called 'Ground Zero' — for a long time prior to my even coming to the company. They were

Jinx

Back in his independent comics days, Brian Michael Bendis wrote and drew a low-sales, high-praise crime series. And despite only producing a handful of issues, Bendis' *Jinx* rates as arguably some of the best work of his career. Set in the gritty streets of Cleveland, Ohio, *Jinx* stars the sailor-mouthed, tough-as-nails Juliet 'Jinx' Alameda, a bounty hunter/bail bondsman who's pretty much sick of her life. She wasn't always like that, though. Time was, she was a proper, sweet gal who got into the business by cutting bonds in the hopes of helping people. That's all in the past, however, as she's now caught up with Dave 'Goldfish' Gold, a wanted man who's hiding out from the law while he hunts down a major score of abandoned mob money that could easily be both their tickets out of town and into a whole new life. Originally published by Caliber Comics, a short run followed at Image until the series eventually just folded under the radar (although Jinx herself did resurface briefly during Bendis' run on *Sam & Twitch*). Recent Hollywood buzz may help revive it, however, as a major motion picture is in the offing with none other than Charlize Theron showing serious interest in playing the lead character.

having a hard time finding the voice for it. There were very dry versions of the Spider-Man story that other people were doing. So Bill came to Joe's office and said, 'I can't find the voice for this. Who would *you* hire?' Joe handed Bill my *Daredevil* script and *Torso* and said, 'I'd hire him. He writes characters. You've already got the story, you just need the characters.' And then Bill read my stuff and called me. He sent me all the stuff he'd done, and I was so grateful to all the other writers because I got to read what they did. And I probably would've done what they had done had I been in their shoes. It was just very dry and almost too respectful in a way. Like they were too scared to touch it. So I wrote the first issue in a weekend, handed it in and said, 'This is how I would write it.' And they went, 'We love it! Do [*Ultimate*] X-Men too!' I was so excited that I said yes to *X-Men* and I didn't even want to do *X-Men*. I was just so happy they didn't fire me.

Did you have any clue how unbelievably popular *Ultimate Spider-Man* would end up being?

I had no idea that the initial announcement would be seen as such a vile thing; it was so bad. I'm coming from independent comics, where your worst villain is ambivalence. Nobody cares about independent comics, so you're just stuck with the crickets. No one hates you. They either love you or they don't care. I was unaware of John Byrne's *Spider-Man: Chapter One*. I didn't know it existed. I wasn't reading a lot of Marvel comics at the time because they just weren't appealing to me. So I was unaware of its existence and the feelings people had towards it. People already felt punched in the face by an idea like this. I just knew that I'd already seen the first issue and it was really awesome. Also it was weird because other creators were shitting all over us. Everyone was like, 'We hate it!' And the only person that liked the idea of it was someone who I had never met before and his name was Mark Millar.

Most of the guys complaining probably had their pitches turned down.

It's not that so much. I was just surprised by the closed mindedness of it. Online, every time we made a move it was like, 'Fuck you!' Now it's like the bigger the 'fuck you' the better the book is gonna do. It's hilarious. Eventually you say, 'Okay, well all my books are doing pretty well and people have expressed pretty positive feelings overall. But *when* will I have enough credit in the bank so I can make an announcement and people don't just jump up my ass?' Because they always jump up your ass, no matter what you announce. I remember when Frank Miller announced *Dark Knight 2* and everybody started screaming and yelling. Let's face it, if he doesn't have enough credit in the bank, I never will. So now I don't worry about it. There's no bank. There's no credit. And that frees you up. It's the same with *The Avengers*. We announced this *New Avengers* idea and people don't even know what it is yet and they're all up in arms. It's the loudest noise I've heard since I've gotten into comics. They're very worried. The first two emails that I got right away — this is so true — the first one, the header said, 'Don't kill She-Hulk,' and the other one said, 'Kill She-Hulk.' Right there it shows you that you'll never make everyone happy.

Is your approach to writing comics different now than it was back in the indie days?

Oh yeah. I've become addicted to the art of collaboration. And it's the thing I most pride myself on. If you read a script I write for [*Daredevil* artist] Alex Maleev or a script I write for [*Avengers* artist] David Finch, other than some verbal ticks, I don't think it even looks like the same person wrote them. I bend over backwards to make sure that these scripts are written for the artist to excel, and not the other way around. Alex has been with me through the whole thing. When I used to write *Sam & Twitch*, I would write the entire book and then draw it, because I didn't know where the writing ended. I would physically draw the pages, hand them to him and say, 'Here, draw these.' I was a megalomaniac freakazoid who didn't know what he was doing. Alex was happy to do it because it gave him less to think about; he could watch TV and draw. Then when he started working with Todd on *Sam & Twitch* after I got fired — Todd was just the opposite of me, he wouldn't even write the script, he would just call Alex up and tell him the story. The resultant panels were bigger and I saw a freedom in Alex's work that I wasn't giving him. It really was a slap in the face. I thought, wow, I was strangling this guy to death.

Besides writing a handful of titles each month, you also tend to stay on a title for quite some time. That's pretty rare these days. Is it something you're consciously trying to do?

I see the value of it in a way that I think few of my peers in the modern age of

Ultimate Spider-Man

In case you haven't heard, there's a new Spider-Man in town. His name's Peter Parker and he's a high school student who gains extraordinary spider-like powers after being bitten by a souped-up arachnid on a class trip. Confused? No, it's not a retro Marvel story. It's the basic premise behind Marvel's highly successful *Ultimate Spider-Man* series by Brian Michael Bendis. Take the three plus decades of continuity you know about Spider-Man and toss it aside. Sure, Spidey's got the same powers and roughly the same origin, but he's back in high school and he's even dating Mary Jane (who knows about his little secret). The names may be the same, but the storylines and origins are all ramped up for the 21st Century. Think of it as if Spider-Man never existed until this series. Clearly Marvel took a big chance with this title (as with the entire Ultimate Marvel Universe) but it's most definitely paid off. Bendis' Spider-Man is a wisecracking, in-over-his-head kid who's having an absolute blast fighting the good fight. And so are fans as they race to pick up each new issue to see how familiar characters (like Kraven, Gwen Stacy, Doc Ock, etc.) will make their debut into this Ultimate Universe.

comics see. Gil Kane and John Romita and these guys stayed on their books and that's why we know their names: because they did these long runs. I would love it if I were forever referred to as the *Daredevil* writer. That's not a pigeonholing; it's a badge of honour. On the other hand, I wouldn't stay on the book if I didn't have anything to say. Writing *Ultimate Spider-Man* is as scary and as exciting as it was the first year of it. And I don't feel like we're done. When it is, I'll leave. I won't just stay on to see how long I can stay on. The biggest thing is, there's this huge value to the writing. I mean, you really get to spend some time with these characters and think of stuff that you wouldn't have thought of if you only did a year or six months.

A lot of my peers love to drop a bomb and leave... and not even deal with the aftermath. I like to drop a bomb and then hang around. *Daredevil*'s a perfect example. We dropped a huge bomb on that book and Joe did say, 'If we let you do this, you've gotta stay.' Kevin Smith killed Karen Page and left. I wanted to drop a bomb and hang around and watch Daredevil try to crawl out of a hole. It seems much more interesting to me. You spend a lot of time showing people Matt Murdock's mindset and then thirty issues later go, 'Oh, guess what? He had a nervous breakdown in issue #8 and he doesn't know it.' You can't do that if you're on a mini-series.

Was there ever any fallout from Marvel at any point from all the bombs you dropped on Daredevil?

No. I mean, I had to present why I was doing it. The biggest one was the identity outing. When I took over the book, I started making a list and I kept calling up [Editor] Ralph Macchio and going, 'Foggy knows?' And then I'd call back: 'The Kingpin knows, right?' You've got this list of every person who knows Matt's Daredevil, including every girl he ever made goo goo eyes at, and this is a huge problem. And at the same time I'm kind of obsessed with secret identities because I think in the modern world they'd be almost impossible. I think it's just absolutely impossible to keep your secret identity because that's a major effort. So I said, 'Why don't we make one of the books in the Marvel Universe about the fact that this guy's been outed? It should be such a powerful statement that it actually affects the other Marvel books. Now you're scared for Spider-Man like you weren't scared in the past. Now it becomes a real danger and a drama.' I presented why it should be Daredevil, and how to do it, so that it's not the Kingpin or some cheesy thing. It's just some guy he's never even met, because that's how it happens. Whenever big shit happens in your life, it isn't someone right next to you that did it. It's someone you didn't even know. So I presented the whole damn thing and I told them why. And this was right around the time the *Daredevil* movie was in theatres, and they could have easily said, 'No, it's time to play it safe. The movie's coming. Just put Elektra in the book and shut up.' But they were like, 'Yeah, let's do it.'

More generally, has an editor ever stopped you from doing something you really wanted on a title?

Yeah, but not a lot. The one reason I work so well with them is that my natural tendencies as a storyteller are very much in line with what Marvel wants. So it's been very easy for me. A perfect example would be the time I wanted to kill the Kingpin in the worst way. I told Joe, 'We have to kill the Kingpin.' So word gets to Ralph Macchio, who's been an editor at Marvel for twenty-five to thirty years. He's been my editor on *Ultimate Spider-Man* since day one, and he's got the greatest history with Marvel comics. He's been there for everything. His name's been on some of the best comics ever made and the [Spider-Man] 'Clone Saga' at the same time. So he's got a lot of knowledge. Anyway, he calls me up and says, 'I heard you want to kill the Kingpin. You know what? They might just let you do it, but I'm gonna tell you *not* to, and I'm gonna tell you why. The biggest mistake Marvel ever made was when they killed Norman Osborn. What happens is, it's cool for the moment, but the minute you're off *Daredevil*, someone's going to bring Kingpin back as like a cyborg monkey or something. So take the Kingpin, stab him, do whatever you want to do with him, but don't kill him.' It really was an excellent point. And I did agree with him when he put it that way.

Walk us through how you write an average issue.

There really isn't an average way. I seem to handle scenes two ways: I either let the conversation go and then I put it away and come back to it and see if it's interesting; or if it's a large action sequence, I choreograph it, I kind of line up my shots and work on it that way. I do know what the issue's going to be. I label the scenes, like what the point of the scene is. That's a big problem in a lot of writing in any medium — people don't know what the point of their scenes are. So I label all the scenes and then start hacking away at them and try to fit all of the scenes I want in that issue into twenty-two pages. Usually I have, like, thirty pages of stuff and I cram it down to size. It's funny, I get criticized for what people consider to be padding, when I think I'm doing the opposite. A lot of times a conversation will happen between two characters and I'll just let it happen. I'll just start typing, regardless of where I was supposed to go with the story. If the characters have altered the story in a more interesting way, I'll go with them. And if I've created a cliffhanger for myself that makes me go, 'Oh my god! How am I going to get out of this?' I will absolutely hand it in. I've written some of my best stuff scared.

How do you come up with the initial story though?

That's a really ethereal thing. It's so hard to discuss. Sometimes it's just an image that creates a whole idea. Then other times I just really want to tell a particular story. One time on *Daredevil* we got really, really dark and I said, 'You know what? It's time for the Black Widow to come back in the book and have sex with him.' And from there you start telling this great Black Widow story. I try to keep it very organic. I think way too many people are structure neurotic. I know how to do structure, but I kind of let go of that if I can.

Does your personal life come through at all in your writing?

Tons and tons. You can't help it. There's nothing about Matt Murdock's life that's similar to my life. I'm not an Irish Catholic blind lawyer ninja. I'm none of those things. But a lot of my high school experiences come through in *Ultimate Spider-Man*. And a lot of my mindset of the world comes through in *Alias* and Jessica Jones' experience. Mind you, I'm not as self-loathing as she is, or as paralyzed by self-loathing as she is.

Speaking of *Alias*, the book was a mature-readers title in Marvel's MAX line, but you ended it and basically started over with the more Marvel Universe-friendly *The Pulse*. What exactly happened at the end there?

Alias was doing really well. It was doing extremely well with trade paperbacks. What happened was I got to the end of the 'Purple' arc and I was surprised to find that I had also gotten to the end of the series. I had gotten to the point of the whole series. That was it, end of the story. It was weird because it had never happened to me before. With *Daredevil* and *Powers*, the story just keeps getting bigger and bigger and bigger. There's no end in sight. With *Alias*, I got there all of a sudden. I called up Marvel and said, 'Gee, I think I'm done.' And Joe said, 'Well if you're done, you can wrap it up. One thing we really wanted out of you, though, was kind of this *CSI* in the Marvel Universe. And we weren't going to bother you with it because *Alias* is kind of already that. But now it's ending, why don't you come up with a way to put Jessica into this new environment, like she gets a new job or something.' The thing is, I love Jessica. I just adore her. So I came back to Joe with *The Pulse*, which made everybody really happy.

And then there was the whole issue of whether it should be a mature readers MAX book or a mainstream Marvel Universe book. And if it's a mainstream Marvel Universe book, then you can have her interacting with more of the mainstream Marvel Universe. To have her interacting with Spider-Man in *Alias* would have been just irresponsible. You just don't want people buying that book who shouldn't be buying it. Jessica may be my greatest addition to the Marvel Universe. I was very happy to do that. So it wasn't a matter of watering it down so much as inching toward what it's become on its own. I love swearing, I would never give it up. But it's a small price to pay to tell stories that actually affect the Marvel Universe.

Does the fact that you used to draw your own work influence the way you write?

Absolutely. Right off the bat, I think I was a much more successful writer than I would've been if I'd just started out as a writer. It's not just the art that I can do, I've done all my own book designs, all my own lettering, a lot of my own colouring. I lettered the first arc of *Powers* myself. I can literally do anything with varying degrees of success. It's not like I'm a genius in all of them but I can physically do them. And literally doing all those things has made me a better writer, because I understand what a comic book can and can't do on various levels. If I were just a writer, that process would've taken a lot longer.

A lot of writers, no matter how good they are, they write a description that says, 'Panel 1: Captain America walks in the room, takes off his mask, takes off his boots, walks to the door, opens the door and takes out a beer.' That's nine panels. And also, because I've drawn my own crowd scenes, I don't feel guilty about making other people draw crowd scenes. I am a crowd scene writer. It's really funny, in *Ultimate Fantastic Four* #6, I wrote to Adam Kubert, '4,000 Ani-Men attack the Fantastic Four.' And what you expect to see is about twelve. He actually drew all 4,000! It's shocking. So I don't ask my artists to do anything that I couldn't do or wouldn't do myself. I know I've heard from every single one of them individually that they're just so grateful that I understand what they need and I understand what they can do. And also I tell them if there's an image in their head that they're dying to draw, to tell me what it is and if I can work it into the script I will. A perfect example is at the end of the *Ultimate X-Men* run that I did with David Finch. I wasn't going to go anywhere near the Sentinels; I just don't think like that. And he said, 'I really want to draw Sentinels.' It started me thinking how that would be a better ending for my story. I think it was the X-Men fighting tanks or something. Sentinels was just better, and that's what people wanted to see more than anything. And if David Finch says, 'I want to draw some Sentinels,' and you go, 'Okay, here are some Sentinels,' you're gonna get some kick-ass Sentinels. They were perfect. They were gorgeous.

Ever have an itch to get back into drawing?

Oh, yeah. I love drawing. It's just, boy oh boy, it is time consuming. And the second I stopped drawing it was like, 'Welcome to comics. Have some money!' For fourteen years, every day I drew for fourteen hours a day. Every day. And

Powers

If Kurt Busiek's *Astro City* is a Silver Age celebration of comics, then Brian Michael Bendis' *Powers* is a Modern Age celebration. Taking a realistic approach to a world with superheroes (and villains), the Eisner-award winning *Powers* centres on homicide detective Christian Walker, who routinely investigates 'super' crime scenes. What makes Walker a bit unique are his close ties to many of the tights-wearing heroes. And that's thanks to the fact that Walker used to pound villains into the pavement as the hero Diamond, until he mysteriously lost his powers. Now teamed up with a rookie detective named Deena Pilgrim, the duo's first job together is investigating the shocking murder of one of the world's most-popular heroes ever: Retro Girl. Subsequent storylines reveal more and more about Walker's mysterious past, while also unearthing some deep-seeded conspiracies between the government and certain superteams. Besides Bendis' patented realistic dialogue, what really makes *Powers* shine is the complete unexpectedness of each turn. Set in his own universe, Bendis can do as he pleases in terms of letting characters live or die, and he's yet to pull a single punch. Just don't get too attached to any one character or they may be the next name on Walker's list of victims to investigate.

then the second I stopped it's like, 'Huzzah!' It's hard to admit that, having spent $50,000 on art school, that I'm just naturally a better writer. I wish I could draw as effortlessly as sometimes the writing comes. Drawing was a tooth-pulling experience. But when I'm writing, it feels right. I wonder if I was actually all along drawing to cultivate the writing. Or I'm just so retarded that I spent fifteen years trying to develop a career and I just had the wrong one. I sent in so many pencil submissions and I have never gotten a pencilling job.

Have you ever had any background in writing?

No. This upsets some people but I have never been formally trained in writing. I'm self-taught. Clearly I spent an amazing amount of time teaching myself how to tell a story. And I firmly believe that you can teach yourself how to do it. But the only way you're going to learn how to write a script is from reading scripts. I analyse comics and movies and plays. If I see something and it works, I will break it down and just analyse why a certain juxtaposition of images works and why a certain juxtaposition of words works.

What tips would you give to any aspiring writers out there?

You gotta do it every day. It's sort of like working out. I write every day. I don't write when I feel like it, I write every day. And a lot of it I don't show to you guys. Literally, it's like weight training. If you don't do it, you get flabby. So you physically have to type or write. When you're up and coming or you've not made it yet, your tendency is to sit around and tell your friends about what you want to write. That's not writing. That's the opposite of writing.

Also, you can't ignore the fact that comics is a visual medium, so what you have to do is find a way to make your script visually interesting to an editor. Either team up with another artist or, if you can draw, draw it yourself. Even Neil Gaiman broke in teaming up with Dave McKean. This has been going on for years and years. It's almost impossible to get someone to cold read a script, but they will read six lettered pages of a comic book if you hand it to them to see if you can tell a story. You're better off submitting like that than you are submitting as a cold scriptwriter.

Where would you like to see your career go from here?

I gotta tell you — and I'm not saying this to be all cutesy — this is so much farther than I thought I was going to get that I keep waiting for someone to say, 'Well, you're done.' Where it's going is really in a good direction. So I would like to continue to do this for as long as I'll be allowed to. Then when I'm not allowed to anymore, I'll just go back and write and draw my own comics.

*   *   *

ED
BRUBAKER

Location means nothing. Otherwise how could you explain the crime-filled writing career of Ed Brubaker? Currently living on a farm in southern California, Brubaker regularly details the lives of tough-talking cops in an unbelievably corrupt city within the pages of DC's *Gotham Central*. Then there's the monthly adventures of a certain cat burglar who skates in and out of the wrong side of the law over in *Catwoman*, not to mention his sleeper hit *Sleeper* for WildStorm, detailing the exploits of Holden Carver, an undercover agent sent to infiltrate a superpowered crime organization... except the only person alive who knows Holden's really a good guy is stuck in a coma. Yep, Brubaker's work is dark, gritty, and there's more than the occasional grisly death. Certainly not what you'd typically expect from a farm boy. But even wilder is the fact that this very down-to-earth writer got his comics start on the alternative side of the industry. Writing and drawing semi-autobiographical comics like *Lowlife* and *Detour*, Brubaker's view of the industry was all black and white. Literally. Until something inside him clicked and the four-colour world of mainstream comics pulled him in.

Have you always been interested in comics?

Yeah, from childhood. When I was two and my brother was four, we were living in Guantánamo, Cuba, because my dad was in the navy. He went into his office and asked all the guys if their kids had any comics they didn't want anymore. He had read comics growing up in the '40s and '50s, so he came home with this enormous stack of comics one day and divided them between me and my brother. Long before I could actually read, I was reading comics. I think the first comic I actually read was the first issue of the *Hulk*. From then on, I don't think a day — or at least not a week — has gone by that I haven't read a comic book.

So your dad got you hooked really early.

His idea was to get us hooked on reading first and foremost, so that we would start reading books earlier than most other kids. My brother followed that path, but me, I was only reading comics. My dad would give me books and I'd be like, 'What? No, comics!' It wasn't until after high school when I was working in book stores that I became a dedicated reader of, well, everything. Comics, though, have been the main dominating force in my life for as long as I can remember.

Were you always hell-bent on becoming a comic book writer?

I never actually thought I'd become a comic book writer; I thought I'd be a penciller. From the time I could pick up a pencil, I was drawing comics. But as I would just make stories up as I went along, I guess you could say I *was* writing, in a way. And then in high school I got into stuff like *Love & Rockets* and *Cerebus* and then Frank Miller. I remember actually noticing the names and thinking, this guy writes *and* draws his own stuff. I always thought Frank Miller was the greatest storyteller going. I was like, 'Oh, man, his stuff is so much more dynamic and you can really follow everything. But the actual art isn't that much more advanced than mine.' So I'd always look at guys like that or early Dave Sim and think, I can't draw this well, but eventually I will. I always liked guys who worked within their limitations really well, because that's what I always felt I would have to do as an artist. I knew I was no Barry Windsor-Smith or John Buscema, and I knew from looking at underground comics that I was never gonna be the artist that, say, Robert Crumb was. I started properly writing my own comics as a teenager really, but I would always get halfway through something and say, 'This isn't good enough to print,' and just abandon it. Even at fourteen, unless it was good enough to print, there was no point in doing it. I never just did them for myself. I always imagined they had to be professional.

Place of Birth:
  Bethesda Naval Hospital,
  Maryland, USA
Date of Birth:
  17 November 1966
Home base:
  Mendocino County,
  California, USA
First published work:
  Gumby 3-D as teenage artist;
  Purgatory USA (as writer/artist);
  'An Accidental Death' (writer
  only) originally published in
  Dark Horse Presents #65-67
Education:
  'Not much'
Career Highlights:
  The Authority, Batman, Catwoman, Deadenders,
  Gotham Central, Lowlife, Scene of the Crime, Sleeper

How did your first published work come about?

During my high school years, I kind of weaned myself off of superheroes and mainstream comics — other than the real standout Alan Moore and Frank Miller stuff — and got more into alternative comics. They weren't even called that then, they were just black-and-whites. Reading *Cerebus, Love & Rockets, American Splendor* and so on, I started thinking, okay, what do I want to do? And what I really wanted to do was just blatantly rip off *Love & Rockets*, kind of write about my own life. I think I spent two or three months putting together samples of what I wanted to do and brought them to a comic convention. I showed a couple of stories I had written and drawn to Dan Vado at Slave Labor. I remember thinking, these guys publish real quality material and they're not so big that they're going to automatically reject me. I left samples with them and they came back the next day. Dan had read one of the stories, really liked it and thought he could publish it. Then I conned the Hernandez Bros. into doing the covers.

What was the book?

It was called *Purgatory USA* and Slave Labor published a sum total of one issue! I actually completed the second issue but there were some business problems — the printer got sold to a new printer who demanded advance payment — and I remember a lot of Slave Labor's line was getting cut, so they canned my books. It ended up sort of morphing into *A Complete Lowlife*, which I did for another publisher.

Actually, when I was right out of high school, my friend Mike Christian and I started working on comics and ended up drawing half an issue of *Gumby 3-D* for Blackthorne Publishing. The guy who drew it shopped at a comic store that I worked at, and he just offered it to us. We were total kids and didn't even realise that he was offering to let us take over this half of an issue because he was behind on deadlines. I'm not sure if we were credited or not. I don't even have a copy of the comic anymore. We just adapted an episode of *Gumby* that they gave us on videotape, along with a bunch of stills they had printed out. I'm fairly certain it was terrible. [*Laughs*] I was eighteen at the time or something like that. Weird; I've been working in comics for over half my life now. But yeah, I never imagined I'd be a writer. I never imagined even then that I would end up writing mainstream comics. You can never plan your life.

What was it like seeing that issue for the first time? And I don't mean *Gumby*.

It was pretty exciting actually. There were three stories in it and one was a really deliberate Garcia Marquez/Gilbert Hernandez kind of riff where I was talking about my mom and the small town she grew up in. I look back at that and go, 'Ee-uw.' But I did a couple of other stories in there that were just personal experience type stuff that were more influenced by *American Splendor*. It came out during the tail end of the black-and-white boom, so it actually sold pretty well. I remember going to a comic convention about six months after it came out and being in a room with somebody who was getting us all high and someone said, 'Oh, what do you do?' And I said, 'I did that comic *Purgatory USA* for Slave Labor.' And everybody in the room was like, '*You* did that?!' I was in exactly the right crowd.

PAGE FOUR
1—Splash panel. Pit Bull shrugs, looking at his feet. In the background, Genocide and Holden are looking down the train tracks. This panel should basically be a wider shot of the scene, focusing more on Pit Bull, and his disappointment. Give us a nice shot of the location, too, it's an isolated area where a train crosses under a small bridge, so our guys could leap down to the speeding train from the bridge, about ten or twelve feet from the bridge to the top of the train, I would say.

> NARR: There's nothing like the chip on the shoulder of an up-and-comer. Guys like Pit
>
> Bull here, just a few steps away from being a serious player.
>
> NARR: Gets his name in the paper once or twice and thinks he's famous. Sets his sights
>
> on the next rung on the ladder, and now that's all he can think about.
>
> NARR: Guys like that can be a real liability on a mission, because they care more about
>
> what the success will mean to them than just getting the job done.
>
> TITLE: THE FIRST MISTAKE

2—Genocide points down the tracks and we see the train speeding toward us.

> NARR: But Tao is considering moving him up, so Genocide and I are stuck with him this
>
> time out, at least...
>
> GENOCIDE: All right, here we go...

PAGE FIVE
1—As the train speeds by, they jump off the top of the bridge, on after another. They're jumping on the last three cars of the train, the non-passenger cars, freight and baggage, with no windows and big sliding metal doors on the side.

> NARR: Still, Pit Bull's alleged talent for trouble may come in handy on this mission
>
> anyway.

2—Holden lands on the top of the speeding train, tumbling a little, reaching for a handhold, and looks back to see Pit Bull leaping off the bridge and Genocide about to land on it, as well.

> NARR: And what is our mission? One of subterfuge more than substance, really.
>
> NARR: Six weeks ago Jeffers Nillsun, the assistance to the scientist who adapted the
>
> technology that made the black hole suitcase bomb possible, went missing.

3—Holden creeps along the top of the train toward the front of the car he landed on.

> NARR: As it turns out, he's been in the custody of Department P.S.I. – a tech-based
>
> covert organization that used to work hand-in-hand with International Operations.
>
> NARR: Today Dept. P.S.I. is planning to hand him over to British Secret Intelligence in
>
> London.

Above: Script page from Sleeper #6. *Courtesy of Ed Brubaker.*

How did an alternative junkie like you make the jump to mainstream comics?

That was more like a long, slow slide. I was about twenty-five and living in Berkeley, California. Eric Shanower [writer and artist of *Age of Bronze*] was a customer at the comic store I worked at in San Diego, and we became friends. He was always real supportive of my stuff. One night he was telling me he was frustrated because he really wanted to draw something contemporary but all his ideas were for things that took place in ancient Egypt or Oz. I offhandedly suggested, 'Well, why don't you let me write something and you draw it?' I remember flipping through one of his books and saying, 'You draw really good midgets. I'll do something that has a midget in it.' I just thought it was a joke, but the next day at lunch he was like, 'Y'know, you really should come up with a story for me.' So I started thinking seriously about it. There had just been this big case in Berkeley of this guy who may or may not have murdered his girlfriend while they were out jogging. I remember thinking about that and thinking about how Eric and I had both lived in Cuba in the '70s, because his dad was in the navy too — he lived there a few years after I did. So I thought, let's do something that takes place in Cuba that centres on a crime.

I wrote up this little one-page pitch that Eric gave to his agent, who sold it to Dark Horse the next day. I actually wrote the whole thing — called *An Accidental Death* — in three days and sent it in. It was a lot of fun seeing someone else draw my stuff, but I still felt like it wasn't my *real* work. The real work was the stuff I wrote and drew myself. But it did fulfil a certain creative vibe and it also got me excited about the whole mainstream side of comics. It got me thinking about other genres and other things I actually wanted to work on, things that I'd never be able to draw myself, even if I wanted to. And then we got nominated for a couple of Eisner Awards and that led to Eric getting me a job writing for Vertigo a year or so later.

And which book was that?

That was *Prez*. I was under the mistaken impression at the time that Vertigo was aimed at teenagers and not at college students and above. So I basically wrote a young adult comic. That was my first DC thing. At that point I was drawing my own comic, working part time jobs, and editor Lou Stathis would call and ask me to pitch projects. I would do a lot of pitches and always end up being told, 'Yours was second or third.' Eventually I just wasn't interested in spending weeks on a proposal and not having anything happen with it. So I gave up and started working at a used book store, reading mystery books all night long. I really started to fall in love with that genre.

Around then, [Vertigo editor] Shelly Roeberg started calling a lot and asking me to do stuff for her. She had been Lou's girlfriend and had taken care of him for the last six or nine months of his life when he was dying from brain cancer. Lou had apparently always said nice things about me, so she really wanted to get me back in with Vertigo. She just kept hammering away at me to give her a proposal. I love Shelly, but she's relentless when she wants something. In my head, I thought there was no way Vertigo was actually going to do anything I wanted to do. So I thought, I'll just pitch whatever I want to do even though I know they're not going to let me do it. I opted for *Scene of the Crime* and limited myself to two days to come up with a proposal and write the whole thing. I sent the pitch in and it was approved by the end of the week. Everything kind of went from there. I met [DC Editor] Mike Carlin when I visited this college in Savannah — they fly a bunch of comic people out every year to talk to the incoming students about the industry. He had read *Scene of the Crime*, loved it, and offered to try to get me some more work at DC. I pitched him [the Elseworlds *Batman* one-shot] *Gotham Noir* the day after I got home and he hooked me up with Sean Phillips, who was already inking *Scene of the Crime*.

So you kept some good friends and continued writing things here and there?

My thing is, whatever job I've had, I've always tried to get into it as much as I can. I've seen a lot of my friends from alternative comics try to break into mainstream comics as writers and I've seen them do the same stumble I did at first. It was thinking that it's not your real work, and not putting as much of yourself into what you're writing for someone else to draw as you put into the stuff you draw yourself. It shows in the final product. It all kind of converged with my deciding that I don't give a shit what *The Comics Journal* has to say about anything. As a teenager it really held sway over me, right up until my mid to late twenties when I realised that being really poor and being able to put out one or two comics a year that barely made any money was really not the life I wanted to lead. Writing was something I was really good at and it came really easily to me. But drawing

Age of Bronze

Who needs Brad Pitt when you've got Eric Shanower? The comics writer/artist has embarked on an epic crusade to tell the entire story of the Trojan War in comic book form. Published by Image Comics, *Age of Bronze* kicked off its lengthy tale in 1998. Drawing from the earliest sources of Greek mythology to modern archaeological finds, Shanower has mixed in various additions of the story that have accumulated over time. With a fresh and modern take, *Age of Bronze* features the story's familiar cast: Achilles, Agamemnon, Paris, Odysseus and, of course, Helen. It may not be the biggest selling comic around, but with two collected volumes to date (and a projected further five to come), there's been plenty of critical acclaim for the San Diego native and his epic story, not to mention a steady flow of academics falling over themselves to praise its authenticity. Previously, Shanower made a name for himself by teaming up with writer Ed Brubaker on 'An Accidental Death', the Eisner Award-nominated mystery based in Cuba that was originally published in *Dark Horse Presents* #65-67 and later collected by Fantagraphics. He's also illustrated numerous graphic novels based on the series of Oz books by L. Frank Baum, as well as various other guest spots around the industry.

was something that didn't come easily to me. So I started thinking, I like other genres too, that automatically dismissing mainstream or whatever takes all the fun out of everything. I had spent a good twelve years without even looking at mainstream comics at all, other than a roommate who was into *Sandman* or something, so I'd read some of that.

Would you actually call *Sandman* mainstream?

Maybe not now, but at the time I considered it mainstream, coming, as I did, from an almost Catholic school of alternative comics where if it was in colour, it was bad. At some point I just made a mental switch to, 'If I'm having fun doing something, someone's paying me well to do it and I'm good at it, then it's either that or working at a gas station. And real work is for suckers.' I'm much more satisfied as a writer now and a lot more accomplished than when I was a cartoonist, where I was constantly procrastinating because I was never really happy with the end product.

Do you find your current company work as creatively fulfilling as your own?

Yeah, in different ways. I wish I owned more of it. And sometimes it gets tiring writing a company-owned character when you have ideas for them and the company tells you no. It's not something you ever encounter when you're drawing your own comic. I've been really lucky that for the most part I've gotten to work with really good artists and I've worked with editors who really understand what I'm doing and just let me do my own thing. It's been satisfying. What I've learned as a writer is that you have so many different creative urges. If you're reading a lot of sci-fi, you'll feel that you really want to do some sci-fi. And if you're reading a lot of crime, you'll have ideas for stuff like that. I've found that the more reading I do, the more urges I get to do other kinds of writing. Lately I've been feeling inclined towards writing essays for magazines.

Do you adopt a different approach with your writing now compared to your comics from the alternative days?

Not that different, honestly. You have to lie to yourself when you're working on the company-owned characters, convince yourself that they're your characters while you're working on them. Which is why I think that writing Catwoman is much easier than writing Batman. There's only one Catwoman comic, but with Batman there's something like eight Batman comics a month coming out. I was always really careful when I was writing *Batman* and then *Detective* that whatever I was doing didn't step on anyone else's toes. I think I worried too much about everything outside instead of just focusing on my book and acting like mine was the most important Batman book. On the whole, my process is still the same, letting the character build the story.

Will you ever write any more heroic characters like Superman or Green Lantern?

I don't know. Probably not Superman, because I never really cared for the character at all. Even as a kid, I always thought Superman was totally — I want to say gay, but I don't mean like gay gay, I mean gay like lame. [*Laughs*] And yet I always loved the *Jimmy Olsen* and *Lois Lane* comics, which were probably far more 'gay'. I thought those were much more interesting, like the *Lois Lane* issue where she takes a pill and becomes black. I read tons of superhero comics. I mean, *Captain America* and *Iron Fist* were my favourite Marvel comics, more so than, say, *Spider-Man*. It really just depends on the character and what ideas I have for them. So far it's been easiest for me to adapt the things I enjoy about my writing for the less superhero-oriented superheroes. But I am writing *The Authority* now, which is about as superpowered as you can possibly get. And that's been a total blast.

What did you find appealing about *The Authority*?

One of the coolest things about *The Authority* — that was more of a subtext when Warren Ellis was writing it — is that it was basically a black comedy making fun of superheroes, and when Mark Millar took over it that aspect came more to the forefront. It was like, okay, now we're not just making fun of superhero comics but we're making fun of *you* for even reading them. So I was looking at that angle, and I had been talking to friends about all the new comics that were coming out either from Marvel or DC, and how they were really just new versions of everything that had come before. Maybe because the fan base is so much older than it used to be, and there's this incessant desire to touch upon everything from the past. It feels like we're constantly looking back: what have we done before? How can we do

Gotham Central

Ever wonder what life on the streets was really like in Gotham City? Sure, it seems somewhat romantic from the Dark Knight's perspective, swooping in to bust heads and scare the living daylights out of cowardly, superstitious criminals. But what about the little guy? What about the poor souls who are out there patrolling the streets every single day and night to ensure your safety? They've got no Batarangs or utility belts or gazillions of dollars to throw around in their war on crime. Nope, they're just average cops trying to make it through another day in Gotham. Think television's *NYPD Blue*, only set in Batman's world with the Caped Crusader making rare appearances. That's the thrust of DC's *Gotham Central* series co-written by crime writer-aficionados Ed Brubaker and Greg Rucka (who alternate story arcs). Formerly just a bunch of generic cops, the Gotham City Police Department's Major Crimes Unit is suddenly filled with real people that you can grab a hold of, like Detective Marcus Driver, who sees Mr. Freeze brutally murder his partner, or the basic clerk Stacy, whose high-point of the day is to switch on the Bat-signal. With hard-boiled mysteries and deep characterisation, *Gotham Central* is chock full of characters that breathe. Unless they're bumped off, of course.

PAGE FIVE

Craig's car pulls into an entrance on a tall cement wall that surrounds some trees and a house in the distance. It's like a country estate.

> NARR(Slam): An hour later, he arrives at his country house, upstate.

We're watching through some trees as Craig opens the trunk of the car and gets out a shovel.

> NARR(Slam): I follow on foot, and when I see him taking out a shovel, I know my hunch
>
> was on the money.

Craig, his coat off, and his sleeves rolled up, is about waist deep in a hole, digging with his shovel. He's been digging for a while. His car is about ten feet away, the headlights shining through the trees to illuminate the spot he's digging.

> NARR(Slam): I give him an hour, then I make a call on my cell-phone.

Close on Craig, digging. He's just stopping, looking down.

From his POV, we see his wife's face, wrapped in plastic, looking up at us from under the dirt. She looks ugly and long dead.

Craig looks sad.

> SLAM(off-panel): You got a few minutes of *freedom* left, Craig...

He looks up from his hole to see Slam leaning against a tree, lighting a cigarette. Totally cool Robert Mitchum pose. Craig looks shocked.

> SLAM: ...Wanna use them to explain *why* you killed your wife?
>
> CRAIG: *What*? Bradley?
>
> CRAIG: But – But – You said –

PAGE SIX

Javier, I'm numbering these panels because I want you to see what I'm picturing. I see the next two pages as both having three tiers. On the first tier of this page, we have three panels, then the next two tiers have two panels each, like traditional old comics.
1–Close on Slam.

> SLAM: Just wanted to see what you'd *do* if you thought the coast was clear. Figured it'd
>
> be something like this.
>
> SLAM: Move the body *off* your property. Dump it somewhere no one'll ever find it.

2–Craig's shoulders give in. He's defeated.

> CRAIG: I'm *that* predictable, am I?
>
> SLAM: I just had a hunch. Now *spill it*, Craig... *Why*?

3–Craig sits down on the edge of the hole, looking miserable.

> CRAIG: You just – You have to see it from *my* point of view, Mr. Bradley...

4–Now we go into a short flashback sequence, as Craig narrates the story. These panels should be like old EC crime comics if you can pull it off (There's a reason the client is named Johnny Craig, after all). The first panel is Craig, working behind a stack of papers at his desk. An old man overwhelmed by life.

> VOICE-OVER BOX: "...You're an old man who life has passed by a long time since. The
>
> only thing you've got is wealth...

Above: *Ed Brubaker script page from* Catwoman *#19, adopting a slightly different style, allowing the artist greater latitude in the page layout. Compare page five with Javier Pulido's layouts, opposite. Courtesy of Ed Brubaker.*

Above: *Javier Pulido's layout of* Catwoman #19, *page five, working from Ed Brubaker's outline, opposite. Courtesy of Ed Brubaker.*

that again and still keep it interesting or make people think it's new? I thought I'd really like to play that up, maybe even use *The Authority* to make some kind of statement about how we've got with comics. Whether it's a very deep one or not, we'll see. I don't think that it necessarily has to be.

How's it going so far?

I've written the first issue, and I'm halfway through the second one. It's interesting. I turned in my first script and the editor, Scott Dunbier, told me, 'Your first page isn't a splash page. *The Authority* always has the first page as a splash page.' And I'm like, 'Well it doesn't anymore.' And it also read 'Part 1 of 12'. So he said, 'It's not going to be three different storylines?' And I'm like, 'No, it's not going to be three different arcs. It's going to be one big twelve-issue thing that has a three-act structure. And each act is sort of self-contained, but it's not going to be three four-issue storylines.' So it's even interesting to play around with the basic structure. The truth is, if Warren hadn't done such a great job in the beginning, I would've never wanted to do the book. He and Mark both left so much to explore in all those characters. It seems like they defined them just enough to make the overall super-arc work without really getting too much into their background and history. So there's really still a lot left to be said about those characters.

More than pretty much any other writer, you really put yourself on the line for your work. You actually arm-wrestled fans as part of a *Sleeper* in-store signing. Was that your idea?

The guy who runs the store, the guy who put on the party at the Isotope in San Francisco, it was more his idea. He had just had Joe Casey in there for a signing and Joe had done readings of his own material in the voices of William Shatner and Elmer Fudd. So this guy said to me, 'You need to have something about this that makes it more than just an in-store appearance or a signing. It's gotta be more of a party.' And I jokingly said, 'What if I arm-wrestled people? If anybody buys the book, I'll arm wrestle them.' And he really loved that and went and promoted the hell out of it. I had no idea when I said it that I'd have to arm-wrestle over fifty people. I couldn't work for a week and a half after that, my arms were totally shot! A lot of people did show up. He sold over a hundred copies of the *Sleeper* trade that way.

The way the industry is right now, you really have to put yourself out there to get more attention for your book, especially if you're doing something that's not Batman, Superman or X-Men. Once the first few issues of *Sleeper* actually come out and I saw the response they were getting I got incredibly depressed about how poorly it was selling. I was worried it was going to be cancelled before we hit #12. I had no idea that Jim [Lee] would decide that, of the comics WildStorm had published in the last few years, it was his favourite and he really wanted to go to the line for it no matter what.

Having Jim Lee behind the book certainly can't hurt.

No, not when he's DC's top-selling artist and the guy who runs WildStorm. I love that. [*Laughs*] In the long run, the attention mainly paid off for the trade paperback. What drove me crazy was that every time an issue would come out, I'd get thirty or forty emails from fans who couldn't find the issue anywhere. Their store would sell out the day the book came out. There's demand for this book that's not being met because the industry is set up really backwards. Before a book ever comes out, its success is judged. If retailers don't order enough copies, that's pretty much it.

How organised and focused a writer are you?

A lot less than I need to be. I used to be very, very organised about work, but what I found happens with me is I'll go through stints where I'm getting a ton of work done and I'm very organised about everything, and then I'll do something stupid like take on a side project because I think I have enough time to do something extra on top of what I'm doing. And that throws a huge wrench into everything because the side projects are inevitably more fun. I kind of allot one week to each thing: do the outline on Monday or Tuesday and then write the whole comic on Wednesday, Thursday and Friday. But I often end up having to work through the weekend. The last six months or so has been a period of playing catch up, and over the next three or four months I'm just trying to get really far ahead on all the books.

The only problem with writing monthly episodic comics is that even if you're not one hundred percent sure you want to do what you need to do that month in

Sleeper

Ed Brubaker must be prophetic. How else can you explain the fact that the writer's sleeper-hit comic of 2003 was called *Sleeper*? Published by WildStorm, the conspiracy-filled title stars Holden Carver, a deep-cover agent with a rather unique superpower: he doesn't feel pain. Instead, he can actually store any pain or trauma and then pass it on to others — kind of like a pain battery. Disguised as the Conductor, Holden infiltrates a metahuman criminal organisation headed by the ruthless criminal mastermind Tao (a character originally dreamt up by Alan Moore). The only problem? His real boss, master spy John Lynch, is stuck in a coma, and Lynch is the only person alive that knows Carver's really a good guy. With artwork by Sean Phillips, the first volume of *Sleeper* was just that... a sleeper. The book constantly sold out, received critical and fan acclaim, and yet was routinely under-ordered. Fans continued to rave about it, while at the same time screaming bloody murder that they couldn't find a copy of the latest issue. Thankfully, WildStorm didn't just look at sales numbers, and stuck with the book long enough for two collections to make an impact and for *Sleeper* to truly wake up.

that comic, you kind of have to turn it in anyway. Sometimes you wake up in the morning, sit down and you can't write. You look at the thing and you look at your outline and it doesn't seem right, it just doesn't fit. And you can't force it. You try and you'll end up with bad comics. I find I go through these real bursts of energy where I'll write two or three comics over the course of a couple of weeks, and then I'll take a few days out to just drive around, go to the movies or read some books. Kind of recharge my batteries.

What I try to do is get up around 8am, read for a little while and look at some online news sites. If I've got the outline written for the week, then I can sit down and start working right away and work through till lunch. Usually if it's a good day, I'll knock off around 3. That's what my actual schedule is supposed to be. But if I don't have the outline written, oftentimes on Monday or Tuesday I just kind of dawdle around the house staring at the walls or seeing what TIVO's recorded. So a lot of times Monday and Tuesday are really wasted and Wednesday through Friday are ten-hour long days. Whatever doesn't get done then, I end up working late at night on Saturday and Sunday.

Do you have an office at home?

Yeah, I have an office in my house. Since I live on a farm, it's kind of weird because there are days when I never even leave the house. I'll just get up and put on my slippers and go into my office and be there until like 4 o'clock in the afternoon.

Do you write full script?

Oh yeah, totally. Well it depends on the artist too. When I wrote for Javier Pulido and when I write for Jason Lutes, I don't do panel breakdowns, I just break down a page and write everything that needs to happen on that page. It's almost more like a screenplay. Then I let them break down the action. The most fun for a lot of these guys is the storytelling. When I first started writing comics, I would do breakdowns of how I saw the action with little thumbnails, because I still think as a cartoonist when I write this stuff. Then I found that the best artists I worked with didn't want someone else to do that part of the work for them. That was the fun part. The actual mechanical part of drawing all the cars and buildings and everything was the least fun part, the stuff they just do because that's the job.

How about doing research for your comics?

I read a whole hell of a lot of true crime and watch a lot of TV shows, all the behind-the-scenes of how crimes are solved. I've gone on a couple of ride-alongs with police. I've actually been in the process for the last few months of trying to get permission to spend time with the local sheriff's department detective unit, but they're real reluctant to let writers be around them because they're worried that you might be a journalist and not a writer of fiction. Most of it is just reading. Greg Rucka has a lot of connections, people he knows who work in the police department and the FBI, so if I ever need some kind of real detail that I can't find online or in any books, I'll call him. Usually, within a day or two, he'll have the answer for me. That's why I want to start doing more of that hands-on stuff myself, so I don't have to rely on Greg to do my research for me.

But I also draw on my background growing up. As a teenager I was kind of a scumbag; after we came home from Cuba I grew up in San Diego and that was a big drug town at the time. When I was in high school we were all really into speed, and I was like a minor league dealer. So I lived around the edges of criminal society for maybe three or four years. I've done some things I'm totally not proud of, but you can't escape what you've done in your life, so I look at that time and take creative inspiration from it. I think almost any good crime writer is somebody who sees the angles. You're in a store and you're thinking about how these employees are totally ripping this place off. I'm always spotting people stealing from work. Having been a person who's stolen from work in the past, I can spot it easily when someone's not actually ringing up my sale. I think part of the fun of crime writing for me is figuring out how you can commit a crime without actually doing it.

What tips would you give to aspiring writers?

The best tip probably would be if you want to write for DC or Marvel or anybody, you have to really be writing for yourself. All the stuff I wrote that got me noticed was stuff that I did because I had something I wanted to express. Just show that you can write characters and write stories. I remember talking to Mike Carlin the first time I met him and saying, 'I don't know if a lot of my skills would apply to DC Universe type of work.' He said, 'Well, *Scene of the Crime* is a great mystery. If you can write mysteries, you can write Batman.' And it never even occurred to me up till that point that he was right. I think a lot of it is really just making the right connections, just like in any business. But once you make that connection, you also have to have the talent and the skill to back it up. So it's a combination of things.

The best advice would be, if you want to write comics, write a story and be willing to put your money where your mouth is. And find someone who's a good enough artist to actually draw the thing. The plain fact is, you can't look at a comic script and tell if they're any good or not. If Eric Shanower hadn't drawn 'An Accidental Death', a lot of people might not have thought it was very good. They might have thought it was really overwritten. Because looking back on it, it kind of is. [*Laughs*] And so is *Scene of the Crime* probably. But it had really small lettering and it had Michael Lark and Sean Phillips doing the art so people read it. If I'm good at anything, it's making people care about characters. I think that's more important than showing me that you know how to write a Superman story. If you can just show you know how to write characters that people are gonna empathise with and want to continue to read about and care about, that's much more important than whether or not you know all of Green Lantern's powers.

*   *   *

MIKE CAREY

No challenge seems too daunting for Mike Carey. With his Vertigo series *Lucifer,* Carey wrangles a main character whose stomping grounds include Heaven, Hell and all of Creation in-between. Not only is the Devil himself a controversial choice for a comic book star (Carey has cheerfully referred to the series as 'The New Adventures of Satan'), but telling original tales with characters birthed by comics giant Neil Gaiman is the surest possible way to invite the rancour of savagely loyal readers. But instead of disaster, *Lucifer* has netted rave reviews as well as several Eisner Award nominations during its run, which is now comfortably past the fifty-issue milestone. Carey hasn't been shy about filling the shoes of other industry legends, taking over the reins of the Alan Moore-created John Constantine in the pages of *Hellblazer,* a character that writers such as Garth Ennis and Warren Ellis have also shepherded. A member of the legion of British writers who passed through UK anthology *2000 AD* on their way to American comics success, Carey's used to following in famous footsteps. But with his talent for weaving jaw-dropping stories on the vastest of scales, it's obvious that before long it'll be Carey's footsteps leading the way.

Was there ever a time when you weren't reading comic books?

I carried on reading comics all the way through high school. And then when I went to university, there was a kind of lull. I lost touch with what was happening in the comics world. Then one day I was walking past a newsagent and I saw a Chris Claremont *X-Men* issue, one of the early ones featuring the Starjammers. I looked at the figures on the cover and recognised almost nobody. I thought, well, *X-Men* seems to have changed beyond all recognition, and out of curiosity I picked it up. I read and enjoyed it, and that got me back into comics again. It was all Chris Claremont's fault.

How long after that fateful *X-Men* issue was it before you decided to write comic books instead of just read them?

A long time, actually. I spent a lot of the '80s trying to write novels — and failing fairly miserably. At that stage I had no concept of planning. I wrote the first chapter and then waited for the second chapter to occur to me. I then wrote the second chapter and more or less carried on until I reached an endpoint. I wrote these huge, sprawling, six and seven hundred page novels that had no structure at all, and then sent them off hopefully to publishers. I occasionally got some positive feedback, but none of them were publishable. It was my wife who said, 'Comics are something that you really love reading. Why don't you try sending in some comic scripts?' And it grew out of that. Someone I knew became the editor of a line of indie comic books, and I pitched some stuff to him.

What was the first comic you actually wrote?

It was something called *The Legions of Hell*. It was accepted for publication but never published. It was a story about a woman with multiple personality syndrome who goes on the run after her husband tries to force her into psycho-surgery; a kind of chemical lobotomy. She believes she is possessed by all the demons in Hell, but it was actually about her relationship with her own inner demons. What she'd done was to segment her personality so that all the different aspects of herself were personified by different demons. When she needed to be angry, she allowed herself to be possessed by the demon who represents her anger, and so on. It was meant to be an eight-issue miniseries, and I wrote three of them. They were accepted for publication by Trident Comics, a comics publishing line set up by the old Neptune Distributors. But they went bankrupt before they published any of them.

How much longer after that until you actually got something published?

I had two stories accepted by Trident. *Legions of Hell* was one of them, and the

Place of birth:
Liverpool, UK
Date of birth:
9 February 1959
Home base:
Barnet, London, UK
First published work:
Aquarius: Promised Land in
Toxic! #30-31
Education:
Oxford University; King's
College, London University
Career highlights:
*Hellblazer, Inferno, Lucifer,
My Faith in Frankie, Wetworks*

other was a superhero story called *Aquarius,* which was very *Watchmen*-esque. I wrote that as a freestanding title, and again they never published it. But they did publish seventeen pages of it in an anthology comic they put out called *Toxic.* So that was the first thing I ever had in print. I never got paid for it, either. [*Laughs*] The cheque bounced.

Legions of Hell doesn't sound so far removed from the themes of your later Vertigo work.

Yeah, it's true. I guess that probably comes from my upbringing. Liverpool is a city where the sectarian divide between Catholics and Protestants is very real and very big in people's lives. It has a very large second, third and fourth-generation Irish immigrant community. There are still, to this day, areas of the city that are Catholic enclaves or Protestant enclaves. My dad was a lapsed Catholic and my mum was Anglican, so I didn't fit in on either side. I grew up surrounded by and immersed in religion but feeling somewhat divorced from it. It's always had a huge emotional hold on me, even though I'm an atheist. I'm a deeply religious atheist. I think my interest in demons and hell comes from those roots.

Which comics influenced you as an up and coming comics writer?

My holy trinity as far as comics writing is concerned is the fairly obvious one of Alan Moore, Grant Morrison and Neil Gaiman. Moore's *Swamp Thing* had a huge impact on me when it first came out. *Swamp Thing* was amazing because Moore was writing horror comics and they were genuinely *horrifying.* They actually left you feeling uneasy; they returned to you in the middle of the night. The images and the ideas in those stories were really scary. Most horror comics just had a twist ending or a story with a lot of implied gore; they were for a quick, cheap thrill and didn't have any real emotional impact. There were moments in *Swamp Thing* that just took the top of your head off. Gaiman's *Sandman* obviously was a huge influence. It's no coincidence that a lot of the work I've done in comics has been playing in Neil's sandbox with Neil's characters. I think he's a superb storyteller who did a lot of things with the medium that hadn't been done before. And Grant Morrison's *Doom Patrol* I still think has got to be the best superhero comic ever produced: anarchic, brilliant, unpredictable, crazy — it's a total and utter mindfuck.

When you read *Sandman* during its initial run, would you think about ways to expand that universe?

No. I mean, I fantasised about it. If someone had asked me then, 'What's your dream job?' I would have said, 'Writing a sequel to *The Sandman.*' But it was only fantasising at that time. The writing I was doing myself at that time was very small, un-ambitious pieces; shorts and things for comics anthologies and so on. So it wasn't a realistic prospect for me.

How long does it take you to write a single issue of a comic book?

It usually takes about a week. That's including half a day to do a page breakdown, which is a discipline I got into through working with [*Lucifer* editor] Shelly Bond, because she always likes to see a scene-by-scene breakdown... before she approves me to go on. Although other editors don't always need that degree of detail, I've found it to be a useful way of making decisions about structure and pacing. So I usually do that first, and it takes two or three hours, maybe half a day. It's a two-stage process after that. Before I write the actual script, I'll rough out the pages. I know other writers do this too; I think Neil Gaiman does it, although he's a much better artist than me. I just do these strange little thumbnail sketches of each page. I drop in the dialogue at that stage as well, or at least the bulk of it. Drawing each panel with stick figures, making a decision about the points of view, what's going to be in the panel and so on, how the panels are going to relate to each other. I do all that before I type a word. That will take about two days or three days. And then the actual typing is fairly quick and mechanical. I can do the typing in about a day and a half or two days.

Do your thumbnails ever get anywhere near the artist?

No, no. They're simply not good enough. Nobody but me could possibly tell what they're pictures of. They're that crude. They're unintelligible scribble. If I'm going into London for a meeting or something, I'll often take my sketchbook with me and I'll be doing this as I'm sitting on the train. People look at me and I'm sure they're thinking, 'What the hell is going on here? Is he an artist? He can't be, he's too bad!'

Neil Gaiman

Had the author of *The Sandman* (and many notable collaborations with artist Dave McKean) simply retired after the completion of his seventy-five-issue masterwork, that would have been career enough for any writer. In *Sandman*, Gaiman completely re-imagined a forgotten DC hero as the Lord of Dreams and created an enduring mythology that has provided a springboard for any number of notable projects, Carey's *Lucifer* being a prime example. But Gaiman hasn't rested on his laurels — and there were many — in his post-*Sandman* career. In addition to a steady output of novels, 2001's hugely acclaimed *American Gods* and *Stardust* among them, Gaiman has penned books for children such as 1998's *The Day I Swapped My Dad for 2 Goldfish* and 2002's *Coraline*. And Gaiman doesn't always leave tinkering with the *Sandman* universe to others: he recently wrote the lushly illustrated graphic novel *The Sandman: Endless Nights*, further expanding upon his creation. The call for Gaiman's talents even extends beyond the printed page — he shaped the English-language translation of Japanese director Hayao Miyazaki's anime classic *Princess Mononoke* for its 1999 American release. Newcomers to Gaiman will of course gravitate to *Sandman*, and rightly so, but there are plenty more strings to his bow.

Could you ever write in the classic 'Marvel style' where you send plots to the artist, then fill in the dialogue afterward?

I'd hate to do that. It just feels wrong, it feels like you're abdicating all control over pacing. It feels like it would lead to flaccid storytelling at some points and unbelievably tight and overstressed storytelling at other points. What I will sometimes do, if I'm working on a particular sequence, is write a note to the artist saying, 'I'm writing this as two separate pages but you can turn it into a spread if you want to.' I'll sometimes throw some decisions back to the artist like that, but it seems to me that the writer has to know where the break points come and how much space is being allocated to each scene. It would just scare me to write in the Marvel style, I think. It'd feel like walking a tightrope without a safety net.

So you're writing panel-by-panel breakdowns?

Yes, it's panel-by-panel. My initial model was Alan Moore, as it was for so many writers of my generation, looking at the published scripts for *Watchmen* and so on. I too also have an anal-retentive personality, and from the outset it seemed quite natural for me, if I was describing two characters drinking coffee, to say what was on the coffee mugs. That wasn't giving the artist any discretion whatsoever. In fact, with those early *Legions of Hell* scripts I actually included maps of the pages with the script to show the panel placement. I even decided how big each image was going to be. [*Laughs*] *Legions of Hell* was offered to Paul Grist [of *Kane* fame] and he turned it down. One of the things that he said to the editor, Martin Skidmore, was, 'Where's the fun in this? I just become a robot if I do this!' Gradually you learn to trust the artist, and you learn that there are certain things that the artist is going to be able to do better than you. And you learn to only specify important details, because if you specify *everything*, then the important details get lost in a welter of complete trivia.

Taking that anal-retentive quality into account, have you ever been unpleasantly — or *pleasantly* — surprised when you see artwork and it's different from what was asked for?

Both. More often, pleasantly surprised. I've had great — and undeserved — good fortune with the artists that I've worked with. I've been really privileged. I've had a few unpleasant surprises. I don't want to name names, but there was a fill-in artist on, um… a *book*… that I was working on, a monthly book. This guy basically had no concept of following the script. It was an absolute nightmare. In two cases, instead of drawing the scene that I'd scripted, he drew a *different* scene that started at the *end* of the scene I'd scripted. I had a police raid on a hotel and it was important that you saw one of these police officers kicking down a door and dragging a character out. Instead what you see is the street outside and a whole bunch of people being filed into a police van. So none of my dialogue fitted! And he would put in what he thought were fantastically artistic details, wonderful symbolic touches, which I hadn't asked for. All the storytelling was fractured out of joint by these crazy little details that weren't contributing at all to the narrative.

PAGE 1 PANEL 1

Tight on the page of an open book. Tight, cramped medieval Latin writing in a German black letter Gothic font. Obviously we only need to see a few lines or even a few words, but something along the lines of the following would work just fine:-

Quis ignorat (sacratissima Maiestas) principalia dona principalibus; principaliora maioribus; et maximis principalissima deberi? Nullus ergo ambigat, cur opus istud, tum nobilitate subiecti circa quod versatur; tum singularitate inuentionis, cui innititur. Tuum est ipsum gratioso animo acceptare, magno fauore tueri, maturoque iudicio examinare: Cum eminenter generosus, potens, atque sapiens videaris.

A hand   the hand of John Constantine, traces the words on the page as he pores over it, translating as he goes. We're looking down on the book as from his POV.

CAPTION: He thought that it would come to them in dreams. But he was wrong.

CAPTION: The dreams were just <u>portents</u>, not symptoms. The symptoms were different.

PAGE 1 PANEL 2

The bedroom of a middle class home somewhere in the USA. A woman in her mid-forties stares down in amazement at a body – male and dead – sprawled on the ground at her feet. She's holding a handgun in both hands, lowered to the level of her abdomen, and she's obviously just shot this man down. He's lying in a spreading pool of his own blood.

CAPTION: There was a woman in Chicago who forgot twenty years of her life.

CAPTION: She shot her husband three times through the chest because she thought he was an intruder coming into their bedroom.

PAGE 1 PANEL 3

A prison cell. A man lies on his bunk, staring at nothing, a trickle of drool running down from the corner of his mouth. Everything in the cell is smashed, wrecked or torn, and there are smears of blood on the walls.

CAPTION: There was a man doing time in a Stuttgart jail who who thought the corners of his cell were going to <u>rape</u> him.

CAPTION: And went from screaming, frenzied paranoia to drooling <u>catatonia</u> within seventeen minutes.

PAGE 1 PANEL 4

A small animal compound   basically just wire mesh enclosures for rabbits and guinea pigs and similar domestic pets. Within the cages we can glimpse the slumped bodies of some of the animals. In front of the cages two policemen are grappling a struggling man to the ground, his face red and contorted as he writhes in their grasp, but his face twisted in an insane, smiling rictus.

CAPTION: Nobody ever did find out what the owner of the Finchley petting zoo thought he was doing.

CAPTION: He swallowed his own tongue and smiled as he suffocated.

Above: *Script page from* Hellblazer *#187. Courtesy of Mike Carey.*

What are your options as a writer when that happens?

I don't know whether this is across the board, but the editors I've worked with at DC are just fantastic in terms of including me in the decision-making. In that case, with the artist I was just talking about, I phoned the editor and said, 'This is utter madness,' and the editor said, 'Yeah, it is a bit weird, isn't it?' Certain pages were subsequently sent back and redone. But that artist was incorrigible and made changes at the inks stage as well, and the comic that was published was still not what I would've wanted it to be. So I exercised my ultimate discretion and said, 'I don't want to work with this guy again.' But [*Lucifer* artist] Peter Gross and I are entirely comfortable with each other, and he'll sometimes depart from the script because he's a great visual storyteller, and can often think of ways of achieving what I want, even if it's not exactly what I specified on the page. Sometimes he'll phone me up and say, 'How about if we do this?' But sometimes he'll just go ahead and do the pencils. There's never been a point where I've thought, 'That traduces my original idea.' Usually I just think, 'Fuck, why didn't I think of that?'

What's your work environment like?

Chaotic. Until very recently, my desk was in the living room of my house, which meant that after 3 o'clock in the afternoon I had the kids running around. The TV's in the room, the game console's in the room — there were a great many distractions. I just recently refurbished what used to be a garden shed into a kind of office/studio space. I work there now, and it's much better, because it feels like I'm clocking in. When I go there, I go there to work, and I work solidly until I clock off again. It's more productive, I think, to keep work and home as separate as you can.

Do you listen to music? Or do you require total silence?

I'll sometimes put music on. But I have to be careful, because what I like best about music is interesting lyrics. If I put music with good lyrics on, then I start focusing on the words and it puts me off my stroke. Generally speaking, I'll just put on a couple of tracks because I feel in the mood for a certain band, but then I'll turn it off again and work in silence for a while. I can't have too much going on around me while I'm working. It just slows me down.

Is writer's block ever a problem for you?

Umm... [*Knocks*] Touch wood, it hasn't been so far, no. I can always come up with ideas. What I'm afraid of, what I'm obsessively afraid of, is something that I've observed in other writers, where eventually you end up recycling the same ideas. You don't realise it, but you end up becoming a sort of pastiche of yourself. I'm not desperately scraping around for new ideas, but I'm always trying to find new ways of telling stories. I try to find different angles to cover the characters from. I'm scared of finding that I'm suddenly trapped in a little pool, recycling the same ideas over and over.

Any deadline trouble?

Not usually, no. There was one occasion when I had to write two issues of *Lucifer* side-by-side in the same week because both Peter and Dean [Ormston] had run out of pages. They both needed work to be fed through to them. I would write a few pages of one issue and then I'd jump to the other issue and write a few pages of that. And that was *really* stressful. [*Laughs*] But generally speaking I'm good at meeting deadlines. I don't think I've ever missed a deadline. And usually I'm a few days ahead of deadline. Again, because of this anally retentive streak that I have, if a deadline's approaching, I just work longer hours. Not working quite through the night, but through most of the night.

Vertigo seems to give writers a lot of freedom, but have you ever wanted to tell a story they wouldn't allow?

I've never been blocked from telling a story, but I'm occasionally censored. There was an issue of *Lucifer* which has a punk band, and I had them singing the lyrics 'George fucking Bush married Tony fucking Blair/The church was made of corpses and the cake was pubic hair,' or something like that. They just changed the names. Instead of George Bush and Tony Blair, they made it something like Bob Rush and Tony Glare, or something. I thought that was pretty weird. It wasn't even a political statement, it was just a piece of nonsense. In *Lucifer: Nirvana,* as it was originally written, there was a scene at the end where the angel Perdissa brings down a 747 on Tiananmen Square, on the Tiananmen Gate. And 9/11 happened while Jon J. Muth was painting that sequence. We had to ditch it and write an alternate scene. But that was perfectly understandable. None of us would have been comfortable if it had gone ahead as originally planned. I very seldom feel constrained in any way at Vertigo.

What qualities do you wish for in an editor?

There are two kinds of bad editor, it seems to me. One is the type who will do nothing, who will just take the script and be a sort of black hole and give you no feedback whatsoever. The other kind of bad editor makes changes for the sake of them, just to prove that they were there. They feel as though they're not doing their job unless they've somehow left a thumbprint on the work, but they're really not thinking hard enough about the script to have a good impact. All their changes are nuisance changes. There was an editor I worked with very early on in my career whose changes would be mind-bogglingly trivial. Like, I had a phone number on the side of a van in one panel, and he said, 'That's the old London phone number. The London phone numbers have changed now. Shall I change it?' And that was his only comment on the script.

A good editor brings out the best in you. With my *Lucifer* and *Hellblazer* scripts, if I look at the first draft and the final published version, I can actually see how the editorial process has worked to fine-tune and to hone the effect I was trying to create. In some cases, early on with *Lucifer,* I would go through four or five drafts. Now Shelly and I have got a really good rhythm going. It's one draft and a polish, basically. To begin with, we had to work really hard to learn each other's methods and each other's rhythms, to the point where now Shelly's interventions will occur at a much earlier stage in the process, at the page breakdown stage or the overview stage. I also do overviews for Will Dennis, on *Hellblazer,* and it's been a long time since I had major structural rewrites to do on a script. We've done all the hard work up front.

Is it rare for your Vertigo editors to tweak dialogue?

Not all that rare, no. One thing that continually dogs me is that I don't always realise that certain expressions are British English rather than American English. And so I'll have a character say something that they wouldn't say in real life, because they're American characters. I'm fortunate, though, because all my editors are Americans and they always pick up on that. When Brian Azzarello was writing *Hellblazer,* he was an American writer and he had an American editor, and so some of his dialogue for John went through unchallenged. It sounded a little odd to begin with, but then he got his ear in. I've also been censored for bad language a couple of times. You're still not allowed to use the 'c' word, even in Vertigo scripts.

Of course, when I use The Endless as characters — we had Death in *Lucifer* #25 and #26 — that dialogue had to be passed through Neil, because he's still

---

Lucifer

Horns, pitchforks and cloven hooves have been the stuff of satanic storytelling for centuries, but there's only one Lucifer Morningstar, as created by Neil Gaiman. Equal parts chilling and charming, Gaiman's fallen angel first appeared in the pages of *The Sandman* #4 in 1989. Morpheus, after a long imprisonment, goes on a quest to recover the tools of his trade. To locate one of these, his helmet, he must venture into Hell itself, and this is where readers are first introduced to Lucifer. The Lord of Dreams bests Lucifer and retrieves his helmet, but Lucifer takes a rather wicked revenge later in the series. In the *Season of Mists* storyline, Lucifer literally closes down Hell and quits as its boss. And, for a kicker, Lucifer sticks Morpheus with the key to Hell, giving him the enormous headache of choosing the next owner of the underworld. As he goes, Lucifer clips his wings and ends up, of all places, running a Los Angeles piano bar called Lux. This is where he remains until Carey's series begins, and Lucifer agrees to undertake a new mission on God's behalf. A huge critical success with a devoted following, Carey's *Lucifer* has grown wings of its own and flown.

concerned, obviously, that when The Endless are used, they're used properly, and they're convincing and authentic. There's one line that I'd written for Death that he asked me to change. I had Lucifer saying to Death, 'You have no claim on me,' and she says, 'I never said I did. I wouldn't have anywhere to put you, anyway.' And Neil pointed out that Death doesn't have a realm. She doesn't have a Land of the Dead where she puts people. The comment didn't mean anything, so I changed that. But apart from that, he was happy to let the dialogue stand.

What kind of feedback do you get from Neil on *Lucifer*? Is it a regular, ongoing thing?

No, not at all. At least not anymore. Basically, Neil told Shelly he's content to let me run with the characters. He doesn't feel like he needs to be looking over my shoulder anymore. Early on, he had a lot of input, both into the first-year plan and into the early scripts, but never intrusive and never in a way that was threatening or unpleasant for me.

What kinds of stories work best for the Lucifer character?

I think you have to be careful with what you allow Lucifer to do. It's hard to put Lucifer into an action scene, because he's certainly not a character who would ever roll his sleeves up and trade blows with anybody. If you get on Lucifer's nerves, you're dead; you just cease to exist. There have been some storylines in which he's played an active role, but generally speaking it's other characters who are doing that stuff and Lucifer is either an observer or he's someone who's set things in motion to begin with. Or he's someone who steps in at the end and stops whatever's in progress.

You can have a story where Lucifer's involved in the action but he's not having to do anything. In 'The House of Windowless Rooms' you have all these incredible machinations with Izanami and her children trying to murder him in various ways that fit in with their tortuous rules of etiquette. And you've got Lucifer always seeing through what they're trying to do and turning it around on them. But there's very little overt action. The character is only one step short of omnipotent, and therefore when Lucifer acts, it's decisively. He's not a foot soldier. He's not even a general, he's the guy above the general.

Do you feel like readers are on Lucifer's side?

Yeah, very much so. He's like Richard III. You recognise that he's a villain, but when you're watching him, you're rooting for him. It doesn't matter how objectionable the things he does are. He is quite easy to sympathise with. I think there are various reasons for that. One is because ultimately, this is a family saga. The central relationship in *Lucifer* is the relationship between Lucifer and God. And that's a father-son relationship. Lucifer is the son who wants to, in a way, become his own author, his own progenitor. He wants to write his own life, write his own story, and he can't. He can't break free of his father's influence. And we've all, I think, to some extent or another, been through that moment in our relationship with our parents.

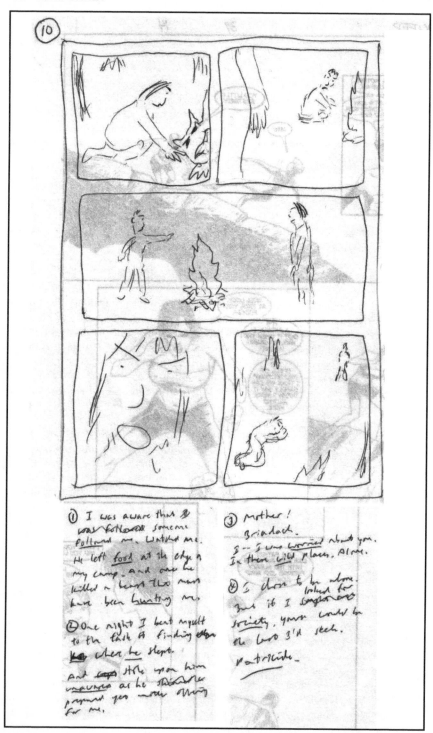

Above: *Mike Carey's thumbnails for page 10 of* Lucifer #56. *Courtesy of Mike Carey.*

Mike Carey
Script: Ultimate Elektra #1, draft2

PAGE 18 PANEL 1

Back to Leander's apartment. Elektra has come inside and both Paul and Leander face her. Leander is distinctly annoyed, and only staying polite because this is both a young girl and a family member. His expression is stern. Paul watches Elektra with the same lecherous interest as before. Bruno stands by as usual, awaiting orders. Elektra is trying to be conciliatory: she holds up her hands, palms out, in either a plea or a "hold it" gesture. She looks anxious and sincere.

LEANDER: Elektra, this is a business address. I gave it to your father, not to you.

LEANDER: And right now is not a convenient - -

ELEKTRA: I'm sorry. I'll be really quick, I promise.

PAGE 18 PANEL 2

Tight on Elektra. She speaks with quiet dignity and seriousness, making her pitch. She knows she's got nothing much to bargain with so she just lays her cards on the table.

ELEKTRA: I want to take over my Dad's debt. I'm going to get a job.

ELEKTRA: I can probably pay you two hundred or three hundred dollars a month.

PAGE 18 PANEL 3

Two-shot on Paul and Leander. Paul just grins, really amused by this. Leander is astonished, disbelieving, affronted.

LEANDER: Is this - - is this a joke, Elektra?

LEANDER: I'm not in the mood for jokes. Go. I'll talk to your father about this.

PAGE 18 PANEL 4

Two-shot on Leander and Elektra. She stays put, more stubborn and dogged now but still painfully earnest. She really needs to convince him. He is still staring at her in a mixture of perplexity and exasperation.

ELEKTRA: No, I mean it. It's making him sick. He can't live like this.

LEANDER: I'm not going to discuss it. Not with a child.

ELEKTRA: Well I'm not leaving until you do.

PAGE 18 PANEL 5

Close-up on Leander's face. He scowls, his patience at an end.

LEANDER: Bruno.

LEANDER: Put her outside, and close the door.

Above: *Script page for* Ultimate Elektra #1. *Courtesy of Mike Carey/Marvel Comics. Used with permission.*
Ultimate Elektra ™ & © 2004 Marvel Characters, Inc.

Every so often I think it's necessary, because Lucifer is a charismatic character and an attractive character in a perverse way, to remind the readers of exactly how big a bastard he is. And how far it goes beyond an attractive roguery. He's not a rogue, he's a monster. I said at a convention somewhere that he's the kind of guy who would set the world on fire to light his cigarette. He simply doesn't have any use for other people's needs. Other people don't figure in his moral universe except as tools to be used. At the end of *Lucifer* #35, that's the realisation that Solomon has. He suddenly has this vision of an intelligence so cold that it sees the entire universe as a toolbox.

When you took over *Hellblazer*, did you feel free to make the book your own right away, or were you concerned about maintaining the status quo?

I'd been a *Hellblazer* fan from day one, so I was steeped in the continuity. I love John Constantine as a character, I think he's one of the greats, and I didn't want to drag him off in a radical new direction. In many ways, what I wanted to do was to restate what I thought were the core values of the book and the character. Brian Azzarello had, I think very successfully, redefined the nature of the book during his run. He wrote great stories in which magic and the supernatural played very, very little part. He was more interested in John as a man who steps out of the shadows into stressful, tense, dangerous situations, ignites them, and then walks back into the shadows. I wanted to put the magic back, because I like John as the laughing magician. I decided to take *Hellblazer* back in that direction, and in doing so I brought back some of the supporting cast from earlier runs, particularly from Warren Ellis' very brief stint on the book. Some people felt that I'd gone too far in terms of incorporating old continuity. On one of the newsgroups I was accused of writing '*Hellblazer* fan-fiction', which I thought was ridiculous. It's important, I think, that when you join a book with that much history behind it, you're respectful of the history. It doesn't mean you can't do new things, but you do it having some awareness of the base that's already there.

What advice do you have for up-and-coming writers?

I think the most important advice is just: if you want to be a writer, write. Endlessly. Just keep on doing it. Because it's one of the many things in life that you get better at by doing it. Someone once said to me that there are three mistakes that a writer can make when they start out: they can aim too high, aim too low or not aim at all. Aiming too high is like sending your first movie screenplay to Steven Spielberg and saying, 'Maybe we can do business.' Aiming too low is writing fanzine stuff and doing it year after year because it's safe and familiar and you're scared of rejection, or whatever. And not aiming at all was the mistake that I made. You send your stuff off to people but you never do any research, so you're sending it to the wrong people. You're narrowing your chances of success, and in some cases, completely eliminating your chances of success.

I blush to say this, but the first pitches I ever sent to DC, I sent to Karen Berger, and they were superhero pitches. This is after Vertigo had been set up.

She had absolutely no point of contact with the DC Universe and no interest in Superman and Batman stories, which is what I was sending her. I just hadn't bothered to think things through or to do the proper research. So know your market. Ideally, know the editors that you're sending your stuff to as well as just the companies that you're sending your stuff to. Look at the books that they're already working on and think about what material you've got that would possibly attract their interest or strike them as worth following up. Check out submission guidelines. Get everything *technically* correct. Take great care about spelling, take great care about paragraphing, and page formatting, and headers and footers and so on. If it doesn't look professional, you may find that it doesn't even get read. If it looks sloppy and amateurish, you could be a genius and still be passed over.

What strikes you as bad comic book writing? Can you give us some examples?

I'm fairly obsessed about dialogue. It pisses me off if I read a book where nobody has a voice, or rather, where everybody has the same voice. I hate clunky exposition. I hate one character saying to another, 'As you probably already know...' and then going into a long spiel about stuff that nobody would ever say in real life. I guess I hate clichés being trotted out without thought. For example, a story that starts with a slow zoom-in, where you see a scene in long shot, and then you gradually zoom in on some characters or on a specific object or whatever, but not particularly because it's a good way of introducing those characters or that object, it's just because the writer's seen

Hellblazer

The 'laughing magician', *Hellblazer*'s John Constantine, has been scripted by a gaggle of writers over his long and storied Vertigo career. Originally the creation of Alan Moore as a secondary character in *Swamp Thing*, Constantine got his shot at stardom in 1987 when Jamie Delano started writing him in an ongoing series. Three years later, with the character well established, Delano exited. *Hellblazer* passed briefly through the hands of Grant Morrison and Neil Gaiman before up-and-coming writer Garth Ennis took over the book (eventually aided and abetted by *Preacher* collaborator, artist Steve Dillon). Delano's cerebral take gave way to Ennis' more grounded, brawling style. Next up, Paul Jenkins swung the title back towards the psychological, a marked departure from Ennis' bone-crunching approach. Warren Ellis followed Jenkins with a brief run that was aborted when he resigned from the book in protest; DC had squashed an Ellis story about school violence they deemed too controversial in the wake of the Columbine shootings in Littleton, Colorado. Brian Azzarello took up the reins after Ellis and injected a healthy amount of dirt and grit into Constantine's trials and travails during his sizeable run. Finally, in 2001, the character passed into the capable hands of Carey.

it done in a movie and thinks it works okay. Usually it's not an effective device. It can be, in the right hands, but generally speaking it's slow and it's clunky and it takes far too much space up on the page. I'm also not a big fan of what's come to be called the 'decompressed' school of storytelling, like fight scenes that take eighteen pages. They just put me to sleep. Just as I listen to music mainly for the lyrics, I guess I read comic books more for the words than for anything else. I like a convincing tone in dialogue. I like clever dialogue. Warren Ellis' *Transmetropolitan* was a book that I adored because it was just so wittily and so sharply written. And Gaiman's *Sandman*, because it's so poetic and resonant.

Would you like to write comic books that aren't quite so serious?

One of my recent books, *My Faith in Frankie*, is a romantic comedy. And it was enormously rewarding. It was a hell of a lot of fun to write comedy. I'd never done that before. There were comic touches in some of the *Lucifer* stories, particularly in *Lucifer* #28, the Gaudium story. But to write a book that was just meant to be flat-out funny and lighthearted was a great new departure for me and I got a hell of a lot of fulfilment out of it.

What books or characters would you still like to take a crack at someday?

Technically, I have done a Batman story — I did a short for *Batman: Black & White* — but it would be nice to do a proper Batman story that had some room to breathe, because he's such an iconic character. Everybody's got one Batman story in them. If it were possible, and I know it's not possible, I'd love to do some stories with Grant's *Doom Patrol* characters. Probably if anybody resurrected that team it would be Grant. He'd probably have to do it himself. But that would be something I'd get a lot of pleasure out of. I have a slight yen to do some of the Marvel team books. The Fantastic Four or the Avengers would be fun to play with because they're such great characters. The JLA, ditto.

Would a *Batman* or *X-Men* comic in your hands follow the same themes as your other work? Free will versus predestination in *Lucifer*, for example?

I'd like to think that it wouldn't. Obviously, in a way, everything you write has got your worldview built into it. But when you take over a continuity book, especially one that's got that much history behind it... you don't start trying to turn it into something else. You bring your vision and your perspective to it. But you don't hijack it. Those themes you described, predestination and free will, they arise out of Lucifer's story because of who Lucifer is, and they also happen to be things that I'm fascinated by. In that case, the story and the characters go hand-in-hand. If you try to use Batman as a vehicle to tell a story that has no point of contact with the character but just ties into your pet obsessions, I think that's probably a very bad way to approach the craft of storytelling.

You're working on a novel again. How have your years of writing comics changed the way you tackle a novel?

Writing comics is the best possible discipline, I think, for any other kind of narrative writing. Every comic is a separate story. And you've only got a hundred and twenty images or a hundred and twenty beats to tell that story in, so you're focused on the bare bones all the time. There's no room for fat, there's no room for self-indulgence in comics. Some of the hardest storytelling I've done was in the *Future Shock*s I wrote for *2000 AD*. They're five pages long. The first page, because you've got to have the titles, has a maximum of five panels. The remaining pages have a maximum of six panels. So you've got to tell an entire story in twenty-nine beats. Andy Diggle once said to me, if you can do a good *Future Shock,* you can do anything.

*   *   *

ANDY DIGGLE

No matter how high Andy Diggle rises in the world of American comics — which looks to be plenty high indeed — his career is forever entwined with *2000 AD*. The British sci-fi comics anthology (home to totalitarian future cop Judge Dredd, and breeding ground for a host of hot UK creators) sparked Diggle's imagination as an impressionable London youth and employed him as an adult, where he capped his tenure with a memorable run as, first, assistant editor and then full editor. After a brief foray into *Hellblazer* territory with a *Lady Constantine* mini-series, Diggle signed exclusively to DC Comics, and he and his rapid-fire, smash-'em-up thrill ride *The Losers* have been netting raves from industry insiders and mainstream press alike. A smartly woven caper book forever jumping from head rush to head rush, *The Losers* staked Diggle's claim on the US comics market. From there, DC entrusted Diggle with rebooting its storied *Swamp Thing* title; after that, the sky appears to be the limit. Diggle says one day he'll again contribute to *2000 AD*, this time as a writer. From reader to editor to writer — Andy Diggle and *2000 AD* will simply never be free of one another!

What was your first published work?

I guess it was *Lenny Zero*. It was my first published work because I commissioned it from myself when I was editing the *Judge Dredd Megazine*. [*Laughs*] I'd been assistant editor on *2000 AD* for a while, working for David Bishop, and when I finally got the editorship of the *Megazine* it was coming up on the tenth anniversary issue. I wanted to get a big name creator to do the cover, but there wasn't any money in the budget to pay for a big name. So as a money-saving scheme I wrote a ten-page filler story myself, and that saved several hundred pounds on the issue budget, which I then put toward paying Frank Miller to do the cover.

So in a way, Frank Miller gave you your first big break.

Yes indeed! So I'm still thankful to him for that. Unfortunately, by the time the artwork came in, I was no longer editing the *Megazine*. It had been handed back to David Bishop because I was now editing *2000 AD* full-time. When the artwork came in, David wasn't very happy with it, and I think expressed his feelings rather bluntly, at which point Frank Miller withdrew the artwork and said, 'Fine, don't pay me, don't use it.' So that piece of artwork never saw the light of day. But the upside was that the story I'd written, *Lenny Zero*, went down very well with the readers. That was the first time I'd worked with [*The Losers* artist] Jock, as well. That collaboration is still going today.

What's the first comic book you can remember reading?

All my earliest memories are of movies, but I know I read a lot of comics as a child. The earliest stuff I remember was the *Asterix* books. I pretty much learned to read reading *Asterix*. I started off following the visual narrative, and then learned to read the actual words later. When I was about five or six, I was really into war comics. I would read *Battle* and *Warlord* and *Commando Picture Library*, all that stuff. Then *Star Wars* came out when I was six years old, and I became a *Star Wars* nut overnight. After that, I completely lost interest in war stuff and everything had to be science fiction. Weirdly, I didn't discover *2000 AD* until several years later, when I was ten. That just completely rewired my brain. It was exactly what I wasn't getting from all the other stuff I was into. I was completely hooked.

When did you decide that writing comic books was something you wanted to do?

Very young. Very young. As long as I can remember I've just generally wanted to tell stories. I wanted to direct movies too when I was a kid. I was very inspired by *Raiders of the Lost Ark* when I was ten years old. I came out thinking, 'I want to

Place of birth:
London, UK
Date of birth:
22 February 1971
Home base:
London, UK
First published work:
Lenny Zero in the *Judge Dredd Megazine*
Education:
De Montfort University, Leicester
Career highlights:
Adam Strange, Lady Constantine, Lenny Zero, The Losers, Swamp Thing

make other people feel the way I felt when I came out of the cinema,' to give people that kind of buzz.

Did you get into comics editing as a path toward comics writing?

It wasn't a pre-planned thing, like, 'The only way into comics is to become an editor, so that's what I'll do.' It's something I just stumbled across, really. I was working at a university in London, doing a fairly boring administrative job, and I'd always wanted to write but I'd never had enough confidence to send my stuff to editors. I'd been teaching myself to write, mostly from screenwriting books, and I'd taken a screenwriting course. I decided, 'Enough's enough, it's time for me to actually bite the bullet and start submitting stuff.' I was running a website for which I'd interviewed various comics creators and so forth, and I'd interviewed David Bishop, who was the editor of *2000 AD* at the time. Through a friend of a friend I heard there was a job going for editorial assistant at *2000 AD*. I thought, 'I've already met David Bishop, so I've got an *in* there,' albeit a very slight one. I applied for the job and ended up getting it — it was that simple. Becoming an editor wasn't something I'd ever had any great interest in doing, but it was too good an opportunity to pass up. I knew that the writers I'd been heavily influenced by as I was growing up, guys like Pat Mills and John Wagner and Alan Grant, had all been editors previously. I'd heard one of them say before that the best possible training for writing comics is to edit them, because you really learn how they work from the inside. But it's not like it was a deliberate stepping stone kind of move.

What was your editorial assistant job like when you first started?

[*Laughs*] My first day in the office, David Bishop pointed to a three foot-high stack of submissions and said, 'Right, your first job is to go through all the submissions and write back to every one of those people.' The slush pile had been building up for years because nobody ever had time to go through it properly. That was fairly daunting because there wasn't a lot of good stuff in there. But you don't want to be completely negative to people. You want to try and inspire people rather than just slamming the door in their face.

What were the most common mistakes you'd see in those submissions?

Not being very good was probably the most common mistake. Because most of the people were pitching for *Future Shocks*, these five-page self-contained stories with a twist ending, everybody would always structure them so that the first four pages were merely building up to the payoff. And because the payoffs were always going to be fairly predictable, it always felt like a long haul getting to that payoff. Nobody ever really seemed to keep adding twists and turns throughout the course of the story. Rarely would they come up with a really compelling hook at the beginning, and then spin it off into something else on page two, and then change that again for page three. Instead, you could see where it was going from panel one. It just became a bit of a slog.

What comic books influenced your writing early on?

Warrior, for starters. That was a very big influence, because it made me realise that comics can be for grownups. That you can have sex and violence in your comics if you want. To a twelve year-old, this was great. Later, as I grew up, I would have to say Frank Miller. *Batman: Year One* is one of the few comics I never get tired of re-reading. I tend not to re-read old stuff, but I recently bought myself a copy of the hardback *Complete Frank Miller Batman* off eBay, and it's now one of my most treasured possessions. The sheer dynamism and the emotional impact, and just the *coolness* of his Batman stuff has definitely been a big influence on me. Alan Moore, obviously. But at the same time, I actually find Alan Moore quite daunting, because he's *so damn good.* I know I'm never going to be that good a writer, and it just depresses me, frankly. You know, 'I can't compete with this!' I'm obviously not saying that Frank Miller isn't a good writer, but I think my head is just wired more like his than it is someone like Alan Moore or Grant Morrison. I do tend to feel slightly jealous of their imagination.

And now you're writing *Swamp Thing,* on which Alan Moore had a legendary run. How do you go about that task?

Well, there's no point trying to copy Alan Moore or his writing style. I guess the signature of his *Swamp Thing* was the fairly lyrical, poetic captions he'd use all the time, and I'm crap at writing that kind of stuff. It's obvious that I'm just faking it if I try and do that. I tend not to use captions at all in my writing, anyway. But I've discovered that trying to write *Swamp Thing* without captions makes it a very different kind of beast to what people are used to with the character. The Swamp

---

2000 AD

Though the fortunes of British sci-fi anthology *2000 AD* have fluctuated over its twenty-five plus years of continuous (weekly) life, one thing remains constant. If you're a British creator and you want to break into US comics, your best bet is via the pages of *2000 AD.* The title has fostered and sent out into the wider world the likes of Alan Moore, Dave Gibbons, Grant Morrison, Garth Ennis, Peter Milligan, Barry Kitson and, more recently, Robbie Morrison and Andy Diggle. Launched in 1977 by IPC Magazines, and devised by writers Pat Mills and Kelvin Gosnell, *2000 AD* blew away the somewhat staid competition at the time with a heady mix of sci-fi, western and dark, dark humour. Its flagship character, appearing in every issue bar, strangely, the first, was Judge Dredd, a fascist future lawman dispensing instant and brutal justice on the streets of a massive, over-populated, crime-ridden city. So popular was Dredd that a second title, *Judge Dredd Megazine,* was launched in the '80s, showcasing the lawman and his world. But *2000 AD* isn't all about *Judge Dredd,* and a host of other memorable series — including *Strontium Dog, A.B.C Warriors, Zenith* and *Rogue Trooper* — have spewed from its bullet-riddled pages.

Thing in my story isn't quite the same as the traditional plant guy. It kind of works better with fewer or no captions because people can't get inside his head, so they're not quite sure what his angle is, whether he's the good guy or the bad guy. When they offered me *Swamp Thing* I said yes because I just wanted to get it back to basics. It had become so entangled in this hopelessly, hopelessly complicated continuity. It annoyed me, frankly. I wanted to fix it. I tend to look at stories in quite practical terms, almost like fixing a car engine. I like rolling my sleeves up and lifting the bonnet of the car and having a fiddle with the engine. The reason I only wanted to do the first six issues was because I thought once I'm finished, I'll have got the character back to a point where they'll have a series where he's Alec Holland, Plant Guy. And his daughter Tefe won't have her powers anymore. We won't need to know all that back-story. And he won't have all these other powers over the elemental forces which Mark Millar introduced, and so forth. With all due respect to Mark, he left Swamp Thing as having become the planet Earth itself, which is a great way to *end* a story, but kind of a difficult place to begin a new one.

You're often credited with revitalising *2000 AD* after taking over as editor. What were the weaknesses of the title leading up to your run?

It had almost tried to become too sophisticated for its own good. *2000 AD* started off as this very pulpy, violent boys' adventure comic with a mean streak of black humour. As all the eight year-old boys grew up with it and were now twenty-eight year-old boys, there was a degree to which the comic tried to grow up too much. It tried to be a bit too clever and a bit too knowing and a bit too ironic. It was

---

Warrior

While *2000 AD* is regularly — and rightly — credited as the inspiration and launch pad for many a successful Brit writer's career, there's another UK comics periodical that could justifiably lay claim to helping shape the comics landscape, on both sides of the Atlantic. Launched by current *Comics International* editor Dez Skinn in 1982, *Warrior* was a monthly black and white anthology title taking the, at the time, radical stance that comics weren't necessarily just for kids. Featuring a startling line-up of nascent artistic and writing talent, including Alan Moore, Steve Dillon, David Lloyd, Gary Leach (also heavily involved in the design of the magazine), Alan Davis, Steve Parkhouse and Steve Moore, *Warrior* was home to a number of intriguing comic strips, from the twisted sci-fi of *Laser Eraser & Pressbutton*, to demon hunter *Father Shandor* and terraced house *Addams Family* homage *The Bojeffries Saga*. But it was two Alan Moore-written serials that would prove the most groundbreaking and influential: *Marvelman* (eventually to become *Miracleman* upon US publication), which took a revolutionary and electrifying real-world approach to a forgotten British superhero; and the chilling near-future fascism of *V for Vendetta*, later collected by DC Comics. The impact of these two stories can still be felt today.

PAGE 5

1) The two remaining missiles SCREAM towards Strange, high above a skyscraper construction site. It's skeletal, little more than a lattice of steel H-girders, with only one out of every ten floors even built --

> CAPTION
> GREAT. MORE THAN JUST HOMING MISSILES - THEY'RE **SMARTER BOMBS** WITH A **SHARED NEURAL NETWORK** --

> CAPTION
> EACH **LEARNS** FROM THE OTHER'S **MISTAKES** --

> CAPTION
> WHICH MEANS THAT EVERY TIME ONE OF THEM IS **DESTROYED**, THE **REST** JUST GET **SMARTER!**

2) Missiles POV. Strange REVERSES in mid-air, FIRING both blaster pistols back at us --

> CAPTION
> GUESS I'LL JUST HAVE TO FIND SOME **NEW** TRICKS TO TEACH THEM --

> **F.X.**
> *BZAM! BZAM! BZAM! BZAM!*

3) His shots hit the first missile and it EXPLODES, causing the missile behind it to detonate in a chain-reaction --

> **F.X.**
> ## BOOM! BOOM!

4) Strange is knocked back by the blast shockwave, tossed sideways like a rag-doll. His jet-pack suddenly cuts out and he's free-falling --

> **STRANGE**
> (jagged)
> *AAGH!*

5) He crash-lands on the rooftop of the skyscraper construction site, his legs flipping up into the air as he SKIDS painfully along on his shoulder, scraping up a dust-trail in his wake --

6) He grinds to a halt, SLAMMING back against a pile of construction equipment --

> **STRANGE**
> *UHFF - !*

Above: *Script page from* Adam Strange: Planet Heist #2. *Courtesy of Andy Diggle.*

constantly kind of winking at the audience, and I wanted to get it back to a slightly less self-conscious 'thrills and spills'. Give the readers some good old-fashioned pulp adventure again, because that's what I thought they wanted. I went for that unselfconscious buzz of energy and excitement which I used to get from it when I was a kid. It's something that me and Jock talk about with *The Losers*. When a page is working we say, 'That's got *Thrill Power*.' And we're only half-joking when we say it. When something's really working, it's got that buzz, when a moment really pays off dramatically. I just wanted to get that back.

Why did you give up the editorship?

I was editor for only a year and a half, at which point I thought, 'Enough's enough.' Again, it's me 'fixing things'. I'd wanted to fix the comic and I felt like I'd done everything I could do with it; after that it was just going to be a steady hum. I'd fixed everything I felt that I *could* fix. And all the other things I *couldn't* fix, from that point on were just going to irritate the hell out of me. Plus, by that point I was starting to think that maybe I could actually get by writing comics. So I decided to give it a go.

How did you pass the torch to the next editor?

When David Bishop hired me, one of the things he said was that he wanted somebody who would question his judgement. And I've got a lot of respect for David for that. He didn't hire me to be a 'yes man'. And he didn't get that — we actually argued quite a lot. There was a certain amount of friction there. But it was good because we could agree to disagree, and even though we both had really strong opinions, we would still admit when we were wrong and change our minds if we were persuaded. But when I hired my assistant, Matt Smith, I wanted somebody who was on the same wavelength as me. It's not that I wanted a 'yes man', but I wanted somebody who I knew that, if I did pass the comic on to him, he wouldn't then undo everything that I'd done with it. He had the same vision of what the comic should be. So I felt quite confident handing it over to Matt when I left. I think he was slightly surprised and taken aback that I left as soon as I did. He was quite nervous about taking over. I don't think he felt that he had a lot of experience. But I think he's doing a fine job.

Do you feel like the comic maintained the changes you implemented?

To be honest, I don't actually read it all that regularly anymore. I think it's largely there. It could probably do with being a bit more gripping. The emphasis could be more on the thrills, the excitement, the cliffhangers. I know it's kind of cheesy, but for me that's always what made *2000 AD* what it is: it's the violence and the humour and the unashamed sense of adventure. I think a bit more of the 'grab 'em by the balls' stuff would be good. But you know, it's fine.

What was your vision for *The Losers*?

It actually changed a fair bit during the development process. When DC first asked me to revamp *The Losers,* I'd never even heard of the characters. I just thought, 'That's a great title for a crime book.' [Editor] Will Dennis told me, 'It's about a platoon in World War II, real hard-luck heroes. What if they all get together after the war to pull a heist?' And I just thought, 'Yeah, sold.' I loved the title. I loved the premise... kind of like the original *Ocean's Eleven* where they're ex-Army buddies. Instantly, before I'd even set the phone down, a story had downloaded itself into my head from Idea Space: Nazi rocket scientists working at Los Alamos and missing Nazi gold and guys in suits calling each other 'Daddy-O'. The next time Will and I spoke he said, 'Garth Ennis is already doing *War Stories* set in World War II, and *American Century* is like a crime book set in the fifties.' We didn't want to tread on those guys' toes, so I said, 'Why don't we just invent new characters and set it in the present day?' So literally, all we did was take the title and throw everything else away. There's a dog called Pooch in the original and there's a guy called Pooch in my book. That's about it.

When did the politics of *The Losers* take shape?

The original pitch was just for a mini-series, rather than the ongoing. And it didn't really have much of a political angle to it... none of the ongoing CIA villainy. It was just a platoon that, in Afghanistan, had stumbled across a cave of al-Qaeda gold that they then stole... and basically became a heist crew back in the USA. It was kind of like *Three Kings 2.* DC liked it enough to turn it into an ongoing, but asked: 'Could I make it a bit more Vertigo?' I decided it needed something to make it a bit more provocative, and that's when I started developing the CIA angle. The first story, 'Goliath', was still going to be a mini-series, but now it was about them ripping off drug money from the CIA. So the idea of the CIA being up to no good was already there in the premise. I thought, how about I spin that off even further and make it even more global in scope? I wrote the first script and that went through about five rewrites. I don't think a single line or panel description from the original first draft actually made it into the final draft. There was a lot of editorial input and cajoling and so forth, which was kind of hard work, but it made it that much better. The fact is, they were completely right. I think if they had published the first draft, it would have bombed. I was grateful to Will for sorting it out.

How much editorial tinkering does *The Losers* undergo these days?

Almost none. It's great. I think they did it just right. I was a new, unproven guy. They didn't know if I knew what I was doing back then. And I didn't, frankly. [*Laughs*] They quite rightly wanted to be fairly hands-on for the launch issue. But every issue after that has had less and less input, until now Will's just happy for me to get on with it and do my own thing. I recently sent him an outline for the next year's worth of stories and he was like, 'Yeah, fine, go ahead, do it.'

Did you make the American government the villain in *The Losers* because you simply needed a bad guy, or because you're trying to get across a political message?

PAGE 11

1) Qatari agents usher the Losers through the double-doors of a plush hotel suite. They are firm but polite. Jensen carries his laptop under his arm.

AGENT

MAKE YOURSELVES COMFORTABLE. YOUR HOST WILL
BE WITH YOU SHORTLY.

2) BIG reveal - the Losers step into a lavish penthouse suite, with a wide open-air bar on the balcony outside. Light and airy, silk drapes lifting in the afternoon breeze. Silk cushions, bowls of fruit, huge sofas...

POOCH

NOW THAT'S WHAT I'M TALKIN' ABOUT. PENTHOUSE
SUITE, BALCONY BAR...
(link)
I WAS MORE EXPECTIN' A **CELL**.

3) Jensen sits at a table and opens up his laptop. He looks nervous. Clay leans over the table, scribbling on a note-pad.

JENSEN

IT, *UH*... IT CERTAINLY IS BEAUTIFULLY LIGHT AND
AIRY... BUT OF COURSE THE DOWNSIDE TO AN OPEN-
AIR BALCONY IS THAT IT LETS **BUGS** IN.
(link)
IN A TROPICAL CLIMATE, ONE MUST ALWAYS TAKE
PRECAUTIONS AGAINST **BUGS**--

CLAY

I HEAR YOU, JENSEN.

4) Close on Clay, holding up a torn-off sheet of notepaper for us to read. On it he has written in fat black letters:

NOTE-PAD

PRESUME AUDIO SURVEILLANCE

5) Sitting at the table, Jensen swivels his laptop around so we can read what he has typed in big black letters.

JENSEN

CLEARLY THESE ARE FINE PEOPLE WE ARE DEALING
WITH, AND I WOULD HAVE NO HESITATION IN
RECOMMENDING QATAR AS A HOLIDAY DESTINATION
TO FRIENDS AND FAMILY.

LAPTOP

WHO ARE THESE DICKWADS?

Above: *Script page from* The Losers #13. *Courtesy of Andy Diggle.*

It was a bit of both, to be honest. It's not a soapbox book. I can't stand using characters as mouthpieces for political views. I never used to be at all political. It was actually September 11th that made me political. I used to wonder, 'Why has everyone got such a big problem with America? America is the good guys,' you know. And then September 11th happened. I can remember sitting at my desk at *2000 AD*. My wife phoned me up. And then John Wagner phoned me up to say, 'New York's burning.' I couldn't get my head around it: why would anybody do this? Why would anybody do something so huge? What is their fucking problem with America?

And so I started looking into it, I started researching it, not just what we get told in the news, but trying to find out: who were these people? What did they believe in? What's driving them? And this led to my interest in America's foreign policy and espionage and so forth. And the more I read about it, the more horrified and infuriated I became, I think. And it pissed me off that I hadn't known this. Britain is just as bad, of course. I'm not pointing the finger just at America. All the shit that we've been up to that nobody knows about, nobody talks about, will turn entire sections of the world against us, make my city a more dangerous place to live because my tax money is going to fund foreign policy stuff that has extremely negative repercussions on a very large proportion of the world — generally a proportion of the world with a different skin colour and a different income.

So I think anger was a big part of it. I just wanted to vent anger. But the fact is, just for simple dramatic reasons, you always want your heroes to be the underdogs. Otherwise, where's the drama? And these days, well, who's the biggest dog around? It's obviously America. It's the biggest dog in the yard. So making the American establishment the bad guys just seemed like a no-brainer. I mean, who else are they going to be? Bank robbers?

As an Englishman living in England, is it difficult to write an American comic book set in America?

Really, I think I have a feel for how the characters talk and act and so forth. We're so completely immersed in American culture. All my favourite movies and TV shows are American anyway. There's a degree to which I'm slightly worried I'm just going to repackage American material back at Americans, if you know what I mean. So I need to make sure it doesn't just turn into a pastiche of my influences. But for the most part, it's not a problem at all. There are occasional moments where I'll realise I've no idea which side the steering wheel on a car is in America or what a street sign looks like or the most basic things. I've got to remember things like, 'Okay, you don't call it a *digger*, you call it a *backhoe*. It's not the car's *bonnet*, it's the *hood*.' But it's easy enough and Will's good for sifting out any Britishisms that creep in there.

I really expected to get some static for coming across as anti-American in *The Losers*. It isn't meant to be anti-American, it's meant to be anti-Bush. It's meant to be anti-hawk. Anti-we're-going-to-kill-you-if-you-don't-do-what-we-say. But it doesn't mean that the Losers aren't patriots. The fact is, the Losers are kind of right-wing conservatives themselves, for the most part. But I haven't actually had any negative feedback at all from that front. I really expected to get some right-wing hate mail. I think Micah

PAGE 15

1) Wide shot to establish the interior of Constantine's sleazy motel room. Constantine lies on the bed on panel left, propped up against the headboard. He has showered and changed, and now he's relaxing, smoking with the ashtray sitting on his chest, legs crossed, zapping away with a TV remote. A bottle of Jack Daniels, a glass and a Duty Free 20-pack carton of Silk Cut cigarettes sit on the bedside table next to him. It's daytime, but it's dark in here with the curtains drawn. Light escapes around the edge of the closed bathroom door in the background. A chair sits in the corner of the room on panel right.

CONSTANTINE
JESUS CHRIST, FOUR HUNDRED CHANNELS AND IT'S
ALL BLOODY ADVERTS. YOU DON'T HAVE TO PUT UP
WITH THIS ON THE B.B.C., Y'KNOW...

2) Move in on Constantine as he turns his head to glance at the bathroom door.

CONSTANTINE
OI, YOU ALL RIGHT IN THERE? YOU'RE TAKING LONG
ENOUGH.
(link)
I'D STEER CLEAR OF THE SHOWER IF I WERE YOU,
THAT SHIT'S JUST ABOUT THE ONLY THING HOLDING
YOU TOGETHER.

3) BIG. Inside the bathroom, everything is rendered in sharp, stark clarity by the unforgiving glare of the overhead florescent light. The grimy Holland-skeleton stands naked in front of the mirror, leaning forward on the hand basin to stare in utter horror at his own reflection. His lidless eyes are wide and pitiful; deep wells of uncomprehending misery.

HOLLAND
(small text)
I'M ... FINE.

Above: *Script page from* Swamp Thing #1, *featuring* Hellblazer's *John Constantine. Courtesy of Andy Diggle.*

Wright attracted a certain amount for *Stormwatch*, and I'm feeling disappointed, actually. I'll have to be a bit more controversial and piss off the right people.

Are you following America's 2004 presidential race?

I don't care who wins as long as it's not Bush. I think he's a very, very dangerous man. I mean, it's not even Bush. He's just some ignorant redneck who does what he's told. It's the guys who are pulling the strings that we need to worry about, but of course we don't really hear so much about them. It is deeply worrying. The biggest stockpile of weapons of mass destruction in the world is in the hands of a reactionary, ignorant redneck.

How much military research do you do?

Most of the research I've done has been into the foreign policy, espionage side of things. Digging up all the dirt on the CIA's history and so forth. It's fictionalised, but it's all based on stuff that's really going on now or has been going on in the past. As far as the military jargon and hardware goes, I tend to pull stuff off the Internet as and when I need it. My brother works for a defence contractor, which helps. If I need to know what the targetting crosshairs of an S.A.M. shoulder-launched missile look like, then I can just ask him.

Are you a stickler for accuracy when it comes to weapons and vehicles and such?

I don't really care about that, as long as it *seems* plausible. The adventures they're having push the limits of plausibility — people being blown out of windows and things exploding left, right and centre — so I'm not really worried if they're carrying the wrong kind of machine gun or something like that. Plus, Jock isn't really a reference freak. There's a beautifully rendered Chinook helicopter in issue #1, but he's not going to worry about getting exactly the right safety catch on a particular model of rifle. Because, you know, life's too short. Who cares? But it kind of annoys me if people make silly mistakes in stuff I'm reading. The classic one being when somebody's pointing a shotgun at you, and they say something intimidating, and then they rack the slide just to make their point. Well, if they pulled the trigger before they did that, nothing would have happened because there wasn't a shell in there! I try and make sure basic things like that are correct, but otherwise it's just window dressing, really. Things like the terminology, I'm sure I've got half of it completely wrong. I don't know anything about military stuff at all, even down to ranks. I'm just kind of faking it and hoping nobody notices!

The Losers is a very cinematic book, and cinematic books are often accused of being drawn-out and 'decompressed'. Do you worry about how that style affects your pacing?

I don't see the link between cinematic storytelling and decompression. I hate decompression in comics. I've never, ever managed to get into manga because for me the storytelling is just way too slow. I'm sure it's a cultural thing, it's because I grew up reading *2000 AD*, where you told a complete story in five or six pages... or sometimes two or three pages. One of the things that would drive me crazy as an editor was, if you've got a six-page story and one entire page is spent with somebody just answering the phone or picking up their car keys, it's like — that's *half an hour of the movie*, right there! You can't spend half an hour of the movie picking up your car keys! What I discovered when I was editing was that by cutting out all the decompressed crap, the more you pare it down and boil it down, the punchier it becomes. The emotional impact of your dramatic moment actually becomes much greater than if the same thing had happened but with four times more panels. Sometimes there are good story-based reasons to slow things down, in which case, fine, but when it's just giving the artist an excuse to draw some lovingly rendered cityscapes, then I'm looking at my watch, like, 'Get on with the story!' People are always telling me that I write very cinematically. But at the same time, they also say that my stuff is quite dense. A lot goes on in every issue. It doesn't hang around.

How long do you intend to write *The Losers*?

I know where my *Losers* story is going to end. I don't know exactly how many issues it's going to be, but I've got it road mapped out and I know where it's all leading, and I'm not really going to take too many tangents off that road along the way. I'm thinking it will probably take three years or so to tell that complete story. But it could be longer. And after that, they can either cancel the series, or conceivably give it to a new writer who could completely revamp the whole thing from the ground up. But I wouldn't imagine they'd particularly want to do that. We'll see.

The Losers

Andy Diggle and artist Jock, fresh from a career-making, attention-catching run on their self-created *Judge Dredd Megazine* series, *Lenny Zero*, left little of the original DC World War II title *The Losers* standing when they agreed to revamp it for modern audiences. As Diggle admits, not much more than the title remained the same for the updated series, which bands together a group of ex-soldiers taking a stand against the corrupt American government they once fought for. In fact, 'taking a stand' might be putting it too lightly; as one character remarks, 'We're talkin' about declarin' war on the Central Intelligence Agency.' After a 'black ops' skirmish, the Losers were presumed dead — a fate engineered by the Agency itself, after the Losers learned C.I.A. secrets they were never meant to know. From the first issue on, it's clear that the Losers are fighting a war where the normal rules don't apply: they steal a medevac helicopter in order to intercept a C.I.A. shipment of heroin and destroy it. It's only by living outside the law can the Losers get any real justice, and Diggle and Jock make sure that justice gets served up at a breakneck, thrill-a-minute pace.

What would you like to write after *The Losers*? Any books or characters you'd like to take over?

Other than doing my own stuff, no, there's not much. I've never really been much of a fan of superheroes. It's not like I got into this industry to write all my favourite superhero characters. But I would very much like to have a crack at Batman. He's a billionaire industrialist, and these are the forces that drive the world. I think there's some interesting stuff that could be done there. Especially pitting him against Lex Luthor, who's *also* a billionaire industrialist. That could provoke some interesting friction. And Batman's just cool. I think Jock would do a really great job drawing Batman. That would be fun. *Hellblazer*, definitely. I think John Constantine's the best character in comics. I don't have a huge amount of faith in my ability to do character-driven stories, although I think I'm getting better. I joke about the fact that the comics I write are basically just stuff exploding, but I know that one day I'm going to want to write my *Magnolia*, something that's a multi-stranded, character-driven piece with no exploding helicopters or dinosaurs anywhere. When I'm at that point, that's when I'll be ready to do something like *Hellblazer* and do it justice.

How would you describe your scriptwriting style?

I write very loose panel descriptions. I've read every different type of script, from the Alan Moore four-page panel descriptions, all in capital letters, screaming at you, to the John Wagner: 'Dredd. Head shot. Grim' kind of panel description. I definitely veer more toward the John Wagner end of the spectrum. Sometimes it will just be, 'Clay. Scowling,' and that's the panel description right there. I try to write in a way that will inspire the artist, so he can see it in his head. But I'm not telling him exactly how it looks, I'm just trying to give him enough information that he is inspired to see his own version of it in his head. Sometimes I'll throw in camera angles. 'Low angle' or 'bird's eye view' or what have you. But me and Jock, we're so much on the same wavelength now that I can just suggest what kind of angle I'm talking about and he will know exactly how to make it pay off. I write my scripts in screenplay format with Final Draft, the screenwriting software. And with a full-page title page at the beginning, the script for a full twenty-two-page comic book generally comes out to about nineteen or twenty pages. Which I guess is fairly tight.

How long does it take you to write an issue?

It varies hugely. When it's all working and I'm just entertaining myself as I'm working, then it's very fast. I recently wrote an issue of *The Losers* in about two days. That was an all-action episode, where you've got a couple of characters battling it out at point-blank range with Stinger missile launchers and people are getting blown out of windows and it's just pure madness. I can write action very, very fast, and I'm giggling with glee as I'm writing it.

Then other times, when I can't see it clearly in my head, and I'm not feeling inspired, it's like pulling teeth. I can basically sit in front of the computer and piss around for two weeks and still end up with nothing that I'm happy with. That is just the worst thing. It sometimes happens when you've had something in development for so long that all the original enthusiasm you had for it has been bled out of you. It's just like rolling a boulder up a hill. You're not quite sure where you're going with it, so you write something and then you realise you're heading off in the wrong direction. You end up deleting an entire day's work and starting again from scratch. Usually after a few days of that, of me moaning incessantly to my poor wife and generally feeling sorry for myself, a light bulb will go on in my head and I'll suddenly realise how to make it work. And I'll scamper off to the computer and get it fixed. But until that happens it's just *miserable*.

What's a comfortable monthly workload?

To do my best stuff, I don't think I can really do more than two comics a month at the moment. I'm still pretty new to all this. I'm still finding my feet and figuring out my working methods and so forth. And I've got a new baby as well, which means I don't have as much time to write as I did. But I'm currently doing three books simultaneously and that, with the baby, is pushing the boundaries of what I'm comfortable with.

What's your daily work schedule like?

[*Pause*] Schedule? I don't have a schedule. I just make it up as I go along. And before you ask, no — it's not down to the new baby. It's just because I'm disorganised. [*Laughs*] Always have been.

*   *   *

PAUL DINI

Paul Dini was a legend in the comic book world before ever writing a single word balloon. As writer/producer of *Batman: The Animated Series*, Dini helped birth the most faithful version of the Dark Knight ever to appear on any screen, big or small. Batman fans turned off by decades of camp or schlock treatments of their favourite hero flocked to the sharply plotted adventures of the new series and its spot-on characterisation of the title character. It's no surprise then that Dini's first Batman tale on the printed page, the 1994 one-shot *Mad Love*, was about as perfect as a superhero comic gets. Already an Emmy winner for *Tiny Toon Adventures* (he'd later win again for *Batman Beyond*), Dini took home an Eisner Award for *Mad Love*. A breathtaking series of highly ambitious, fully painted collaborations with artist Alex Ross cemented Dini's comic book credentials, while in the cartoon world he followed *Batman* with runs on *Superman* and *Justice League*, as well as a big-screen animated *Batman* movie. Recently, he's found the time to nurture his very own comic book universe, that of *Jingle Belle*. The book's heroine, Jingle, is daughter to Santa Claus himself... a fitting creation for the writer who's given superhero fans so many amazing gifts.

Prior to your TV career, did you have aspirations to write for comic books?

Both the desire and opportunity to write comics came *after* I was working in television. Before that, I really didn't have any idea how comics were produced. As far as I knew, the comics industry was a closed and locked door to most outsiders, which in some ways I believe it still is. I thought the odds of actually getting published in comics were so astronomically high that it wasn't even worth trying. At that time, though, there was starting to be more interaction between the fans and the professionals, and by going to the San Diego comic cons in the early '80s, I did get more of a taste of how comics were produced. But by then I was already writing television and I was more interested in doing animation than I was in doing comics. It wasn't until the early '90s, when I had started on the *Batman* animated series at Warner Bros., that I developed any sort of real interest in doing more than reading comics. And that was only because a job was more or less offered to me on a plate.

How did *The Batman Adventures: Mad Love* one-shot, your first work for DC, come about?

I'd actually written one other comic book before *Mad Love*, an Elvira story for Claypool Comics. I did that for my old friend Richard Howell, who's an editor at Claypool. That was sort of fun, and it's really how I got my feet wet, doing that story for him. Also around that time, Bruce Timm and I were working very closely on the *Batman* TV series — along, of course, with an entire team of other people — and we both had a fundamental interest in comic books. We liked them a lot. We'd have lunch on Wednesdays and go to the comic book store together. This one occasion, we were at a meeting with [DC publisher] Paul Levitz, talking about Batman stuff, and I think either he or Scott Peterson, who was the editor of *The Batman Adventures* comic at that time, said to us, 'If you ever want to do an issue of the book, we would love to have you guys do one.' And we just said, 'Gosh, that sounds great.' Before we knew it, we were working on the premise for the *Mad Love* comic book. We wanted to do a story that featured the Batman animated characters in a setting that was a bit different, a little more adult, certainly darker than we were doing on the show at that time. DC liked the outline an awful lot, and they gave us a shot at the book itself. We were very, very pleased with the results, and that got me more interested in the idea of doing other comics work. The unfortunate thing, at least as far as my schedule goes, is I'm not able to do comics work very often. Holding down jobs on several TV shows leaves me with precious little time to do more than the annual issue of *Jingle Belle*, and a few other things.

After years of writing for animation, how was comics writing different?

There are similarities between the two writing styles, and there are big differences.

Place of birth:
New York City, USA
Date of birth:
'A long time ago.'
Home base:
Los Angeles, California, USA
First published work:
Elvira: Mistress of the Dark #1
Education:
Emerson College, Boston
Career highlights:
Batman Adventures: Mad Love,
Batman: War on Crime, Jingle Belle,
JLA: Liberty & Justice, Shazam:
Power of Hope, Superman: Peace on
Earth, Wonder Woman: Spirit of Truth

For *Mad Love*, I adopted a kind of shorthand of the style in which I would write a TV script. One of the things that made working on *Mad Love* so much fun was that Bruce was right down the hall from me, so I was able to run into his office with new ideas for the script. He would say, 'Put that in, that sounds good.' Or if I had an idea he wasn't sure about, he'd say, 'Well, put it in, but I'll probably take it out later.' It was a really unique way of working, and I don't know if we could repeat it. Even though there was a script, and Bruce worked from it to a great degree, he largely used it as a departure point. There was a scene where the Joker is in his lair, and I had indicated that while he was thinking and trying to come up with a plot, he's going around on a little carnival ride. Bruce read that and just said, 'Ah, that's stupid. It's hard to draw and it breaks up the pacing. Let's just have him working at a desk, like he's totally obsessed with this.' So I would put in little flourishes like the carnival ride or things that I felt were fun, and Bruce would yank it back to the meat of the story. Ultimately, I learned to write to an artist's strengths and let Bruce concentrate on the drama of the story and the intensity of the emotions. Mind you, I think it was as much a learning experience for him as it was for me.

Were you surprised at how well received *Mad Love* was?

I was frankly delighted… and kind of shocked. I thought, wow, our first time up at the plate and we hit one out of the park. That's not too bad. I was sorry that we couldn't repeat it right away. It would have been nice to sit down and knock out a comic book series, maybe our own take on Batman in a run of like twelve issues, or just something completely new. But it just didn't work out that way. The shows kept us pretty busy and still do. We do have the *Harley and Ivy* book coming out, but again that was actually something we planned a year or two after *Mad Love*, and it just took us forever to get around to finishing it.

Why do you think Harley Quinn was such a hit with fans, first in the animated series and then in *Mad Love*?

I think the readers see something very accessible in Harley, something that they don't necessarily get with characters like Catwoman or Talia or Poison Ivy. Take Catwoman for example, she has a love-hate relationship with Batman that's been very established for almost as long as the character herself has been around. She's this foreboding character who's also sort of a male fantasy figure. Poison Ivy is this seductress and people like her as far as a villain goes, but she's pretty much bad through and through. When Harley came along, she didn't read quite as your standard villain. Sure, she's definitely in the villains' camp, but she's sort of a good girl gone bad. I think the fact that she's got a friendly, fun demeanour makes her lovable instead of formidable. There's also something attractive to people about the girl that hangs out with the bad guy and finds something in him to love. Harley has a soft spot for this creep that she really shouldn't be hanging out with at all, and that gives her an innocent quality. Makes her kind of stupid, too, but I think it's the innocence of Harley that fans respond to.

There's also a lot of visual appeal to Harley. She's pretty to look at and I think the primary black, red and white colors on her work phenomenally well, almost on a psychological level. Mickey Mouse is the same colors, incidentally. Then there's the unpredictability factor. You're never sure what Harley's going to do. I think there's a softness to her that characters such as Poison Ivy, Catwoman and Talia just don't have. A lot of women fans find her fun. Others don't like her very much; they think she's a doormat who keeps coming back for more bad treatment. Originally I looked upon that as the tragic failing of the character; she did have that terrible personality quirk. I didn't want to say that it's something that only happens to women. I wanted to say that every person meets this one other person at some point in their life that they're attracted to, and they become a total clown for them. So that's the essence of Harley, she's my own cautionary lesson turned into a character.

It seems like a lot of thought went into Harley beforehand. Is that par for the course when you're creating new characters?

Harley Quinn was, like a lot of characters, kind of a happy mistake. I put her into this episode called 'Joker's Favor' purely because the Joker needed some henchpeople. But then I thought, why shouldn't henchpeople include a girl? I bounced it off [*Batman* producer] Alan Burnett, and he agreed, thought it would be good to have a girl working with the Joker. And then I got to thinking, what kind of girl should she be? At first I was picturing a standard girl goon, someone who was attractive and might wear some sort of sexy outfit and say, 'Yeah, boss,' a lot to the Joker. But I decided that wasn't for me, wasn't any fun. I'd seen too many other characters like that. So then I got thinking, what about

Batman Animated

Prior to the 1990s, the cartoon versions of Batman weren't exactly inspiring glee in comic book fans. The bright colours, simple plots and cornball gadgets featured in *The Batman/Superman Hour* and *SuperFriends* were still drawing upon the cheesy Batman from the 1966 live-action TV series — a far cry from the Dark Knight comics fans had come to love. But the Batman of the public consciousness changed from camp to cool in 1989, when director Tim Burton's live-action movie proved to be a box office smash. In 1992, *Batman: The Animated Series* hit the small screen. Visually striking, with bold blacks devouring the foreboding cement jungle of Gotham, the series had real dramatic weight right from the opening credits. And the Batman of this world was all business, a true vigilante whose visage once again terrified evildoers. The look of the series was due in large part to the character design and model artwork of Bruce Timm, Paul Dini's future collaborator on *Mad Love*. The stories themselves were often Dini at his very best, boiling Batman down to the bare essentials: a driven avenger carrying out a very personal war on crime. Comic book fans finally had an animated Batman they could call their own.

something that harks back to the funny gun molls and henchgirls that they used to have in the *Batman* TV show in the '60s? Every villain that showed up, there was always a girl in the gang. And what if I give this one some actual personality? So I came up with the idea of a girl who wore a jester's costume and I thought Harley was kind of a cute name. It can be tough for a guy or cute for a girl. And Harley Quinn, it just seemed natural to make a pun like that.

A lot of Harley was based on my friend [actress] Arlene Sorkin, whom I'd known a long time. At that time she was appearing regularly on TV, and she had this impish personality I wanted to capture. I'd even seen her dressed up as a jester on an episode of *Days of Our Lives* that she was in. I called Arlene and said, 'Do you want to do the voice of this new character on the show?' and she said, 'Sure.' Overall, Harley just seemed to work well in 'Joker's Favor', and I began bringing her back in other episodes. She added this nice quality for the Joker to play off, and she kind of caught on with the viewers. It's like the way characters such as Daffy Duck or Bugs Bunny catch on. Nobody really sat down and created Daffy Duck as we know him: the manic character who can go from being a total hooting screwball to a jealous, egotistical, scene-stealing jerk. Sure, those are all elements of Daffy's character now, but nobody sat down and came up with that exact character. Originally, he was just a duck that came in, made some noise, and annoyed Egghead in an early Warner Bros. cartoon. Later on, someone probably said, 'That duck's funny, let's bring him back.' And the more they used him, the more they found other funny things to do with him and other ways to expand his personality.

What about assigning personalities to characters who were already well established, like the Joker?

I'm sure other people have their own take on the Joker, but for me you should never know too much about him. Many writers have done him, and a lot of them have been really good, but for me personally there's always something phantom-like about the Joker. Too much of a revealing look behind the make-up and he would stop being a clown, and you need him to be a clown for at least part of the time. I don't mean the sad clown, I mean the out-of-control clown, the clever clown, the trickster, the menace. But at the same time he also has to be a very entertaining and funny guy. To know too much of the Joker's back-story, I felt, would have hurt the character. I didn't want to humanise him in the way that we humanise characters like Clayface and Mr. Freeze, but I found I could put him in human situations with Harley that kind of stretched him in a funny way. Like the fact that he relies on Harley not only as a member of his gang, but also as the one who feeds the hyenas and sorts out his sock drawer, things like that. It's as close to a domestic situation as the Joker gets, and it's funny to see him having to deal with all that.

Comics so often get bogged down in continuity, yet the stories you write, both in comics and on TV, are very accessible for newcomers. How do you ensure that?

If there's any secret to the way I look at comic books, it's that I see them as sort of tall tales or folk tales. You can pick up a story about a character from mythology, or a character in a fable or folk tale, and they kind of read the same way. I

PAGE THIRTY-NINE

Panel One

Jing speaks to the lemmings, who have landed in the snow and are digging their way out
of the snow or shaking it off them. Jing points to the three or four wolves, who are now
happily flying and turning flips in mid-air.

JING: Look, I know you want to help but I need big, strong animals, like those wolves!

WOLF#1: Hey! This flying stuff is all right!

WOLF #2: Yarrf!

Panel Two

The lemmings adopt know-it-all attitudes as they sneer at the off-panel Jing.

LEM: Ho, ho! Is to laugh! Silly Jing-girl can't trust wolves!

LOU: Them think with tummies, and have attention span of gnats!

Panel Three

Jingle is just as ready to show off her know-it-all attitude as she starts to explain to the
lemmings:

JING: Old school misconceptions! Modern studies have shown that wolves are loyal,
intelligent creatures, just as trustworthy as sled dogs or…

WOLF #1 (Off, interrupting Jing): Look, boys!

Panel Four

The lead wolf points up into the sky where a flock of Canada geese are flying in a "V"
formation. The other wolves react with hungry delight as they follow their leader after
the birds.

WOLF#1: Canadian honkers!

WOLF #2: Aaaoooww!

WOLF #3: We eat!

grew up reading a lot of those type of tales, and there's a comfortable familiarity with them. These are archetypal characters and you pretty much know what they're going to do. I think that our take on the *Batman* animated series in general, and in books like *Mad Love* in particular, was not so dissimilar. Here's Batman, here's Alfred, here's the Batcave, here's Commissioner Gordon in jeopardy. Here's a mad villain with a scheme to kill the Commissioner, here's Batman saving him, here's the villain trying something else to kill Batman. And here's the wrinkle we throw in, in that it's not the villain, it's actually his henchgirl who comes up with the plan. Even if you only have a passing knowledge of who Batman, Commissioner Gordon and the Joker are, you can get into that story. You're not asked to deal with a recurring storyline about somebody else on the police force who you may not be very familiar with. Or stuff like, who happens to be Robin this month? Isn't that the kid that Bruce Wayne adopted years ago? Well, yes and no. There's been other kids that he's adopted since then. You don't have to deal with all that baggage in order to enjoy *Mad Love*. The only element you have to process, or you did at the time, was possibly who Harley Quinn is. But even if you don't know who Harley is, you're still able to follow the story.

Was your collaboration with Alex Ross on the fully painted Justice League books different to working with Bruce Timm?

Those books took a long time to do. Those took me about as long to write as it did for Alex to paint them. I would just block out big chunks of the year where I'd be working on one or other of those books. Rather than me just give Alex a script, it worked out better if we worked from a detailed outline, one that we would usually write a year before the book came out. That way he would thumbnail out the book and break down illustrations, and I would take those and start scripting. When the big drawings came in, I would tweak the script and add more detailed text. That worked out best as far as Alex having an immediate input into the writing, and also it juggled in with my schedule a little bit better.

When you're writing for Alex Ross, what's on your mind as far as playing up his strengths as an artist? Are there stories that you naturally want to tell with him, or stories that you tend to steer away from?

We spend a lot of time talking about the stories... what we want to see in them, what we don't. I'll make a case for certain things, and Alex will come in with very strong opinions about what he wants to show and what he doesn't. For instance, I never shy away from a good old superhero/supervillain mix-up, while Alex was very committed to the idea that if the four great superhero characters we'd chosen for these solo books — Superman, Batman, Captain Marvel and Wonder Woman — have any worth at all they can stand on their own. In other words, the story should be about how this iconic superhero relates to mankind, rather than one where they're facing off against their worst enemy. These are characters that, over the sixty years they've been in existence, have come to symbolise something for mankind. Wonder Woman, for example, is the classic female heroine. Whether you've read her comic book or not, you know that image of her charging into battle wearing her outfit. She means something on a visual level. It's the same with Superman, though possibly less so with Batman and Captain Marvel. But certainly these four are the ones who got the ball rolling as far as superhero characters go. They're very iconic.

In his original stories, Superman was more concerned with helping the common man, both as reporter Clark Kent and as Superman, than he ever was with fighting his enemies at that time: Lex Luthor, the Ultra-Humanite or whoever. Superman was more like a cause for social change, and I think those early tales are the ones that resonated with Alex the most when it came to doing the *Superman: Peace on Earth* story. We decided to put ourselves back in that place before there was a Lex Luthor, before there was a Mr. Mxyzptlk or Kandor or Krypto the Superdog and see if we could go back to making Superman an iconic character who helps mankind. I think we did a pretty good job with that first story. With Batman, we wanted to do a story where he's more concerned with street crime than fighting the Penguin and the Riddler. Wonder Woman was somebody who, as a warrior in modern times, is trying to find a place in man's world. She comes to see it more as the human world rather than just a battle of the sexes. And to do that, the goddess has to get off her cloud and go down and meet with the common man. That may or may not be everyone's favourite interpretation of Wonder Woman, but it was the one that worked for us. Do gods rule us, or do they walk among us? It's a more interesting story, I think, if they walk among us.

Do DC characters lend themselves more towards that type of storytelling than Marvel characters?

Alex Ross

It's easy to get carried away when expounding upon the incredible career of illustrator Alex Ross. By taking the two-dimensional world of superhero comic book art and transforming it into a lavishly realistic universe with his peerless painting ability, Ross added a depth and weight to the medium previously undreamt of. In 1993 Ross took the comics world by storm with the mini-series *Marvels*, written by Kurt Busiek, which portrayed superheroes from the point of view of the awed average citizens they protect. Fans fell in love with Ross' painted format, in which the amazing, real-world detail — down to the last wrinkle of Spider-Man's costume — somehow made the iconic heroes all the more fantastic. Ross then teamed with writer Mark Waid for *Kingdom Come,* a landmark mini-series that offered a futuristic take on the DC Universe. After that, the traditional comic book page could no longer contain the breadth of Ross' vision; his series of giant tabloid-sized one-shots commemorating the 60th anniversaries of Superman, Batman, Captain Marvel and Wonder Woman were grand in every way. When tackling such enormous projects, Ross found a writer worthy of the task in Paul Dini, and their collaborations mark some of the high points of Ross' astonishing career.

I think they do. I think with the Marvel characters it isn't so much about their powers as it is about their personalities. The Fantastic Four is a dysfunctional family. Their individual powers are kind of beside the point. I think you could change each of their powers, and as long as you retained their personalities you would still be able to tell an interesting story. Sue could be the strong one, Reed could have waterpower, Johnny could turn to vapour and Ben could be an alligator. It's the family dynamics that matter. You could change everything about them and it would still read as a family that has to put their differences aside to work together. That said, there is something kind of wonderful in the way their powers worked out. Johnny is the hothead: he bursts into flame. Reed is always trying to be the peacemaker, so he's malleable. Sue tends to fade into the background, invisible. Ben is the brute, so he's the rock monster. But it's their personalities that really propel the story. Spider-Man could have just as easily been Cockroach Boy. The good news is, you get to be a superhero. The bad news is, you're a creepy superhero. He's super-powerful, but he's also kind of a bug in real life, too. That's the charm of those characters. *X-Men* is all about the awkwardness of your teen years; you don't know who you are yet. You have potential, but you imagine the rest of the world looks upon you as some sort of a freak. The Hulk is like the id repressed by intellect, the side of yourself you have to hide. The Hulk is just this shot of unbridled rage that boils up to the surface now and then. Everything's so strait-laced: you have to be good, you can't express contrary opinions, you have to mind your temper. And the Hulk is the character that says, 'The hell with that, I'm going to go out and smash something.' The Marvel characters are all born out of the psyche or human emotions, whereas the DC characters are more born out of an ideal, I'd say.

Do you write comics for DC characters more because you prefer them, or because you already write for DC characters on television?

I think there's a familiarity between myself and the DC Universe. They're the characters I know the best. Marvel has approached me a couple of times about working on a few assignments, and for whatever reason — more time than anything else — it's never worked out. I've talked to [Marvel editor-in-chief] Joe Quesada about it on many occasions, and he just says, 'We've got to get you over at Marvel on something.' Overall, though, it's easier for me to juggle in a script here or there for one of the DC editors than it is for me to forge a new relationship with Marvel. The door's always been open and for that I've always been grateful. It just hasn't worked out. But, like any fan, I'm sure I have a Spider-Man story in me, or a Fantastic Four story. One of the things that's happened in recent years that's changed my outlook is I've been given the opportunity to create characters of my own. As much as I like the classic characters I grew up with — and I'll always have that fondness for them — when it comes down to finding the time to do a script, I'd rather be doing a story with my own characters than someone else's.

Speaking of which, tell us about the genesis of *Jingle Belle,* your creator-owned comic at Oni Press.

Jingle Belle came from kind of an interesting place. It was not so much a desire to do a Christmas book — although I certainly love Christmas, possibly more

Above: *Paul Dini preliminary sketch for the Rick Mays-drawn* Zatanna: Everyday Magic. *Courtesy of Paul Dini.*

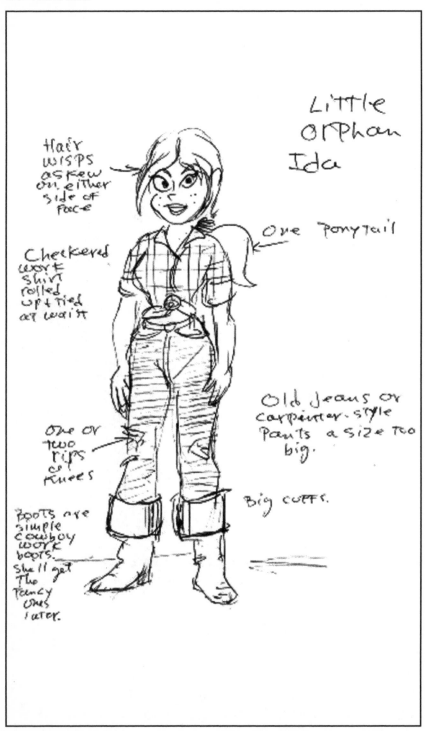

Above: *Paul Dini character design for* Mutant, Texas. *Courtesy of Paul Dini.* Mutant, Texas ™ *and* © 2004 *Paul Dini.*

than anybody I know — it was more that I'd always thought I'd like to write about a holiday character, just to see if I could write something like *Frosty* or *Rudolph*, or akin to a Rankin/Bass special. And then I began thinking about father-child relationships, especially in regards to the way I'd seen them here in Los Angeles. Often I'd be thrown into the company of some very well known people — filmmakers, writers or actors — whose careers have meant things to a lot of fans, and I'd see the way they react in their home lives. You have this iconic father who means the world to a lot of people, especially young people, yet at home, how does their kid see them? Then I started thinking about Santa Claus. If he had a kid, what kind of a child would they be? While I was sketching, I came up with the idea: what if Santa had a rebellious teenage girl who was kind of a spoiled brat? Her dad could give her every great toy in the world, and probably has. She's somebody who ages much slower than a regular teenager, and she's so over the Christmas stuff by now, and has to live it twenty-four/seven. She'd be like, 'I hate having to dress like an elf, I want to go out at night. I want to go meet some Eskimo boys. I want to get some time off the North Pole.' And yet she's kind of stuck there. Pretty soon I had this fun dynamic, and I just started creating this little world around it.

With *Jingle Belle* you have no boundaries — you can do whatever you want. That's not true of most of your other writing. How does that affect you creatively?

As far as *Jingle Belle* content goes, it's absolutely unbridled. I can create whatever I want. But you have to remember the Spider-Man rule: 'With great power comes great responsibility.' Or at least *some* responsibility. I look back at some of the early Jingle Belle stories and there were times I just said, 'It's fun to make her a bad-ass,' and pretty much gave in. So she'd be swearing or getting it on with guys and stuff like that. I thought, how far can I push this? And then, how far do I *want* to push this? At what point does the character become unlikable? I've done stories where I think I may have gone too far with Jingle Belle or she was more of a brat than she should have been. At the same time, this is a creative process. I'm not going to scold myself over things I did then. I'm not going to apologise for them either. I might have to do some soul-searching if the stories are ever reprinted in a mass-market trade paperback for a wider audience, and she's running around calling people 'assholes' or swearing or yelling at her dad. I'd really rather not go in and change those stories, it'd be better just to not reprint them. I hate that, when creators go in and change their old stuff.

Is there more or less satisfaction writing *Jingle Belle* than writing DC-owned characters?

There's every bit as much satisfaction in writing a good *Jingle Belle* story as there is in anything I've done for anybody else. She's my girl. And Harley's arguably my girl too, but at the end of the day, Jingle comes on home to my house, whereas Harley is part of the DC Universe. I'm lucky in that every time I have a chance to revisit the Batman universe, whether it's in a comic book or now, in the new *Justice League* show that Bruce and I are doing, I always find that there's a new Batman story inside me. And it's the same every year when I go to tell a Jingle Belle story.

Do you feel the restrictions you have on the animated series force you to be more creative?

I think swearing, for example, is an easy way out for a lot of writers. I look back at some of the early *Jingle Belle* stories and think it would have been more creative to come up with something funny rather than something that was just rude. So that's what I challenge myself to do now, when I think that way. In a lot of cases, swearing is more an extension of the writer's own laziness, or his own willingness to shock, than it is an actual attempt to create character. One of the faults I see a lot in comics is that I'm not reading a character, I'm reading the writer being clever. It annoys me when I see characters using jokes or puns or allusions that only the writer would know. In this case, the character isn't a character, he's a hand puppet, and the writer isn't even making any effort to disguise himself underneath the table. It's just, 'Look at me, I'm having my character make clever statements about a movie I saw a month ago,' or whatever's running through the writer's mind. It's not the character talking, it's Writer X playing to his fans again. That really bugs the hell out of me.

What advice would you give to aspiring comic book writers?

As a rule, I'd say a good writer is also a good reader. So if you want to be a writer, make sure that you're reading. And don't read just comic books. There are a lot of different ways to craft a story, and not all of them involve Magneto and the evil mutants attacking again. Read comics, read what you like, but be

Jingle Belle

A twisted take on Christmas lore which somehow still seems to keep all the magic and wonder of the season intact, Paul Dini's *Jingle Belle* is straightforward holiday cheer for grownups. The star of the show is the title character, Jingle, a pixieish resident of the North Pole who happens to be the teenage daughter of the one and only Santa Claus. Eternally young, Jing has long since grown weary of the whole Christmas scene and has to find new ways to amuse herself, no matter how her actions might enrage dear old Dad. Sure, sometimes she's screwing up Daddy's famed naughty/nice list or turning the elves' workshop into the site of one hellacious keg party, but Jing comes through in the crunch: she's also taken over her father's Christmas Eve toy run when Santa was incapacitated with the flu. Published annually by Oni Press, the title has attracted an all-star roster of guest artists, from Jeff Smith and Jill Thompson to Frank Cho and Sergio Aragonés. Dini might pay the bills with his superhero fare, but it's obvious he enjoys his romps in *Jingle Belle*'s Christmas wonderland with the same passion he has for any Caped Crusader.

aware that there are other things out there that will bring a broader perspective to your writing.

Are there superhero clichés that you try to avoid at all costs?

When we were writing the *Superman* show, it got to a point where any episode that began with Clark and Lois at an event, I would just throw out. For me it's like all of Metropolis is at the big opening of something or other and Clark and Lois are always there covering it. I'd say, 'I want you to start this script over again,' and they'd come back with, 'But you didn't even *read* the rest of the premise!' The fact is, I didn't *need* to read the rest of it. I knew that as sure as you're born, a big villain is going to attack, and Clark's gonna duck out and go into action as Superman. He'll send the villain packing, and the villain's going to go off somewhere, reveal his whole plan to some flunky or somebody he's threatening, and Superman's gonna come back and find him at the end. That happened in at least ten different scenarios, all of which I'd kill from the outset. If I see Clark and Lois at an event, it's like they're just waiting for Metallo or whoever to show up. Let's not open with this because it leads down one easy and rather lazy storytelling path. What if maybe we open with Lois at home and she can't find a dress to wear? It's something different. What if we open from the villain's point of view? There are so many other ways to break a story without having reporters going like robots to the opening of the opera or whatever, and oh look, here's the villain, and Superman goes into action. That is the biggest trap I had to deal with on shows like *Superman* and to some degree on *Batman*. If you have a social gathering and Bruce Wayne is there, *just wait*, the villain will show up any second!

What other comic book cop-outs irk you?

The big sin of a lot of comic book writers is that they start thinking all they have to do is rehash the character's origin or little bits of plot history and stretch it out for ten issues. And at the end of issue ten you get, 'Oh-ho, here's Mystery Villain, who's been manipulating things behind the scenes! Now I'll find out — oops, he got away.' And then, after you've had all ten issues collected in a hardcover, you bring Mystery Villain back for twelve more installments — and it's equally inconclusive. I hate these inner monologues where the hero's constantly telling the audience, who knows their origin, what their origin is, or what their relationship is to the other characters in the book. It becomes the biggest shell game in the world, because you're not even getting a story. Continuity is a very easy dodge too. In some cases, in the ongoing adventures of a superhero, all you have to do is play the continuity card.

Are there any characters you're still dying to tell stories about?

I think I've gotten a chance to write a lot of the characters that I really, really liked as a reader and fan, and I think anything else would be gravy at this point. Like I said, I think I have a Spider-Man story in me that would be a lot of fun, or a take on Dr. Doom or Captain America that I might like to do someday. But right now there's nothing in the back of my head that's forcing me to tell those stories or keeping me up at night. I really *wanted* to work with Alex Ross and tell those one-shot iconic character stories. I *wanted* to write at least a one-shot about Zatanna, largely because I liked the character. I felt I had something fun to say about her.

I do really like writing *Jingle Belle*. Equally as much, if not more, I like writing about Ida Red and the *Mutant, Texas* characters [for Oni Press]. I like to tell stories about the creatures and the people that live there. [Sheriff] Ida Red is about as pure a heroine as I could come up with. There's very little cynicism in her. I also like the mayor of Mutant, Texas, because he's insane. He's kind of an amalgam of a lot of people I know down in Texas who are these very passionate, opinionated and well-meaning boobs, but there's something very funny about them at the same time. I think if you look for parallels between the mayor and the guy who's running the country right now, you'll see they're kind of similar. I would like to do stories with the mayor in that are a bit more political and make statements about the world through the *Mutant, Texas* characters. I think of the places like Dogpatch [in Al Capp's comic strip *Li'l Abner*] or Walt Kelly's Okefenokee Swamp [in *Pogo*] and realise I've barely begun to scratch the surface of the *Mutant, Texas* characters. I think I'll be writing an Ida Red story long before I'll be writing another Batman story, simply because those characters are the ones that are pushing their way out of my brain at this moment.

*   *   *

GEOFF JOHNS

Retro is in again thanks to the '80s-inspired storytelling of Geoff Johns. You can't look at the writer's recent *Avengers* run at Marvel or his current work on the revamped-yet-again *Teen Titans* for DC without reading a heavy influence from two decades back. But you'll also notice something refreshing about Johns' comics: they're filled with heroes. Real heroes. In a time where most of the industry's spandex-clad characters are running around in grim, gritty, crime-themed stories, his heroes are standing tall in bright, flashy costumes, fighting the good fight. It's as much a nod to comics' 'Silver Age' of the '60s, as it is Johns' pure love of the classical ideal of the superhero comic. A sort of step back to a more innocent time before *The Dark Knight Returns* and *Watchmen* opened up the industry's eyes to a darker, more realistic world. Johns, a former movie industry production assistant (for big-budget films *Conspiracy Theory* and *Lethal Weapon 4*), made the jump to comics at DC, first with *Stars & S.T.R.I.P.E.*, and soon after with *JSA* and *The Flash*. He was even instrumental in bringing back Hawkman, a fan-favourite character who'd been MIA from comics for seven long years. Yes, Geoff Johns is not just any ol' comics writer; he's an old-school comics fan.

Did you read a lot of comics as a kid?

I was a pretty big comic fan, yeah. My brother and I got into them around 1983. We'd go to my grandmother's house in Detroit, and she'd have a box of my uncle's comics up in the attic. They were mostly from the '60s but we thought they were brand new. We didn't know any better. I remember later going to the dime store with my brother and we saw all these comics on the stands, and I was like, 'Oh my God, they still make these!' I guess I really got into comics when *Crisis on Infinite Earths* was coming out back in the mid-'80s. I remember picking up *Crisis* #4 and not knowing what the hell was going on. There were so many great characters, though, that it really didn't matter. My favourite character was always the Flash, and I particularly remember collecting *Flash* and *Crisis*. Then, literally like three months later, Flash dies. But for some reason it didn't bother me. I just said, 'Oh well, I'll just collect old *Flash*es.' So I started buying the old stuff. And then when I found out at the end of *Crisis* there was a new Flash, I was totally cool with that too. As long as there was a Flash I didn't care. So I also got into that new stuff. I kind of grew up in the post-*Crisis* world.

That time period seems to have heavily influenced your work. Would you consider your style somewhat old-fashioned?

Well, I try to combine the old-fashioned and the modern, without throwing away what the old-fashioned is. I don't have any interest in writing heroes that aren't heroes. I like the heroic ideals. I really do. I like characters that rise from the ashes and still kick ass and fight no matter what, just because it's the right thing to do. So yeah, I guess my style is a bit old-fashioned, certainly in ideals, ethics and morals, and maybe even in the presentation as well.

That old-fashioned, even 'retro' feel is probably most prominent on *JSA* and *Teen Titans*. Were you purposely trying to recreate the great runs both books enjoyed back in the '80s?

I guess I've tried to take what I liked about those books then and modernise them. If you look at *JSA*, it still feels like the *JSA* of old, but almost all the characters are brand new. I mean, you have characters like Star-Spangled Kid, Sand, Atom Smasher, Mr. Terrific, Dr. Midnite and Hourman... but they're all new versions of those characters; they're all a little bit different than their predecessors. I think Mr. Terrific in particular is a very strong character. Our aim is to make *JSA* familiar but different, to make it feel like this is our generation. Same with the *Titans*. If you look at the *Titans*, there's obviously a harkening back

Place of birth:
    Detroit, Michigan, USA
Date of birth:
    25 January 1973
Home base:
    Los Angeles, California, USA
First published work:
    Star Spangled Comics #1
    (March 1999)
Education:
    'I have a degree in Media Arts
    and Film from Michigan
    State University.'
Career highlights:
    *The Avengers, The Flash,
    Hawkman, JSA, Teen Titans,
    Stars & S.T.R.I.P.E.*

to the [writer] Marv Wolfman/[artist] George Perez era. Part of the reason is that I truly believe those characters were some of the last to come out of DC that have the potential to become iconic. Cyborg, Raven and Starfire particularly have what it takes — especially now with the animated *Teen Titans* series — to really become lasting DC icons and so it'd be stupid not to use them. And then we bring in the new wave of young kids like Superboy, Robin and Wonder Girl and try again to give it that classic feel. But at the same time this isn't exactly the Titans from the '80s. Or even the '60s. It's almost like back in the '80s, the new kids were Starfire, Raven and Cyborg. And now they're the old kids and the new wave is the next generation of sidekicks.

Did you always want to be a comic book writer?

No. Actually I wanted to draw. I can actually draw pretty well, but not great. When I was really young, I drew my own characters. But then in high school and college I got more into film. I kind of got sucked up into that world, but I still read comics. It's funny, in college I think I even got more into buying comics than when I was a kid, because my roommate was into comics too. There was a CD store right above the comic shop that would buy old CDs for like $5. So we'd sell old CDs and then go downstairs and buy comics. Even back in high school, my friend and I would take our lunch money for the week and buy a box of Ho-Ho snacks at the grocery store. We'd eat one Ho-Ho a day and at the end of the week we'd have six bucks left over. Back then, comics were a dollar, so we'd go to the comic shop on Friday after school and buy six comics. It was an exciting time.

Teen Titans

Over the years, there have been plenty of superteams, but few have been made up entirely of youngsters. Originally a team of superhero sidekicks, the Teen Titans have grown out of the shadows of the big boys to earn their own spotlight. The book's latest re-launch under the direction of Geoff Johns further cements the Titans as one of DC Comics' premier superteams. With a nod to Marv Wolfman and George Perez's hugely popular *New Teen Titans* from the '80s, Johns has recaptured the chemistry and magic of that decade's team and updated it for today's comics fan. Titans Tower is home to the latest Titans roster, consisting of Superboy, Robin, Wonder Girl, Cyborg, Beast Boy, Starfire and Kid Flash. Just about the only one missing from the classic '80s run is the mystical Raven… and even she's shown up in Johns' tenure. As have fan-favorite villains Deathstroke and Brother Blood. Plenty of action, mystery and intrigue are mixed with the soap opera-like qualities that affect all teenagers. And that's exactly why these Titans are still so popular today. In fact, they've even spawned their own animated series on the Cartoon Network featuring the same basic lineup but done in a more light-hearted anime style.

THE FLASH #182 – G. Johns   33

PAGE TWENTY.
PANEL ONE.
High angle, looking right down to the street. Dozens of stories up. Cold throws
Chillblaine off the balcony – he screams.

1. CHILLBLAINE: Wait! Wai--

2. COLD: Good-bye, KID.

PANEL TWO.
Cold blasts his cold-gun towards the alley ground below – creating a heap of tall RAZOR
SHARP ice spikes…Chillblaine falling towards them.

3. SFX: KRNGGTTT!

PANEL THREE.
On Chillblaine – screaming, falling right towards the ice spikes. The ice spikes glitter as
the moonlight strikes them.

4. CHILLBLAINE: AAA--

PANEL FOUR.
Low angle, looking up at Cold. Grim. No smiles here. This was not a victory. The
ripped up drapes whip in the wind behind him.

5. SFX (CHILLBLAINE BEING IMPALED): SHRRRP!!

PANEL FIVE.
Tight on Chillblaine – a profile of his face looking straight up. His eyes still open. Blood
seeps around him.

A SMALL WAFT OF STEAM RISES FROM HIS MOUTH – his dying breath.

[NO DIALOGUE.]

PANEL SIX.
Exact same as above, but the STEAM IS GONE. He's dead.

[NO DIALOGUE]

PANEL SEVEN.
Exact same panel as four, but Cold is gone. The drapes continue to whip in the wind.

[NO DIALOUGE.]

Above: *Script extract from* The Flash *#182. Courtesy of Geoff Johns.*

How'd a snack cake-eating kid make his way into comics professionally?

First came the movie career. After college, I saved up around $1,500, and being an idiot I thought that was enough to move out to California. My friends and I rented a U-Haul, got an apartment off the Internet and drove out west. I came to LA with $1,500 in my pocket, which was probably not the smartest thing I ever did, but it actually worked out fine. I had decided I wanted to be a screenwriter, because in college I had really gotten into screenplays. I thought I'd get a job in special effects first because I had the experience with all these programmes in multimedia. About two weeks in, my friend got an internship down at Fox Studios and was telling me how great it was. So we decided maybe getting an internship would be a cool way to get a foot in the door. We sent out hundreds of letters and I had lots of informational interviews — I wouldn't actually ask for a job, I would just ask to come in and talk to them. Richard Donner was my favourite director, and I knew they were doing *X-Men*. So I called up his office and asked if there were any internships, and they transferred me like eight times and finally someone said an intern quit this morning, could I come in tomorrow?

Is that what you'd call good luck or good timing?

It was certainly timing. Unfortunately, it was also unpaid, so not so good. I remember later reading that Stan Lee did the same thing breaking into comics. Anyway, I took the job. If they wanted me to deliver something on the lot, I'd always run or take the golf cart. Everywhere I went, I'd just move fast. If they needed anything, I'd do it. I didn't care what it was. Eventually, if they needed something fast they knew they could come to me. About three or four weeks after that I got a job as a production assistant for the office, and I actually got paid! And that was just the best time in the world. Soon after, they decided to go into production on *Conspiracy Theory* and Richard Donner needed a new assistant. The people in the office knew me, recommended me... and he offered me the job.

When I shot *Conspiracy Theory* in New York, I met a bunch of people from DC Comics. They had just sent over copies of their Paradox Press book *The Big Book of Conspiracies*. I called up the editor who'd sent the books over and invited him to the set. He brought a lot of people with him and I asked them as many questions about comics as they asked me about the film. I remember one guy said, 'Do you ever write? You should write something for us.' I was so busy with my day job, I don't think I turned in a proposal for about a year and a half. I turned in a *Stars & S.T.R.I.P.E.* proposal right after we were done with *Conspiracy Theory* and were about to start on *Lethal Weapon 4*. And I think three or four months into shooting *Lethal Weapon*, I got the phone call from the editor who said, '*Stars & S.T.R.I.P.E.* has been approved for a monthly series.' I couldn't believe it.

And that snowballed into more comics work?

This was where I really got lucky. Before *Stars & S.T.R.I.P.E.* even came out, I had met James Robinson and David Goyer, because they were gonna use the Star-Spangled Kid in *JSA*. When James left *JSA* about a month later — before that

The Flash #210 – Geoff Johns   28

PAGE SEVENTEEN.
PANEL ONE.
The Flash suddenly races on to the scene, birds flying every which way to get out of the Flash's way.

The Flash has to zig and zag between the birds.

1. CAPTION (FLASH): Didn't expect all these BIRDS. Have to slow down.

2. CAPTION (FLASH): I don't want to hit one. It'd punch a hole right in me.

PANEL TWO.
Double Down spreads out his arm and throws back as shirt – his skin peeling off, transforming into razor sharp cards all around him. A smile on his face.

Birds are still flying all around in chaos.

3. DOUBLE DOWN: Flash? ACES.

4. CAPTION (FLASH): Jeremy Tell. DOUBLE DOWN. After a losing streak at the Flying Pig Casino, Tell murdered a winning gambler in the parking lot. A deck of cards in the man's jacket flew out at Tell.

5. CAPTION (FLASH): The cards burrowed into his skin. BECOMING his skin.

PANEL THREE.
The razor sharp cards fly by the Flash, some slicing into his suit and drawing blood. One of the razor sharp cards slices open a dove in the way.

6. CAPTION (FLASH): No one can quite explain why or how. They theorize the cards are magical on some level. Tell says he was CURSED.

7. FLASH: HNN.

PANEL FOUR.
The Penguin aims his umbrella at Double Down, squawking. He fires bullets from the end at Double Down.

8. PENGUIN: Watch my BIRDS, you NITWIT.

SFX: BRRRATTTT!

9. CAPTION (FLASH): Like most ROGUES he blames his predicament on someone ELSE.

Above: *Another extract from a* Flash *script, this time from Issue #210, featuring the Penguin. Courtesy of Geoff Johns.*

issue even came out on the stands — I got a call from editor Pete Tomasi, and he said, 'Do you want to co-write *JSA* with David Goyer?' So I got lucky, but again it was partly timing. I think timing's a lot in life. *Stars & S.T.R.I.P.E.* got cancelled and then I got *Flash*. So I was doing *JSA* and *Flash*, and still working for Donner. It was crazy. I worked every day and I wrote at night. Eventually I got offers for more and more work, and Donner was about to take another year off from shooting, so I decided that was the time for me to leave the movie business.

Was it a tough choice choosing comics over movies?

It was particularly hard leaving Richard. I'd learned so much from him. The cool thing was, he'd have me in on every story meeting and I got to be there the whole time from the beginning to the end, from pre-production to post-production. So I learned a lot about storytelling and how to work with people. He used to always say, 'It's not about ego. If someone has an idea, I don't care who that person is, even if they're a grip on the set, if they have a good idea and you don't use it, you're stupid.' And he's right. It's the same thing with comic books. If someone has a good idea for a story point or a character, it's dumb not to use it. It's a collaborative effort.

How did you convince DC to finally bring back Hawkman?

I think at that point it had been seven years since the character's last appearance, and the plan was, 'Okay, let's figure out how to bring Hawkman back.' A lot of people had thought about it, but nobody really wanted to do it. Originally the return of Hawkman was going to cross over into *JLA*. David Goyer, Pete Tomasi and I all just said let's do it without them. Let's just do it. We *really* wanted to bring Hawkman back. All three of us really liked the character. So we pored through the old stuff and just spent a whole weekend figuring it out. We thought that because there had been so many different incarnations of Hawkman, it was almost like there had been different reincarnations. That idea played thematically with what we wanted to do, so it was easier to swallow. They kept giving Hawkman new lives, so we said, fine they're all *past* lives. He's a reincarnated guy. Let's go with the original and tie it into Thanagar. Let's just bring in the elements we like from every era of Hawkman and put them all into one character. The base premise works. Will they reinvent him again? Yeah, someday. But I think this one will last for a while. I really do. People like the character.

You've got three monthly books on your plate currently. Are you pretty structured with your writing?

Very. I have a pretty rigid schedule. I have an office I go to. I get there around 9am and I'll leave around 6pm or 7pm. Sometimes I'll work at home on the weekend, but even then I have a schedule. I always know what I'm doing in any given week, and I always concentrate on one specific title. I have to. I couldn't, say, write five pages of *JSA* then write five pages of *Flash*. To me that'd just be sloppy. That's telling me that I don't know what I'm doing with the story. If I start to do that then I don't know where I'm going. When you know where you're going with a story and a script, you'll want to finish it all the way to the end because you can't wait to get to that part.

How it works is I generally plot ahead inside my head. I know what the story arcs are. We have *JSA* plotted through to issue #80, so I know pretty much what happens in each upcoming issue. I then spend about a day plotting each issue specifically, page by page. And then I can write about five pages of actual script a day after that. So all in all it takes about a week. I write full script. I can't write the Marvel plot method. For me it's a little bit nebulous. If there's that one line of dialogue and it deserves its own panel, you've got to know that line of dialogue's gonna be there. The dialogue's as important as the visuals in my mind. If [artist] Rags Morales picks up a *Hawkman* script and sees a six-panel page and wants to do it in four, and can, then fine. If he wants to do it in eight panels, then fine. I don't have a problem with that. Scott Kolins used to add panels all the time on *Flash*, so a six-panel page became ten. He'd pull lines out that he'd want to do a reaction shot for and he always made it work, largely because he's such a good storyteller. The guys I work with are pros. I'm the screenwriter and they're the director, so they're gonna figure it out.

How closely do you work with each artist?

Every artist I'm working with knows where we're going for the next year and a half on their particular book. They know every storyline. They know the characters. They know everything because it's their book as much as mine. I feel they should

---

Hawkman

In terms of comics continuity, Hawkman is the Poster Child of confusion! With so many different incarnations, re-launches and origins, Hawkman's always been a mess. For a start, there's Carter Hall, an archaeologist with a strong love for Egyptian history. Then there's Katar Hol, an extraterrestrial police officer from the planet Thanagar. There's even a 'merged' Hawkman, a variant of Katar Hol who combined with the Golden Age Hawkman and Hawkgirl into a totally new Hawkman. Get the picture? For seven long years, DC Comics just, well, put Hawkman on hold... until Geoff Johns brought him back, first in the pages of *JSA* and then in a new *Hawkman* series. Rather than do away with all the previous Hawkmen, Johns pulled it all together with one simple idea: reincarnation. Hawkman and Hawkgirl are reincarnated warriors who use a material from the planet Thanagar called Nth metal to fly. Thanks to this metal, they are reborn again and again, destined always to fall in love. Except this time around, Hawkgirl has no memory of their relationship, and despite Hawkman's constant advances, she basically refuses to love him. For all his brute strength and determination, Hawkman must now learn the virtue of patience.

always know what we're doing, what we're planning. They should feel comfortable that we know what we're doing. In the case of Mike McKone, he can't draw every issue of *Titans*, but if he knows every storyline coming up, he can know which ones he really wants to do. So we don't have problems with scheduling.

But honestly, once I hand a script off, I'm pretty much done as far as my involvement goes. I get paid and the finished pages look beautiful. We don't really go back and forth on a script once it's in. Artists will give me feedback if they have problems or questions or anything, and I might do a slight tweak on a script or a rewrite. But beyond that, once we talk initially, it's pretty much hand off and go time. I've got to start on the next one. I trust them. As long as they trust me — they know what I'm doing and where I'm going — then I trust them because I know they're gonna execute things properly. I've been really, *really* lucky because I work with a number of great artists. I don't have any problem with them reinterpreting a scene as long as the story gets told.

Do you think visually or even sketch things out as you're writing?

Yeah. I draw actual thumbnails that nobody ever sees and then I throw them away after I'm done. I have no use for them, so I just toss them out. I actually have a system set up where I have my thumbnail pages laid out ready. It's a weird mathematical thing… I have a grid composed of six mini-pages on a page, and I take those and divide each mini-page into panels. That's about a full day's worth of work right there. I look at the six pages, divide them up into panels, write the script and I'm done. It's kind of a good system.

How do you handle writer's block?

There's always days where you don't get in the mode of writing or you don't feel like writing, but I don't call that writer's block. I just call that an off day. Writer's block is where you can't even come up with an idea. If I'm having a hard time on one title, in terms of the plot direction, I just switch. That's another advantage of working on several books. If I'm on *Flash* and I can't figure out what to do for the next scene, then I'll switch gears and say, you know what, this week I'll work on *JSA* instead, because I know exactly what's happening on that book. And by the time I get done with *JSA*, I'm ready to go back to *Flash*. I try and stay far enough ahead of my deadlines so I don't have to be tied down to any one monthly schedule. I usually have about an extra month's leeway, so I can do that. I can go from *Titans* to *JSA* and then go back to *Titans* and not worry about it. But if I don't know where I'm going with a story, it's always on the plot breakdown. It's never on the script. So it's always that first day.

You've done your fair share of team books and solo character titles. Do you need a different mindset for each?

Yeah. A solo book's a lot different to a team book. The latter is hard because you have to juggle all these various characters and so it takes longer to write. It takes me a lot longer to write an issue of *JSA* than to write an issue of *Flash*, just because

Teen Titans #5 -- Geoff Johns   23

PAGE SEVENTEEN.
PANEL ONE.
Starfire and Kid Flash gather around Cyborg. Cyborg kneels down, putting his fingers on a small puddle of blood where Raven was.

1. KID FLASH: Who was that?

2. STARFIRE: A friend of ours. A former Titan.

3. CYBORG: Something TOOK her.

PANEL TWO.
Superboy flies above Wonder Girl, Beast Boy and Robin. He's holding Deathstroke's ripped up mask.

4. SUPERBOY: Looks like Deathstroke beat it too.

5. WONDER GIRL: And JERICHO...where'd she send HIM?

6. BEAST BOY: Knowing Raven...it wasn't any place GOOD.

PANEL THREE.
Tight on Kid Flash. He looks over at Cyborg and the other Titans.

7. KID FLASH: Wait. So did we...WIN or WHAT?

8. ROBIN: If we did --

PANEL FOUR.
At least the bottom half of the page -- but if you can expand this panel to the bottom 2/3rds, terrific. Nice and desolate. A question mark ending.

Longshot of the destruction. The Titans Tower is in the background, almost dividing the panel in two. On the left, Kid Flash, Wonder Girl, Robin and Superboy -- on the right, Cyborg, Starfire and Beast Boy.

A team still divided.

9. ROBIN: -- we sure as Hell DIDN'T do it TOGETHER.

Above: *Disharmony in the ranks in* Teen Titans #5. *Courtesy of Geoff Johns.*

there's so much stuff going on with every character in *JSA*, and as soon as a different lead character talks, you have to switch mindsets completely. With *Flash*, you're always inside Flash's head. Even if you cut to a scene with the Rogues, you're still in Flash's world so you're seeing it through his perspective most of the time. With *JSA* there's so many different perspectives. *Titans* same thing. You've got to cut back and forth between all these very well defined characters. I like both. I love team books because it's a challenge and it's fun to write so many diverse characters. The thing about team books is that it's all about interaction, it's all about how the characters respond to each other, how they deal with the problems together and apart. I like that a lot.

In a weird way, I sometimes think of *Flash* as a team book. We have the Rogues, who we've really been trying to flesh out over the last few years, and I think we've been pretty successful. They're definitely a team. And then we've got the Flash's supporting cast, characters like Linda and the cops, and even the city itself, which we've been working really hard to define. The city is all about movement, just like it is with the Flash himself. It's all about people building stuff that moves. It's about the hard work ethic. We tried to take everything inside Flash that's important and mirror it in the city. But the Flash is still the lead character, so overall the solo mindset applies. One other thing about Flash that makes writing him different: no other character can fight ten villains at once on their own. It's always a big, big deal when Superman takes on four guys at once, but the Flash does this every single day. He's always fighting eight guys. It's been like that since the '50s. And that's one thing that makes Flash special, that he can fight all these guys at once.

That business about defining the city, making it like a supporting character in the book, we did the same thing with St. Roch in *Hawkman*. But there we didn't have as much time to really delve into its origins. So with St. Roch we're trying to make it the embodiment of mystery, of different cultures, history and everything else. There's one line where we said that the weird thing about St. Roch is that if you look in any history book, in any atlas or anything, there's never a date that says when it's founded. Nobody remembers when it was founded. Just one day it was there. And that's kind of like Hawkman to me. He's been around forever.

How does writing alone compare to co-writing a book?

Co-writing is really fun, especially when I work with somebody I like. The process is a little bit different, but it's still fun. When David and I worked on *JSA*, we'd have dinner and then basically plot the script, page by page and write it down. Then we'd write up kind of an outline for it — a page-by-page outline — and just divide it in half. Usually with *JSA*, we do it literally in half like that. Occasionally, though, we'll do it by scene. I like working with people, that's why I like comic books, film and TV. I sit in a room and I work, but I still like working *with* people. At the end of the day, that's what makes everything fun, it's other people. I'm not too into the isolated environment. I'm on the phone a lot. I talk to my editor, I'll talk to my artists. Friends come meet me here for lunch all the time. There's hardly a day I'm in the office where I don't talk to anyone, and there's rarely a day where I don't see anybody.

How would you define a good editor?

Everyone will tell you something different. Some people will tell you the role of an editor is to stay out of your way. I don't agree with that. I think their role is to help guide the ship. They're the ones who are in overall charge of the book. They're the ones who are overseeing the whole thing. Editors are essentially like movie producers. To me, a good editor is someone I can bounce a story idea off and they'll give me positive feedback. A good editor will give me constructive notes on a script. I'm not one of those, 'I don't want anybody giving me any notes on this script,' guys. Like I said before, it's not about ego. If Pete Tomasi has notes on *JSA*, they're always good notes. That's it. End of story. There's no discussion. They're just good notes, and I use them to make the story better. A good editor always knows when to step in and when not to.

You recently went exclusive with DC. Does that mean you're happy with them?

Absolutely. I could not be happier with DC Comics. It's insane how well it's gone. DC's just my home. I started there and now I know everybody there. I'm comfortable with them. They let me do what I want to do and I just have a great time. Going exclusive with them wasn't an easy decision, but at the same time it was. It just felt natural. I'm having a lot of fun there. The guys over there are some of my best friends and I like the DC Universe a lot.

Which comic writers have influenced you the most?

Besides the Silver Age greats — who I think influence everybody, even if they don't know it — I really, *really* liked John Ostrander. I thought he was terrific on *Suicide Squad*. Great concept. Great execution. I liked Peter David on *Hulk*... I was really into that series when he was working on it, and you've got to respect that twelve-year run. I mean give me a break, even if you didn't read it or like it all, you have to respect that. Mark Waid was a huge influence on me when he took over on *Flash*. It was just amazing. I remember being in college when that 'Return of Professor Zoom' story came out and I was just floored. It was the best storyline he did in that book. It's plainly one of the best stories I ever read.

How have comic conventions been for you?

I love conventions. I actually got engaged at a panel. My wife proposed to me at San Diego in 2001. We had been dating for a while and she wanted to ask a question during the panel. I was like, 'What's it gonna be this time? How's she gonna harass me this time?' And she proposed. I was like, 'Yeah, let's go!' I had spent the last three or four months sort of hinting that I was going to ask her, and I was going to ask her that Christmas and she beat me to it. She reads a lot of comics and it's funny because she has opened up my tastes quite a bit to different books. She buys a ton of independent books and she's really a pretty good barometer for comics and accessibility.

How much research do you do for your stories?

I've got a *lot* of books, from forensics to animals to the universe itself. One example is when Wally West [the Flash] became a police mechanic. I went out and bought about six books on police cars and restoring police cars and just mechanics in general, so I could talk knowledgeably about how an ignition works, or how brakes work, or what kind of electric wiring system's in a '97 Ford, stuff like that. It's the same with medical research, the technical language I need for Dr. Midnite's dialogue. It just rounds out the story more. If a reader knows their medical facts or the details about a certain type of jet engine or anything like that and you get it wrong, it takes them out of the story. And I don't want to take anyone out of the story.

Is there any character or title you're dying to get your hands on?

There's probably not a single superhero icon I don't want to write. I really love the characters I'm on right now. I love Green Lantern. I love Superman. I love the Hulk. I'd really love to do Spider-Man. The Shazam Captain Marvel. The Legion of Super-Heroes. Mister Miracle. Green Arrow. Batman. I can probably go ahead and list every character in the DC and Marvel Universes so I won't bother. But essentially it's that.

So will you be taking on another title anytime soon?

I'm on three monthly books right now, so for me 2004 is gonna be pretty quiet. 2005's gonna kick my ass though. I've got a couple of projects in 2005 that are gonna

The Silver Age

Back in the 1940s, DC Comics' output consisted largely of fairly straightforward adventures, featuring by-the-numbers tales of Superman, Batman, Hawkman, Green Lantern and numerous other do-gooders. But with the advent of the Cold War, fears of Communism crept into the world — gasp... even the comics world — and censorship became a serious issue. Many superheroes, bar the most popular characters, just faded away. As the climate cooled, however, comics entered a 'Silver Age', a sort of Renaissance for the industry. Historians agree that 1956's *Showcase* #4 officially kicked off the Silver Age, with its tale of an all-new Flash (Barry Allen). More revised characters continued to pop up with a new look and in many cases, new secret identities. For continuity's sake, DC would later explain the Golden Age (as the previous era was dubbed) characters as having lived on an Earth from a parallel universe. Marvel Comics added momentum to the Silver Age in the early '60s, adding a more personal, human touch. Silver Age comics may be generally regarded as a bit cheesy, hokey and just all-around silly fun, but with their more realistic heroes and a healthy dose of science fiction, they were a big step up from the wooden characters of the Golden Age.

be pretty monstrous. But it's good. I get to recharge my batteries now. I just want to keep any superhero book I'm writing a fun, entertaining read. That's my goal.

What's your advice to any aspiring writers out there looking to break in?

Just write. That's the biggest thing. I meet people every day who say, 'I always wanted to get into writing,' and I ask them: 'So have you done anything?' They invariably reply, 'Well, I have this story idea but I haven't actually written anything yet.' That's the first thing. Before you start saying how do I get in, write. You've gotta write. If you have an idea for a four-issue *Batman* story, just write it. Don't just keep pitching it, write the thing. You'll get practice, you'll get better. Give it to friends to read and see what they think and try to get better at it. Just keep writing. The hardest thing about breaking in as a writer is that you can't just walk up to editors or whoever at a convention and say, 'Hey, can you check this script out?' It's really hard. And if you look at my story, how I broke in, it's completely backwards. There's no right way. It's the same thing with movies. There's no right way to do it. I called up an office and got lucky with an internship. Is that how you get in? No, not really. If you want to write, start writing.

What's your favourite issue that you've written?

Probably *Flash* #182, detailing Captain Cold's origin. I like that one a lot. I like that character. I like his attitude. The whole thing isn't even necessarily about the nuts and bolts of why he does what he does. It's how he thinks. The fact that he doesn't think he's a murderer, and he is, is just ridiculous to me.

Do you think you'll still be writing comics twenty years from now?

I hope so. Obviously there are different generations of comic book writers that come in and out. I'd like to still be doing comics. We'll see what happens. Right now I'm enjoying the ride.

*　　　　　*　　　　　*

BRUCE JONES

A self-proclaimed 'old fart', Bruce Jones made his name back in the '80s with sci-fi and horror comics such as *Alien Worlds, Twisted Tales* and even the jungle-bound *Ka-Zar*. But with the release of his cinema-inspired creator-owned series *Somerset Holmes*, Jones seemed to virtually vanish off the face of the comics world. Sure, a few scant projects would surface here and there years later, but it wasn't until recently that Jones not only jumped back into the comics ring, but grabbed it by the throat. With a violent, street-level attitude, he started to explore Wilson Fisk's origin in a new *Kingpin* series for Marvel. His brooding, methodical and conspiracy-filled work on *The Incredible Hulk* propelled the comic from the slums of the Top 100 back up to the penthouse. Oddly enough, he did it with very little help from the Jade Giant himself. The Hulk clearly takes a back seat to the on-the-run Bruce Banner in Jones' issues — a move that fans either love or loathe. Under exclusive contract with Marvel, the writer's come a long way from the industry of old, a time when he would spend his days running around with legendary artists Bernie Wrightson, Mike Kaluta, Jeff Jones and Barry Windsor-Smith.

You're known today primarily for your writing, but you originally broke in as an artist, right?

Yeah. The first stuff I did was largely illustration work for science fiction magazines. Back in those days, the science fiction crowd and the comic book crowd hit off each other creatively. You'd be at somebody's house or a party, and that's where the comic book thing kind of crept in. Everybody was always looking for work and somebody would say, 'Well, so and so is hiring over here, or they need an artist over here.' Half the time it was science fiction projects and half the time it was comic book stuff. You just kind of went where the dough was.

Were you a big comics fan growing up?

Well, y'know, I'm an old fart, so when I was a kid there were a lot more comic books around and I think just generally more of the populace was reading them.

Comics were in every corner drug store and pretty much everywhere you went. Except book stores, which is where they are now. Strange, huh? So yeah, I read them. I read a lot of other stuff too: science fiction books, fantasy. I was just a reader. You'd go over to your friend's house and there'd be a stack of comics lying there. Everyone was just reading comics. I particularly remember I used to like *Tarzan*, because they had this artist named Jesse Marsh who was great at capturing animals. I was eclectic in my tastes, really. I liked the science fiction comics, the pulps. What happened to the pulps? I mean, my god, the newsstands used to be choked with pulps. I think in fact someone said comic books actually replaced the pulps. I don't know. Maybe it's just part of an ongoing change in society.

So everyone read, but were you a collector?

I don't think anyone collected then. There was no collector mentality. We just threw them away. We didn't have video games and Xbox and stuff that my son has. We had TV, but no cable; there were basically just three channels. Of course we had movies, but I think people in general just read more and I think reading in general has been in decline. I don't really know why. Probably TV. Everybody wants to blame it on TV. [*Laughs*] I'm kind of getting tired of that. There must be another reason. I guess like everything else, it just goes in cycles.

Growing up, did you ever think you'd be working in comics?

Well, I certainly had aspirations to be a writer and an artist, mostly an artist. I wanted to draw; I loved to draw. I really got more into the writing of the comics because I wasn't crazy about the scripts I was given. I just thought that they were kind of dumbed down. I was doing illustrations for science fiction magazines, and of course you'd have to read the story first. Then I'd read the comic book stories and they just didn't seem as good to me. And I thought, well why can't these be

Place of birth:
   Kansas City, Missouri, USA
Date of birth:
   31 October 1945
Home base:
   Overland Park, Kansas, USA
First published work:
   Illustrations for *Fantastic*,
   Amazing and *Analog*
Education:
   University of Kansas
Career Highlights:
   *Alien Worlds, The Incredible Hulk, Ka-Zar,
   Kingpin, Somerset Holmes, Twisted Tales*

better? I don't know if I made them better or not, but at least I tried. And it was more fun doing my own stuff. That way I could draw what I wanted to draw.

What was the first thing you actually wrote for comics?

Gosh, I think the first thing I actually wrote was for a magazine called *Web of Horror* that was published around the time Jeff Jones, Bernie Wrightson, Mike Kaluta, Barry Smith and I were all running around together. I can't remember which one of us stumbled onto the guy that was publishing it, but they were doing the kind of science fiction stuff we liked. I remember Jeff did the covers, and Bernie and I did some interior work, and there was a science fiction writer named Terry Bisson who was editing the book, so he was right in there with understanding what we liked to do. I showed him some sample pages that I'd just done: dinosaurs or something, I don't know what it was. And he looked at it and said, 'Well, how does it end?' I didn't have an ending for it so I made up something on the spot, and he said, 'Well that sounds good. Yeah I'll buy that.' I had to go home and finish the damn thing. [*Laughs*]

So how'd you get from dinosaurs to superheroes?

I didn't do very much superhero writing because I didn't really read that stuff. I was working for *Warren* magazine, which used to publish a lot of horror and science fiction, and I was writing and drawing for them. Then the editor left and — as is often the case — suddenly you're without work. But when she went over to Marvel she kind of took me with her. She inherited a couple of titles, one of which was *Ka-Zar* and the other one was *Conan*. I had been reading Robert E. Howard so I was up on that stuff. It was either that or something I was doing for Roy Thomas at the same time, which was also Howard stuff: *Red Sonja* I think. I don't remember who called first, but I think it was right around the same time.

I also did some war stories for DC with Joe Kubert. But those were mostly things I drew. You kind of went where the money was. Y'know, at conventions, kids come to the table and say, 'How do you break in?' And I always tell 'em the same thing: move to New York and then go up to the offices and hang around. Eventually what happens is some editor can't meet a deadline because some artist drops out or some writer drops out. And he hands you the script and says, 'Well, when do you think you can do this?' Everyone I knew, that's how they broke in. I don't really know whether that's true anymore.

I think security's a little tighter these days at Marvel and DC.

Yeah, probably. But back in those days, all the doors were open. Everybody was very friendly. We used to go up and pester them until they got so sick of seeing our faces and would just give us a script to get rid of us. That was great. You'd walk in and Neal Adams or Jack Kirby would be sitting around. At DC there was a kind of luncheon area, but really it was just a place to hang out in. It all was very friendly and family oriented. Yeah, I still don't know any other way to break in except to knock on the door and say, 'Here's my stuff, look at it.'

You were a pretty big name in the '80s but suddenly vanished, only to recently return to rave reviews. What happened?

What happened was, I was doing work for Marvel but I wasn't under contract. I got an offer from an outfit called Pacific Comics out in San Diego. I was living in the Midwest and had been thinking about getting more involved in film work for quite a while, but I realised I was never gonna do it unless I got out to California. My wife and I moved out to San Diego, and I got my own packaging deal for Pacific Comics. I did several books for them while I was also doing work for Marvel, and it just got to be really kind of crazy. There was too much work to try to do all of it.

Brent Anderson — who I had worked with on *Ka-Zar* — and I did a comic book called *Somerset Holmes*. It was specifically set up with an eye toward getting somebody in the movies to take a look at it. And that's exactly what happened. A director called us and said he wanted to make the film, and that sort of got me into the film and TV business. And then things got *really* crazy and I had to make a decision. Finally, I called up my editor at Marvel and said I'm gonna have to leave. I remember regretting it in some ways, but I didn't really have a choice. So I just kind of disappeared from comics and concentrated on TV and movies and then novels, and really dropped out for quite a while.

What did you do for TV and the movies?

I work with my wife April on the TV stuff, and one of the first things we did was a

The Early Years

He may be winning over new fans on his recent conspiracy-filled run of the *Incredible Hulk*, but Bruce Jones is no stranger to comics. Starting out as an artist working mainly on sci-fi and horror titles, Jones soon made a name for himself in the '80s as a comics writer. Highlights include: *Alien Worlds* — a sci-fi anthology series published by Pacific Comics and Eclipse Comics, featuring original tales by Bruce Jones and a bevy of big name artists including Dave Stevens, Jeff Jones, John Bolton, Mike Mignola, Richard Corben, George Perez, Brent Anderson and Art Adams; *Twisted Tales* — a horror anthology series published by Pacific and Eclipse, featuring thought-provoking yet horrifying original tales by Jones and other writers, plus high-profile artists like Richard Corben, Mike Ploog, Berni Wrightson, John Totleben, John Bolton and Butch Guice; and Marvel's *Ka-Zar the Savage* from 1981–1984. Jones kicked off his twenty-eight-issue stint on that book with issue #1, alongside Brent Anderson (*Astro City*), who remained as artist for most of the run. *Ka-Zar the Savage* saw the jungle hero joined by his ferocious saber-toothed tiger Zabu and the saucy yet dangerous Shanna the She-Devil. Story highlights included a lengthy Spider-Man guest-appearance and the supposed death of Ka-Zar!

show for HBO called *The Hitchhiker*. It went into syndication and ended up running endlessly. We got a lot of cheques on that. Then, back in the '80s and '90s, the networks got very involved in making their own kind of movies, so I wrote a lot of that kind of stuff. It's very easy to make a living selling movie scripts, but it's very hard to actually get what you sell up on the screen. You can make a living one of two ways; either by re-writing other people's failed work or by just writing scripts that never make it to the screen. I went through a period where I was probably making more money then I'd ever made in the comics business, but I wasn't doing anything that anyone was seeing. So it looked like I'd vanished. Hollywood's very seductive. Once you get your Writer's Guild card and you get in, the pay is *very* hard to turn down.

After a spell doing movies, how'd you jump back into comics?

Actually, after the movies I started writing novels. I wrote a series of thrillers for Doubleday and Dutton and got very wrapped up in that. Then I got a call out of the blue from [editor] Axel Alonso, who was with DC/Vertigo at the time. He remembered my *Creepy* and *Eerie* stuff from back when he was a kid — which made me feel old — and he said, 'We're doing these horror titles for Vertigo, would you be interested?' I always loved that genre, so I said sure. Then, when he moved over to Marvel, he gave me a call about the *Hulk*.

He just pitched you *The Incredible Hulk* clear out of the blue?

Yeah. And I turned it down. I said, 'I just don't think I can do that stuff because

Somerset Holmes

Talk about your hard luck. First she gets amnesia, and then someone's out to kill her. Only thing is, she has no clue who's after her or why they want her dead. And if she doesn't find out fast, her past will be the least of her worries. That's the basic premise of Bruce Jones' six-issue mini-series *Somerset Holmes*, set in modern Southern California. Published by Pacific Comics (with Eclipse Comics publishing issues #5 and #6 after Pacific went bankrupt) during the big independent comics boom of the mid-'80s, the story seems a bit more like a suspense film than a comic book. And for good reason. Jones and his wife April Campbell teamed up with artist Brent Anderson (fresh off his *Ka-Zar* stint with Jones) to create a cinematic-style comic with one goal in mind: get Hollywood to take notice. They wrote the screenplay themselves to save it from typical butchering, and then succeeded in catching some attention. As the script was continually optioned, cheques just kept pouring in. But unfortunately the film itself sat in limbo, never making it to the big screen. Comics fans can still find the original series in back-issue bins, as well as the Eclipse graphic novel collecting the entire series.

I haven't kept up with it at all.' I hadn't been reading Marvel stuff for the longest time and I had no idea what was going on. When I was working at Pacific Comics, everything was Chris Claremont and he was king of the world. But even then I didn't try to keep up with all that continuity, and I told Axel I didn't want to start now. Fortunately, Marvel's decided that continuity was one of those things that had become a problem. It was hard to get new readers because they were expected to remember things that happened twenty years ago. So when I said I didn't know anything about the Hulk they said, 'Great, that's exactly what we want.' And that's kind of how I got the job.

But you initially turned down *Hulk*?

I don't know if I ever officially hung up the phone, but I pretty much told them I didn't think I could do it. I think Axel offered me a short Spider-Man thing first and that was fun. I think the Hulk just came across his desk while we were working together and he just asked me if I'd be interested in doing it. He said, 'I want to do something new too. I want a completely different approach because frankly the book's not selling at all. We're wide open to ideas.' That was when I got interested.

You had some huge shoes to fill, considering Peter David's decade-plus run on the title. Did you find that intimidating?

It didn't phase me because I wasn't particularly aware of Peter's work or that he had made a big hit. When I came to it, the book was in trouble and they were grateful just to have somebody that had kind of a different take on it. Once I got into my run I started hearing about Peter David, and I thought, uh oh, I'm in big trouble now. I deliberately tried not to go back and read his issues, because I didn't want that stuff creeping into my work.

How about the *Hulk* TV show, was that an inspiration at all?

When Axel and I first talked about the book, what he had in mind was something between *The Fugitive* and *The X-Files*, but he wasn't pushy about it. I liked both, so it sounded like a cool way to go. So no, there wasn't that much of a conscious effort to ape the *Hulk* TV show, but there was a conscious effort to think of it in terms of *The X-Files* and *The Fugitive*.

Your run on *Hulk* has sparked either high praise or huge criticism, largely due to the lack of 'screen time' you give the Hulk. What's your take?

To me, the story's everything. When Banner's on the screen, as far as I'm concerned the Hulk is on the screen because they're the same person. Sure, after I began writing the book and it started getting popular, all that criticism started coming in. One interesting thing I found out — the most popular issues are the ones *without* the Hulk. I started getting some pressure from somebody — maybe it was myself — to put some more Hulk in and when I did the sales dipped a little bit. So draw your own conclusions.

I've been to conventions and gotten the flak. I think I was in Chicago and I was signing books. There was this long line, and I was feeling great because it stretched all the way back to the wall, and then some kid walked up. Nice looking kid, very intelligent-looking. My head was down, I was signing something. 'Mr. Jones?' I said, 'Yes.' He said, 'Are you Bruce Jones?' I said, 'Yes.' 'Bruce Jones, the guy that writes the *Hulk*, right?' I said, 'Yeah.' He said, 'WHERE'S THE HULK?!' at the top of his lungs and just walked off. Everyone was kinda stunned and I thought, 'Oh boy.' So what're you gonna do? You can't please everyone.

The thing about the Hulk is, he's such a powerhouse and so dramatic, whenever he's given screen time he is just so much *there!* That, and Banner's supposed to be a fugitive on the run. I just felt like I had to be very careful about how often the Hulk made an appearance, because he would always wreck something and that would alert the cops and everybody else. It immediately put kind of a different spin on Banner running around being this reclusive fugitive. If this guy's wrecking buildings, everyone in the country is gonna know about it. The other thing I felt was: the Hulk's a more interesting character if you build up the anticipation of his next appearance and not just see him beating somebody up every issue. One thing I do know, the 'Hulk hitting the next villain' approach had already been done and I didn't just want to repeat it. The conflict the character experiences as Banner is far more interesting.

Do you write full scripts?

I've always worked that way. I write it all out like in a movie script with the panels, dialogue and the action. My way of thinking is: that way at least the artist can see exactly what I want the reader to see. If the artist doesn't want to do it, that's fine, though occasionally you'll run across one who'll just pick up the script and kind of give it a cursory read, then throw it in the trash and start drawing. I guess maybe because some artists are used to working the old Marvel plot way. In that case, you have to go back in and figure out, 'Oh my god, what am I gonna do with this?' But that doesn't happen very often. I've been extremely lucky. My god, look at my run on *Hulk!* There hasn't been a bad artist in there.

I try to make the direction in a script very, very clear. I set it up like you would with camera angles and try to describe everything so the pacing and the action is *extremely* deliberate. And then when I'm done, I'm done. If the artist follows what I've written, to me you're gonna have a good comic book. If he doesn't follow it, that's up to him. And of course the really great artists will sometimes come up with an idea that's better than your idea and actually improve on the script. Of course, that's more than welcome because it just makes you look good.

Did comic book writing come easy to you because of the screenwriting?

Actually, the screenwriting stuff came easy because I'd already done the comic book writing. They complement each other. Having said that, a comic script is not a screenplay and it's not the other way around either. They are very different animals. But they're certainly more alike than, say, a novel and a comic.

Above: *A sketch of a rather fetching female vampire. Courtesy of Bruce Jones.* ™ *and* © *2004 Bruce Jones.*

You've written books, comics, movies, TV scripts. Which do you prefer?

I like 'em all. They're all different challenges. Movies, TV and comics have a lot in common, in that it's a collaborative effort and you're always working with someone else. When you're working on a novel, you're kind of alone. That's got its good side, because it's all yours, but then when it bombs you really look bad! The healthy thing about TV and comic book scripts is that you are forced to kind of keep your ego in check, because you know that you're just one part of a larger process. You do your job as well as you can, but then the artist has to come along and do his part. You're working together on something. In a way it's more pleasant because you're distancing yourself from it.

How long does it take you to write an average issue?

If I can get five solid pages done every morning I usually feel pretty good, and then the rest of the afternoon is gravy. Sometimes I'm working way ahead and there was a point where I was actually working with three different artists. That was nuts. The paychecks were good, but it was bad because three different artists mean three different storylines. I don't think that's wise. For me, anyway. Maybe Brian Michael Bendis can do it, but I just can't give my best if I'm trying to do three separate plots at once.

Do you have any sort of schedule to help you stay focused on your writing?

The Incredible Hulk

Kermit was right: it ain't easy being green. Especially when you've also been grey, then green, then grey, then smart, then stupid, then smart again, then a Las Vegas bouncer, then… well, you get the picture. Just as there've been numerous incarnations of the Hulk, there have also been a number of key creators involved in his history. Stan Lee specialised in big, smash-'em-up action stories. His and Jack Kirby's version started as a grey-skinned brute who surfaced every sundown. The character soon changed to green and transformed whenever Banner's stress levels got too high. Under John Byrne's direction, the Hulk and Banner were physically separated into two beings, and Dr. Banner finally married Betty Ross. The most prolific *Hulk* writer, with over 100 issues to his name, was Peter David. His run on *Hulk* was filled with a ton of humour, as his Hulk retained Banner's mind intact for the most part. Also, Betty died of gamma radiation poisoning and the Hulk reverted to grey for a while and wore snazzy suits as a Vegas casino bouncer named Mr. Fixit. In Jones' run, the Hulk takes a major back seat to Banner, who's continually on the run from the law and a number of super secret organizations.

I do now. I didn't when I was younger, because when you're younger, you're younger. I used to sit at a drawing board and be up till 3 o'clock in the morning with the television on. Watching a TV show and drawing. I can't do that anymore. I try to work mornings because I'm at my freshest, and also I have kids, and by 3 o'clock most of the year the kids come home from school and my son wants me to play Xbox with him or something. Usually the attitude of the house changes then.

I don't crack a whip on myself, but it's usually the first thing I do when I get up. I have breakfast and pretty much hit the keys. Sometimes you have a great day and you're through by 12 o'clock or 1. Sometimes you have a not so great day and you're not through till 6. It's the way it goes. I've found over the years I've become easier on myself. I let myself forgive myself if I don't do as much work as I feel I should. That's because I've found when I try to force the work, the next thing you know you're re-reading it and boy you might as well not have bothered at all it's so bad. For some reason or other you just didn't feel like writing that day and those things happen. There's nothing you can do about it, so why feel guilty?

Has your background as an illustrator helped you with your writing?

I think it's helped me tremendously, but then I'm probably not the person to ask. I think anyone who is an artist and then becomes a writer has got a leg up on those who just start out as writers. I think most comic book writers are at least somewhat visually oriented or they wouldn't be attracted to the field. They'd be writing novels or short stories or something like that. I don't think being an artist is something you have to be to write comics, but I think it's certainly an advantage.

Do you ever get the itch to start drawing your own stuff again?

I'm not sure I'd want to get back to the tedium of drawing individual comic book panels. I would, however, like to get back into doing the more illustrative stuff I used to do. I would like to be drawing figures and scenes that aren't necessarily anything to do with storytelling. The storytelling aspect of comics is such a huge part of the art. When you're just drawing something for the sake of drawing it, you can do things that you don't have to worry about. I really enjoy doing that.

What about a creator-owned project?

Yeah, I think about that a lot. I think I probably will do that. I just don't know who with and I'm not sure exactly what. I think Brent and I were one of the first to cross over into movies — I mean, *Somerset Holmes* never actually got made into a film, but it came very close. It certainly got optioned a lot of times. I practically lived off that comic out there. It only ran for six or eight issues, but man did it get optioned like crazy. And that was when nobody was optioning comic books! Now I see all these guys are selling their comics to the movies for a million dollars, and yeah that certainly gives you pause. I don't necessarily think that's an excuse to start doing it, but it must be nice.

How much of your personal life comes through in your work?

I think it all comes through to some degree. I think the best ideas come from inside of you, whether you're aware of it or not. I never consciously try to do it, because then it always looks forced. Mostly, I'm just trying to tell a good story. I guess I'm conscious of the fact that I put things into my scripts from maybe something that I've read — some book on science or some news item that I think is important — but only if I think it makes for a good story. I think there's a certain percentage of all writing that can be used as a teaching tool, but it's entertainment first and foremost.

Exactly how do you conduct your research?

Well, if it's a character or villain or something from the Marvel canon that they have an interest in reviving, then they'll send me a lot of that material or I'll get it online. It's so easy just to go online and find any of that material. I finished a Stephen Hawking book a couple of months ago. A lot of that stuff is so technical it's almost impossible to get into a story, but there are certain overall aspects that you can use. It's more the philosophy or the impact that science has had that I try to get in there.

How about writer's block? What do you do when that beast strikes?

I've never had it. I know people talk about writer's block, but I have no idea what that really is. I'll tell you what I *have* had, and it may be what people call writer's block, but I just recognise it for what it is to me. There are moments or hours or sometimes days — rarely weeks — where I just don't feel like writing. To me, that's perfectly normal and I've got a million other interests to fill that time. It only becomes a problem when you start to think, if I don't get this written eventually I'm not gonna get paid! So you have to consider that and you get motivated. Other than that, I just let my mind go in the millions of directions that it wants to. Maybe the reason I don't have writer's block is because I'm always reading about something else, some new angle or idea, and that kind of feeds into my stories. I've read about people who are buried under writer's block, and I have to ask myself why those people even want to be writers? If it's not enjoyable, why do it? Anybody can write. I think writing *well* is what's tough.

Besides the Hulk, are there any other characters you'd like to get your hands on?

I'd like to do Batman. I think that would be a lot of fun. And I think I'd like to do the Punisher. I wouldn't mind doing some more Wolverine stuff. Yeah. There's a dark side of Bruce Jones. Which is the only side. It depends on the editor and what they want too. You can get yourself in situations where you think it's a great idea and you get, 'Batman would never say that,' or, 'So-and-so would never do that.' You run into editors like that, but I also understand

Above: *Another page of the story 'Sea Serpents', which was originally published by Richard Corben. Courtesy of Bruce Jones.* ™ *and* © *2004 Bruce Jones.*

why they're doing it. There is the constant conflict between what has gone on before/what the fans expect and trying to cover new territory. It's an endless tug of war, and in the two years or so that I've been back working in comics I've actively seen it happen.

At Marvel now they're trying harder then ever to look at both categories of comics reader. Largely, I think, because they're in book stores and they know that the casual adult reader might go over and grab one. He doesn't know anything about the history of Spider-Man or whatever, so it has to be accessible to that person. But the comic companies are also aware of the fact that there's a hardcore group of enthusiasts, many of whom have been reading comics for thirty years. They know their Spider-Man or whoever and that's exactly how they want him. I don't think anybody can truly reconcile these two categories any more than they can explain why manga is slowly pushing regular comics off the shelves! Every time I go to a Borders there's three more racks of manga and two less shelves for comic books. It's depressing in a way. I don't get it.

So you're not a big manga fan I take it?

The weirdest thing happened to me. I was at a convention about six months ago, sitting down at a table signing and doing my thing, and all of a sudden I hear all this screaming. I thought, 'God, what is that?' I look way down and at the end of the other table is this guy, sitting and talking to the fans. I know most of the people in the comics business but I don't recognise him at all. Who the hell is he? There's this *huuuge* line of people and all this excited screaming and yelling. Then it suddenly dawns on me, everybody in that line is a girl! Finally, I couldn't stand it any longer and I got up and moseyed down just to see what was going on. It turns out this guy is the voice of one of these *Yu-Gi-Oh* characters. He had like 25,000 fifteen year-old girls and they were going apeshit for this stuff. That was the first inkling I had that something strange was taking place.

Y'know what's really exasperating for Marvel and DC? They're trying so hard to produce a good product. You know, print it on good paper and glossy stock and have it carefully coloured, and all of a sudden here are these masses of young girls going in there and reading black and white pulpy paper things that you have to read backwards. It's leaking into our culture. This is worse than 1941 and Pearl Harbor. [*Laughs*] Nah, I'm just kidding. I love the Japanese.

If you're not reading manga, what are you reading these days?

I read everything Brian Azzarello writes. I follow him from *100 Bullets* to *Batman* to whatever. Like me, he's been blessed with very, very good artists. I have to admit that as much as I love Brian's stuff, I also really like the artists he works with. I know that I wrote some stories back in the Warren days that nobody ever talks about, but I thought were some of the best stories I ever wrote. It's just that the artwork was less than, shall we say, terrific. People tend to remember the art. After a while you begin to see a pattern — invariably the stories you sort of get famous for have terrific artwork. And I'm as guilty as anybody else. I'll see a comic book or a story that has artwork that puts me off, and frankly I won't give the story a chance. That's not fair to the writer. It's a collaborative medium, that's the bottom line. I guess the other side of the coin is there may be artists out there that have such a huge following that they could just draw the phone book and people would like it. And that doesn't seem right either.

How has it been working exclusively for Marvel?

It's been good. They have a pretty open mind and I think that's because, like I say, they've been trying so much to bring in a larger readership. I think they've realised to some extent that if you just keep appealing to the hardcore fans it's like a snake eating its own tail. So they've been more and more inclined to take chances. They certainly took an enormous chance with me. I can't believe the latitude they gave me. So that really hasn't been a problem. They've been great.

And your relationship with editor Axel Alonso seems to be going great as well.

We've very symbiotic. Even over at Vertigo we kind of had a way of thinking alike. And Axel has terrific instincts. Axel, much more than I, has a feeling for the commercial end of it. He has great instincts for knowing what might be tricky territory and what might be something the fans are gonna go crazy over. So we try to meet somewhere in the middle because we don't just want to do crass commercial junk.

*　　　　　*　　　　　*

MIKE MIGNOLA

Mike Mignola's artwork is so mind-blowingly good, with its big, inky slabs of nightmarish beasts and thunderous action, it's easy to forget he's *writing* the stories as well as drawing them. The tales in his signature work, *Hellboy,* which he's doled out in tantalizing spoonfuls for more than a decade now, are told in a manner unlike any other comic book on the shelves. Mignola's visuals speak volumes; as one gets drawn into a *Hellboy* story, it's more *experienced* than it is read. The multitalented New Yorker entered the business doing time on superhero books for Marvel and DC he rarely enjoyed. When comics superstars such as John Byrne and Frank Miller migrated to upstart publisher Dark Horse in the mid-'90s, Mignola followed, with the singular intention of bringing *Hellboy* to life. Numerous awards, as well as industry-wide respect, followed. *Hellboy* recently took its turn in the spotlight of pop culture when director Guillermo del Toro turned Mignola's creation into a big-budget, live-action movie, which will likely draw in a multitude of new readers. Those readers are in for a treat: Mignola's fusion of kinetic art and endlessly surprising storytelling are a bigger blast than any mere movie could ever be.

When did you first start reading comics?

You know, I don't remember reading comics as a little kid. I do remember my cousin had certain issues of *Fantastic Four* and *Doom Patrol,* and that they were fascinating to me, but I don't actually remember reading them. I was probably in junior high school when I seriously started reading comics. Around that time Marvel was reprinting things like the Kirby *Fantastic Four* stories and *Thor* and I started picking those titles up. *Conan* and the Kirby *Fantastic Four,* I remember specifically reading those, and that's what led me into seriously collecting comics for a few years.

Did you at any point start creating your own comics back in those days?

I never did. Strangely enough, I'm not one of those guys who actually made up stories and drew comic book pages. I don't know that I ever really thought that I'd be drawing comics professionally. I just wanted to draw monsters, and I wanted to do pin-up art. When I was in art school I started seriously thinking, 'Where am I going to find a job drawing monsters?' I didn't know much, but I knew there weren't a lot of jobs for guys who just wanted to draw monsters. I started looking at comics, and quickly realised that I was never going to be good enough to actually draw them, so I thought maybe I could break in as an inker. Once I got out of art school, I geared myself toward breaking in to the industry as an inker, but — as it turned out — I was a really horrible inker. So that didn't last very long.

So because you were a horrible inker, you moved on to... pencilling?

Yeah. Isn't that funny? But that's really the way it happened. When I went up to Marvel, I had lots of samples of pin-up stuff and cover images, and one of the editors up there, Al Milgrom, who's a fantastic guy, I think he really wanted me to try pencilling. But I was too lazy and too scared of it. So he gave me inking work, and the inking work really crapped out. I plainly just wasn't any good at it. I remember him coming up to me at a convention after the inking was pretty much over, and he said, 'Are you ready to try pencilling *now?*' So my first pencilling job was a Sub-Mariner story for *Marvel Fanfare*. Before that I had done maybe two or three sample pages just on my own and never shown them to anybody.

Were you happy pencilling superheroes when all you really wanted to do was draw monsters?

It turned out that I really enjoyed storytelling. The superhero stuff, eh, some of it I liked, some of it I didn't. I hated doing *Alpha Flight,* I hated every second of

Place of birth:
Berkeley, California, USA
Date of birth:
16 September 1960
Home base:
New York City, USA
Education:
California College of Arts and Crafts. 'People think I majored in basket weaving. They're not far off.'
First published work:
The New Defenders #116 (uncredited, inked five pages)
Career highlights:
The Amazing Screw-On Head, Bram Stoker's Dracula, B.P.R.D., Chronicles of Corum, Fafhrd and the Gray Mouser, Hellboy

it. I hated waking up in the morning when I was drawing *Alpha Flight*. It was so much a real superhero comic, and I just wasn't cut out for it. A lot of those first couple years of doing stuff for Marvel, the feeling was, 'This just isn't what I do. It doesn't feel natural and I'm not having any fun.' There were maybe a couple of issues of *Hulk* that I enjoyed working on — though one of them was a nightmare! — and *Rocket Raccoon* was actually a lot of fun. But when I got into things like drawing Superman, I *knew* I shouldn't have been drawing Superman. I went through my career for years looking for jobs where there'd be at least *something* in there I could show off with or do a good job on. I was basically looking for books that had monsters in them. But in those early years, I was not an 'in-demand' guy. It never would have occurred to me to go in and say, 'Right, I want to do *this* kind of book.' I basically had to do what I was asked to do.

That changed after three or four years at Marvel. I went to First Comics and did this fantasy series, a Michael Moorcock thing called *Chronicles of Corum*. Because I wasn't working for Marvel and I wasn't working on an established character — even though Michael Moorcock had created it, I came up with all the visuals — I started feeling a little bit more like nobody was looking over my shoulder. Nobody was going to say, 'Hey, that's not what the Hulk looks like!' I started feeling a little bit more comfortable with what I was doing. When I went back to Marvel and DC after doing the *Corum* book, I was like, 'I think I know what I'm doing, guys. If possible, leave me alone and let me do it.' There was definitely some confidence in me that wasn't there before. Not that I necessarily did great work when I came back from *Corum*, but at least I started feeling that maybe I had some real perspective on this stuff.

Chronicles of Corum

Based on the books by author Michael Moorcock (best known as the creator of fantasy character Elric), First Comics' *Chronicles of Corum* provided an early showcase for the artwork of up-and-coming Mike Mignola. *Corum*, published intermittently in a dozen issues from 1986–1988, explored the sword-and-sorcery world of Moorcock's frequent hero, the Eternal Champion, a fighting force so powerful he could go toe-to-toe in battle with the gods themselves. But *Chronicles of Corum* wasn't the only fantasy prose Mignola turned into dynamic comic book art; he also illustrated four issues (for Marvel's Epic imprint) of *Fafhrd and the Gray Mouser*, based on the writings of Fritz Leiber, starting in 1990. Mignola even got a chance to draw the character that started his love affair with fictional and legendary monsters when he lent his artistic skills to Dracula, first for a series of Topps trading cards in 1992, then in four issues of Topps' *Bram Stoker's Dracula* comic book in 1994. Though Mignola's earliest published work was a mishmash of assignments from companies great and small, his skill at illustrating the fantastic — which would come in plenty handy for *Hellboy* — was evident right from the start.

Did you feel more passionate about the work after *Chronicles of Corum*?

I had always been passionate about drawing comics, but it was a struggle for me to actually draw stuff. I'm not a real natural artist. I did a *Dr. Strange/Dr. Doom* graphic novel that I enjoyed a lot, but unfortunately I didn't really get a chance to finish it the way I wanted to because I overbooked myself. I took on this giant DC project, *Cosmic Odyssey*, at the same time, and then suddenly Marvel was clamouring to have the graphic novel done. Mark Badger ended up inking it. Originally I was supposed to ink that book myself, and while Mark did a great job it would have been nice for me to see it all the way through. But, little by little, as I became more established in the business, I was more careful about what I did or didn't do. I drew this Batman *Gotham by Gaslight* book, which was no fun at all, but it was something I felt was really necessary to show what kind of material I should be doing. Having finished *Cosmic Odyssey*, I had finally gotten superheroes out of my system. There were just so *many* superheroes in it, I thought, 'I'm done with this.' From *Cosmic Odyssey* on I think you see me, little by little, figuring out what I should be doing, and finding the kind of jobs to best suit what I do.

Where did your fascination with dark stories come from?

I read *Dracula* when I was in sixth grade. I don't remember exactly what it was about that book, but I just decided, 'That's it!' I remember it as a conscious decision, almost a discovery; this was *exactly* the kind of material that I wanted to be reading. Which, I guess, was weird. I'm not even sure what it was about *Dracula* that spoke to me in such loud terms, but there was really no going back once I'd read it. Everything about that book appealed to me. *Dracula* steered me toward other supernatural literature and those other books in turn steered me toward folklore and mythology and all that stuff.

Did you gravitate towards telling monster stories because you liked drawing them, or did you draw monsters because you liked the stories?

It's sort of a 'chicken or the egg' thing. One of the first stories I plotted appeared in *Batman: Legends of the Dark Knight* #54. Somebody at DC said, 'Come up with an issue of *Batman*,' and my immediate thought was to do something supernatural. I was very happy with that Batman story, both artistically and in terms of the subject matter. I knew then, if possible, I wanted to continue doing those kinds of stories. So when it came to doing *Hellboy*, I already had the subject matter and I had the stories I wanted to do; creating the character was secondary.

With supernatural stories, the subject matter and the imagery is really densely interwoven. I certainly had no interest in writing a novel, say. I just couldn't do it. When I plot stories, what matters most to me is that there's certain key imagery I want to visually put down on the paper. It's not as simple as, 'I want to draw this monster' — though there certainly have been stories I've done that revolve entirely around, 'Oh, I've always wanted to draw this monster' — it's more that there are certain themes, certain sequences, certain locations, whatever it is, that are definitely visually-driven.

What inspired your move from the Big Two to a creator-owned book?

Having done the *Legends of the Dark Knight* issue and knowing that I wanted to continue creating stories like that, I briefly thought, well, I could keep on making up horror stories and cramming them into issues of *Batman* or *Wolverine* or whatever, and kind of bounce back and forth between Marvel and DC doing stuff like that, or I could just make up my own thing. That seemed much simpler, and from a business point of view made a lot more sense. And anyway, I had done Batman, I had done Wolverine... in fact, I had done a little bit of everything in mainstream comics. It had got to the point where I didn't want to keep repeating myself, and I thought, well, one thing I haven't done yet is to put something down on paper that's one hundred percent mine. I knew you couldn't do creator-owned work at Marvel or DC, so Dark Horse seemed to be the natural place to go. About that time, both Frank Miller and John Byrne were doing creator-owned stuff at Dark Horse and Art Adams and I had both been talking about going that route. In fact, there were a whole slew of guys in the same boat at the same time and so it was a simple choice. When I told [Dark Horse publisher] Mike Richardson what I wanted to do, I didn't tell him what it was, I didn't tell him what it was about, I just said, 'I want to do *Hellboy*' — that's it — and he said, 'Fine.' So the whole process was very smooth.

How fleshed out was the Hellboy character and the *Hellboy* universe before you started that first mini-series?

Honestly, at that stage I really had no idea what I was doing. All I'd come up with was an image of the Hellboy character and a rough idea what the subject of the first mini-series [*Seed of Destruction*] was going to be. My original idea was, 'I'll turn my rough ideas over to John Byrne and he'll flesh the whole thing out into a proper story.' But every day, over various conversations with John and as I thought about the series more and more, I would add another piece to the Hellboy jigsaw, then another piece and another piece. So by the time it came to sit down and actually draw *Seed of Destruction*, I had come up with the entire plot. I don't want to minimise what John did at all, I couldn't have done it without him, but I don't think he ended up contributing any actual plot elements to the first mini-series.

When it was time to do the actual book itself, I was like, 'Okay, John, I've got the plot, now I'm going to draw it,' and once I'd drawn it, I had to do a real rough typed script so John would know what the hell was going on. Over the course of the four issues, I scripted more and more and more, so by the end, John really didn't have that much to do. I remember by issue #4, he would write certain dialogue that I would just edit out. And I thought, 'Oh man, that's a real ballsy thing for me to be doing. He was nice enough to script this book, and here I am editing his work.' When John and I first discussed *Seed of Destruction*, we talked about the writing style and what the tone of the book should be, and should we have this running internal monologue of Hellboy's thoughts, because we wanted this pulpy, *noir* kind of thing going on. I realised somewhere in the course of that first story that maybe this wasn't such a good idea after all. I think actually that was when both parties realised that I should probably just be writing the book myself. At some point during *Seed of Destruction*, I just suddenly thought, 'I know what this book should sound like.' I learned a lot on that first mini-series.

Having a writer like John Byrne backing you up sounds like a great safety net, just in case.

I couldn't have done it without him. I couldn't have worked with that much white paper. I needed to know that somebody was going to come along and do the *real* work. I could write dialogue as long as I knew somebody was going to come along behind me and turn it into *real* dialogue. Like I say, I don't want in any way to downplay John's role. I went into that first mini-series saying, 'If I write it myself, it will be *odd*. I want somebody who's written a lot of mainstream comics stuff to make *Hellboy* more accessible.' But that said, there were lines John wrote where I said, 'Huh. Sounds like mainstream comics, and that's what I *don't* want.' I think I had some odd turns of phrase that John corrected, and I came back with, 'Yeah, but you know, I liked it better when it was *odd*.' What I finally realised was, 'Gee, if I like it better the way I had it, then I should just write the comic.'

What are your strengths and weaknesses as a writer?

That's a tough one. I still don't consider myself a 'writer'. I think my strength as a writer is knowing my limitations as a writer. Most of this is just a chickenshit thing on my part. I try not to stick my neck out and write stuff I don't know how to write. I can write dialogue because I listen to people talk, but I'm certainly not

John Byrne

Writer/artist John Byrne has worked on just about every big-league character in the world of superhero comics over the past three decades. But in the minds of fans, his classic run on *Uncanny X-Men* along with writer Chris Claremont will forever be the multitalented creator's greatest legacy. In fact, *Uncanny* was just one of many long and legendary runs as Byrne tackled the titans of the comics world, and not just a few of them — sometimes it seems like there's no title in modern comicdom that Byrne hasn't shepherded. *Fantastic Four, Superman* and *Wonder Woman* all received overhauls from Byrne, and each time his knack for boiling down heroes to find their core appeal, then building them back up again with pitch-perfect characterization, left the books in far better shape than he'd found them. Byrne turned creator with *Next Men*, moving to Dark Horse, whereupon Mike Mignola sought his counsel as he began mapping out *Hellboy*, his first stab at a creator-owned comic book. In the end, Mignola says he found his own direction for the character, but with a veteran of John Byrne's calibre watching his back, Mignola was always on solid footing, no matter what.

PLOT

BPRD# 4

⑫

- Pages 16-17

-- top of Page 16 -
we zoom in on
bad guy as he talks
more about Frog creatures -
- Panel 2 - Abe says BPRD
will round them up
- Panel 3 - We see a
bunch of frog guys
Hop/Running through a
shallow creek with wood on either side - BPBD
Helicopters are seen above - through the trees.
- Panel 4 and 5 - Closer on one of the frog guys -
as he comes toward us he looks more human.
- Panel 6 - Back view of people (actually frog-creatures)
walking away from us across field. In backgrand
we see road, maybe town in distance -
-- Top of 17 - one of
the human looking frog creatures
hitch hikes while others stand
a way off - maybe a car
is slowing - Panel 2 -
dried up dead guy behind
wheel of car - he had
misfortune to give them a
ride -- has the same
marking as old lady at end
of "Seed of Destruction" Chapter 3.

PAGE (16)

① ② ③ ④ ⑤

PAGE (17)

① ② ③ ④

Above: *A page of Mike Mignola's plot for* B.P.R.D.™, *A Plague of Frogs #4. Compare the top thumbnail to Guy Davis' pencils, facing page. Courtesy of Mike Mignola.* B.P.R.D. *and* Hellboy ™ *and* © 2004 Mike Mignola.

Above: *Guy Davis' rough pencils for* A Plague of Frogs #4, *with Mike Mignola's word balloon and caption placements. Courtesy of Mike Mignola.* B.P.R.D. *and* Hellboy ™ *and © 2004 Mike Mignola.*

someone who's going to sit there and write a big prose passage about, I dunno, what the wind smells like. Ray Bradbury can do that, Neil Gaiman can do that; me, I know my greatest strength is my artwork, so as much as possible I will downplay the words and try to convey atmosphere and mood with pictures. I'm happiest being in control of the whole process and being able to make decisions like, 'I'll let the art tell the story here, I'll let the words tell the story here.'

When does *Hellboy* work best? And have you ever tried to tell the wrong kind of story?

There are two Hellboy stories I've done that really, really don't work. Both are cases of me not having done enough homework. There was this one story called 'The Corpse', which worked out great, because it was largely based on a particular Irish folktale, which I researched thoroughly and padded out with a bunch of other weird details from English folklore. There's a richness to that story, coupled with my perspective on the whole thing and my sense of humour. That story was *loaded*. But when it came to actually putting 'The Corpse' out in comic book form, I realised it was too short. Off the top of my head, I came up with an overall title: *The Corpse and the Iron Shoes*. So then I had to come up with a story called 'The Iron Shoes', one that was only six pages long. I knew that there was this particular kind of creature and I thought, 'Well, I could give it big iron shoes and call it the Iron Shoes,' and I just *did* it. Looking back, I probably should have spent a couple more days reading English folklore, because the end product just didn't have the authority, the weird details, that you get from actual folktales. That was one of the worst Hellboy stories I've done. There was just nothing to it.

I did this one Hellboy story recently, featuring a Malaysian vampire. I'd wanted to draw this creature for years, but I'd never found any actual folklore about it, other than, 'There's this creature, and this is where it comes from.' At that point, I shouldn't have done the story, or at least I should have taken that monster and put it into another story altogether. But instead I put Hellboy in Malaysia, and he encounters this creature, and… he fights it. End of story. There was just nothing to it. I didn't bring enough of my own sensibilities to it. I've done plenty of stories that don't seem to make any sense, but they're fun, or they're playing up an aspect of my personality. I think where *Hellboy* works best is either when it's so much *me,* or it's based on some other source, like a folktale or a fairytale. The stuff that's sort of half-ass, in-between, is the stuff that doesn't work.

Once you have an idea in mind, how do you begin to turn it into an actual story?

Most of my stories come about in very different ways. I've been reading supernatural stuff since I was in sixth grade, so that's like thirty-five years, a long goddamn time. So I've got a good general knowledge of the subject, but I also have a terrible memory, so I have dim recollections of certain things. A lot of the Hellboy stories, I'm putting them together in my head based on things I remember, from things I read a long time ago… maybe an image I saw, a creature I've always wanted to draw. So when it comes to actually doing the story, when I have enough of a general idea, maybe two or three good images and some kind of a beginning and ending in mind, then I sit down and pull out the books and start looking for specifics.

A good example would be the second *Hellboy* mini-series, *Right Hand of Doom*, where I knew I wanted to do something with vampires. I already had the gist of the story, which was: Nazis get the body of this vampire and they're going to bring it back to life, and a bunch of shit's going to happen. So I was able to structure the basic plot and then get down to the in-depth research. I knew right from the outset that I didn't want to do standard Hollywood-type vampire stuff and so I came up with this actual mythology about the goddess Hecate and snakes and wolves and owls. The idea was to bring in as much traditional but non-stereotypical vampire material as possible into this particular tale. That's really where I have the most fun, doing that kind of homework. Another example would be the story I mentioned previously, 'The Corpse', where there was this Irish folktale that I had read years before and had always wanted to adapt. When I sat down to do the Hellboy story, I said to myself, 'First I'll re-read that folktale and then I'll read a bunch of other related folklore and see if I can sprinkle some of that in there as well.' And that's more or less how this stuff happens.

With a story in mind, how does it start making its way onto paper?

Initially, I don't write anything more than just a couple notes here and there. In a lot of cases, I haven't even written notes, I'll tend to just run the stuff over in my head for a long period of time. Little by little, certain stories will come to the forefront, and then eventually I'll say, 'Okay, everything else can go into the background and I will pull this one particular theme out.' I focus all my energy on it, all my thoughts on it, and then I just thumbnail the whole job. Over the last couple of years, I've gotten into the habit of writing down notes as certain things occur to me; a little bit of dialogue or a particular image. Sometimes I lose those notes. Sometimes I actually put them in a filing cabinet. But mostly it's all in my head.

More and more now, I put a little extra emphasis on the writing as I'm doing my thumbnails. There was a time when I just did the thumbnails and had no idea what anybody was going to be talking about. That led to some really weird problems on the whole *Wake the Devil* mini-series. I don't know that I had any idea what was going to be happening on a particular page or series of pages, other than, visually, 'Hellboy will do this, he'll walk into this room, and then this creature's gonna come up out of the floor, and blah-blah-blah.' What happened was, when I then sat down to script the book, I knew Hellboy was going to encounter this character, but I had no idea that character would then start yakking on and on about him being the Beast of the Apocalypse. That's how the whole Beast of the Apocalypse thing happened in *Hellboy*. I had nothing for these two characters to say to each other. So, of course, the one says, 'Hey, guess what, you're the Beast of the Apocalypse!' I'm like, 'Holy shit, I never saw that coming!' As a result, the end I had in mind for that mini-series, the actual space I had thumbnailed, was too small. I couldn't end the mini-series without coming back in and addressing that whole Beast of the Apocalypse situation. So nowadays I try to have some idea of what the hell guys are talking about when I'm doing my thumbnails.

With the thumbnails done, how do you turn them into finished pages?

Once I've done the thumbnails, I then do a lot of research for my locations and things like that. Ideally, if I've got the time, I like to do my thumbnails and then spend some time with a sketchbook and various photo references. It's almost like I do set design. I never spend as much time on this as I should, which is a shame, because the more time I spend doing designs for characters and locations, the better the end result. If I just do my thumbnails and then rush straight into drawing and make stuff up on the page, it's never quite as good as if I gave it a little bit of extra thought beforehand.

When do you start seriously thinking about the dialogue?

I draw very slowly, and part of the drawing process now is, 'What are these guys saying?' It's become organic and very necessary to the drawing process to consider the dialogue. By the time I've finished drawing a page, I probably have as much as eighty or ninety percent of the dialogue written. There might be two or three different versions of it written on the same corner of the page, but at least I have a pretty good idea of what I'm doing. Then, once I've drawn the book, I can go back in and script the whole thing pretty quickly, because the rough version already exists on the original artwork. Another part of the

Hellboy: Beast of the Apocalypse

New to *Hellboy*? Never fear. Mignola's loath to bog down his stories in too much continuity, so neophytes should have an easy time picking up on the saga to date. In Mignola's words, Hellboy is 'the world's greatest occult detective,' a paranormal investigator unafraid to mix it up with the things that go bump in the night. One of the reasons for his bravery is the fact that Hellboy's a nigh-on indestructible wrecking machine with a big stone fist, and getting into a slugfest with him would be ill-advised. Hellboy works for the Bureau of Paranormal Research and Defense, and the crimson behemoth isn't even the strangest character the organization employs. In *Wake the Devil*, Hellboy learns that he's the Beast of the Apocalypse, pulled from Hell by Nazi scientists as a means of bringing about a fiery end to the Earth. At the heart of this sinister plot... none other than the Russian prophet, Rasputin, who it turns out is even more unkillable than his countrymen had thought. The Beast of the Apocalypse stigma has hung over Hellboy ever since, but luckily for readers, it hasn't kept him from doing what he does best: kicking the snot out of evil.

SCRIPT

BPRD

Plague of Frogs #4   (8)

— Page 16

① They are the new children of the old gods. And the human race ... will pass away. (Priest)

② I ... did ... this. (Priest)

③ More BPRD agents are on their way. They'll round up your creatures ...   (Abe)

④ Some ...   (Priest - off panel)

⑤ " Not all ... "   (caption)

⑥ " Many will escape ... " (caption)

⑦ " They will not be recognized for what they are..." (caption)

— Page 17

① " They will do what they must to survive..." (caption)

② " They will be drawn to the secret places ..." (caption)

③ " They will remember the old songs ..." (caption)

— Page 18

① " And they will sing ... and prey ..." (captions)

② " Prayers not heard in a million years on this earth ..."   (caption)

③ " And the old gods will wake ..." (caption)

Above: Script page for A Plague of Frogs #4. Again, compare the script for page 16 to Guy Davis' pencils and Mignola's initial plot. Courtesy of Mike Mignola. B.P.R.D. and Hellboy ™ and © 2004 Mike Mignola.

dialogue process I look on as a designer, so I'm designing certain images with those word balloons in mind. There are actual occasions where I've written dialogue in just because, in a particular panel, it will look good to have a balloon there. The art and the story at that point are so much hand-in-hand that I can't easily separate doing one thing before the other. That's why I couldn't ever imagine going back to working with another writer. I remember when I first started writing my own stuff, and I started getting the hang of it, I was suddenly thinking, there's so much I can do! I have so much power because I'm completely controlling all of this stuff. I felt like I'd stumbled into this whole new world of infinite possibilities, of which I've only explored the leading edge. There are so many more things you can accomplish creatively when you're in control of every stage of a comic book.

Since you have control over your own creation, what role does your Dark Horse editor, Scott Allie, play in all this?

My editor, my long-suffering editor, has the misfortune of me calling him every single day and saying, 'I was thinking of doing this! I was thinking of doing that!' And basically he just ends up as a sounding board for all my bullshit, crazy-ass ideas. And then I have to beg him to be honest with me. I know editors out there who just go, 'Yeah, it's fine! Everything's great!' Scott, even though he won't necessarily *say* he doesn't like something, I can tell from his tone of voice when he's not too impressed. Scott's also very good at getting me to fix certain problems. Plenty of times I've said, 'Listen, just tell me what's missing.' And he'll say, 'Well… just think about it.' And in some really weird, interesting, subtle way, he'll let me know what's lacking. As much as I'll say, 'I don't know what else I can do!' he somehow gets me to go back and rethink the material and add in what it needs. I remember on one of the mini-series he just said, 'It needs a Mignola moment.' Meaning, something that doesn't make any goddamn sense, that's only there because I thought it was an interesting image or idea. It needed to be something that was purely drawn from my subconscious. It's nice to have an editor who knows how I work. I don't know how I could ever do the book without him. I need somebody there who can kind of read my mind and who won't let me embarrass myself. Mind you… Scott did let me do that Malaysian vampire story!

How quickly — or slowly — do you work?

Once upon a time, I could draw about a page a day. And the script for that just adds a couple of days. But these days, I've become so fanatical about the way I work that I'm constantly rejecting pages or I'm rewriting pages endlessly. And it just seems that it takes me *forever* to get this stuff done. This latest mini-series was a nightmare because I plotted it three different times. Part of the problem was that I didn't have a gigantic chunk of uninterrupted time to just draw it from beginning to end. What happened was, I started drawing it, and then I had to go to Prague to be on the movie set. So while I was in Prague, I had a chance to look back on the first eight pages I did and say, 'Eh, they don't really work. Wouldn't it be better if the story was *this*?' So I came back from Prague, sat down to draw the thing again with a new plot in mind, did twelve or thirteen pages and said, 'Mmm, yeah, you know, that's not really working either.' So I scrapped the whole thing *again*. I think the problem now is it was much easier to do this when I didn't think anybody was looking at it. The more exposure *Hellboy* gets, the more pressure I feel for this stuff to be *really* good. And my problem has always been, the stuff is *never* good enough. What I need to do is get back into that frame of mind where I can say, 'It's good enough. Let's move on to the next one,' instead of working and working to make it *perfect*. Because it's never gonna be perfect.

Did the comic-book-to-movie process of the big-screen *Hellboy* teach you anything about storytelling?

What I realised about my work is that I am very shy of doing any kind of emotional development with characters. I would never have characters sit around and talk about their feelings. Over the course of ten years doing the comic, I think you see certain relationships between certain characters, but it's only done by the way they speak to each other. It's never done as full-on, talking about their emotions. It's just, 'Well, these guys relate to each other in this way, because there's some *unwritten* relationship between them.' You couldn't be that subtle in the movie. Mind you, it was great that we had ten years of the comic to draw on in making the movie. Overall, the more I can say about the movie, 'It's a separate animal from what I do,' the easier it is for me to distance myself from it and just say, 'Oh, that's fine, because that's del Toro's *Hellboy*.' My first meeting with Guillermo, I told him, 'Make it completely different. Make it as different as you want. Make it your thing. I've done my version.' And even though he made it much more faithful to my material than I ever thought he would, it's still his thing. So I don't torture myself by looking at stuff on the screen and going, 'Ohh! It was different in the comic!' or 'I would have done this or that differently.' I drew some mental line and said, 'His thing's over there, my thing's over here.' They relate to each other, one is drawn from the other, but they're separate entities. When I look at the movie poster, I go, 'Oh look, it's del Toro's new picture.' I don't say, 'Oh look, there's *my* new movie!'

In the comic book, are the characters' emotions less important to you than the story itself?

Well, more and more, the comic *is* going to be about Hellboy's feelings. It's just done in an extremely slow way. The problem is, as a writer, and as a person, I'm very shy. The one scene I actually did in the comic where Hellboy talks about his feelings on being the Beast of the Apocalypse, it's very strange in the way it's presented. Hellboy is definitely not looking at the person he's talking to. I think that scene is so telling about the way I deal with emotional things, and the way I deal with saying something that might be embarrassing. He's in shadow and he's looking off into space. The character of Hellboy is so much like me. I know that if I had to have that kind of serious conversation, I couldn't look at the person's face. That's probably one of the clearest cases where my own body language was in that character.

I find the Hellboy character extremely interesting to explore, because I've kind of written this guy into a corner. He's got this really weird problem of being the Beast of the Apocalypse and I find that so fascinating. As I move beyond the first ten years of *Hellboy* and into the next ten years of *Hellboy*, I really want to explore some of those things. I want to wander through the folklore more, but there's definitely a story arc that involves Hellboy's mother and his relationship to his mother, and then there's a story arc that involves his relationship to his father and whatever siblings he may or may not have had in Hell. And I think there's even a slightly autobiographical thing that fits into the way I deal with those kinds of relationships. I've never really had the emotional commitment to the supporting characters that I've had to Hellboy. They were always just kind of decoration around Hellboy himself. The Hellboy character contains so much of my own personality and certain physical characteristics of my father, and it's largely made of everything that I've ever really liked. He's always going to be the most intensely personal character to me.

What advice would you give to someone who wants to write comics, given that you never intended to write comics at all?

'Write what you know.' Or in my case, it's 'Write what you really care about.' I couldn't write a Western, because I don't give two shits about Westerns. Writing, to me, is such a personal thing that I can't imagine sitting there and writing material that I just didn't love. That seems to be the only formula that works for me. I couldn't fake it if my life depended on it.

*   *   *

MARK MILLAR

There are two separate-but-equal parts to the career of Mark
Millar. On the one side is a résumé that includes A-list mainstream
superhero titles, from the all-ages *Superman Adventures* to *The
Flash*, as well as top-selling runs on Marvel's rebooted 'Ultimate'
universe *X-Men* and *Avengers* titles. On the other side of the fence,
there's the thorny thicket of controversial books such as *The
Authority* (Bad language! Extreme violence! Homosexual
superheroes!) and *Chosen* (no less than Millar's take on the Second
Coming of Christ). The Scotsman cut his teeth, like so many of the
comics writers populating the UK, in the pages of sci-fi anthology
2000 AD. From there, he plotted a long and steady course up the
ladder of American comics throughout the '90s. The 21st Century
brought fame, as a pillar of Marvel's smash-hit Ultimate
community, and fortune... Millar's creator-owned collection of
titles, released under the MillarWorld banner, have netted big
paydays both in sales and in subsequent Hollywood movie deals.
Millar's feet remain firmly planted in both sides of the comics
world, and whether his stories are family-friendly or for grownups
only, readers just can't get enough.

When did it first occur to you that you'd like to write comic books for a living?

As a little kid, I used to make my own comics. Whenever you read an interview
with any writer or artist that seems to be everyone's secret origin. We'd all get A4
paper and a staple gun and make little books that we'd try and sell to people. I
remember that for a long time I didn't even realise photocopiers existed. I'd sell
my comics to kids in the neighbourhood, but each one was kind of how monks
used to write bibles a thousand years ago: completely handwritten. There's still
lots of them lying around the house. If I'm ever really famous, I can sell them on
eBay. I hadn't looked back at them in quite a long time, but I did so recently. It's
things like Cyclops blasting Spider-Man to pieces. It's the kind of stuff that these
days a social worker would look at and get really scared. It honestly looks like
something that child abuse victims come up with! [*Laughs*] And yet I had this
lovely, happy childhood. I first became aware of actual comics when I was about

four, and as soon as I finished reading the first one, I got a piece of paper and a pen and started copying the pictures. It's in the blood. It's been there right from the start, probably like everyone else in this book.

When did you make your first attempt at a comics career?

Originally I wanted to be a writer and an artist. When I was thirteen, DC had a thing called the *New Talent Showcase*. It was organised by Dick Giordano as a means of finding new blood for DC. He had his brother-in-law, Sal Amendola, head up this department. I remember sitting in the ass end of nowhere in Scotland, getting the latest issue of *Superman* and seeing, 'DC would like to find new writers and artists.' So I put together samples on schoolbook paper, drawn and hand-lettered over the lined paper. It looked like absolute shit. I wrote and drew this eighteen-page Superman story and sent it in to Sal Amendola. Six months passed, and every day I used to run downstairs to see if there was anything back from DC, and one day I got this brilliant letter, that I've still got. It was probably a form letter, but because it said 'Dear Mark' at the top of it, I assumed that the giant document the guy had written was just for me. I found it incredibly encouraging. It gave me lots of advice about both the writing side and the art side. Even though at school I was encouraged to have an academic career, always in the back of my mind, I thought, well, I've got a letter from Sal Amendola. And he's a real American and could actually, possibly, get me a job at DC at some point. That was always this little dream in the back of my mind whenever I was studying.

What were you studying?

I always had this artistic side, but I was pushed into sciences at school. If you show

Place of birth:
   Coatbridge, Scotland
Date of birth:
   24 December 1969
Home base:
   Glasgow, Scotland
First published work:
   The Saviour
Education:
   St Ambrose High School,
   Coatbridge, Paisley University
   (dropped out in final year)
Career highlights:
   The Authority, Chosen, Spider-Man,
   The Ultimates, Ultimate Fantastic Four,
   Ultimate X-Men, Wanted, Wolverine

any kind of academic flair, you get pushed into chemistry, physics or mathematics. The arts were seen as more for people who were fairly un-academic and slightly gay, as they said at my alma mater. It was like, 'You don't want to go into that. Here, go into some hard science and be a man, you little fuck.' So I ended up going and doing a degree I wasn't very interested in. But then an opportunity came up when I was nineteen: there was a small publishing venture in the UK, and they were looking for writers. Well, that just seemed like my 'get out of jail free' card. I could give up the course and go do comics work. I dropped out in the final year of my degree, and my family was going nuts. They were saying, 'Look, comics isn't actually done by real people. And anyone who does it, doesn't make any money whatsoever and, let's face it, they're probably retarded. You're insane. Go back to university and finish your degree.' But I had this real love for the medium. It was a time when Alan Moore and Frank Miller and this next wave of guys like Grant Morrison and Neil Gaiman and Pete Milligan were coming through, so I was inspired. I just desperately wanted to get in on it and do this for a living. So I went from what was a relatively secure setup, a degree where I'd be pretty much guaranteed a job, to being penniless and desperately trying to hawk my wares around the independent comics scene in the UK for a number of years.

What was the first work you were able to get published?

The very first thing that I did was a book called *The Saviour*. I thought it should be something quite big, so I launched it as a sequel to the Bible. I got in the local newspaper, saying, 'You've seen Matthew, Mark, Luke and John, well here's the final chapter of this thrilling story.' We managed to do quite well with that. We won a couple of awards and that kind of kicked off the comics career for me.

How did you start trying to break into the American comics market?

Growing up, the American market — geographically, even — was so far away that it seemed almost impossible to break into it from here. But then Alan Moore was picked up by DC when I was around twelve years old, and I spotted that he'd got there via *2000 AD* in London. I watched it happen with the next generation of guys, like Neil Gaiman, Grant Morrison, Pete Milligan, Jamie Delano, and it was suddenly becoming a well-worn path that led to American comics. I never really had any great love of *2000 AD*. In fact I had no interest in it at all, I'm ashamed to say. But I worked there for about three years, just trying to get the attention of the American market. And maybe hone some kind of skills, although most of what I did was terrible.

What was the first thing you wrote that was printed in the American market?

The very first thing I did was *Legends of the Dark Knight* [#79], for [the late editor] Archie Goodwin. Archie was the first person at DC who gave me much attention. He liked a couple of the proposals that I'd sent, but I think he knew I wasn't ready yet. He was always very encouraging, but never really bought anything. But he'd always give me good advice, and he did pick up this one Batman story. What happened next was a classic Charlie Brown situation. I'd wanted to work for DC since I was four years old, and all of a sudden I sold my story to them. I was so excited. I told everyone.

And when the thing came out, they'd spelled my name wrong! It was just heartbreaking. [*Laughs*] But I was in! It was tremendously exciting. I just assumed that I would immediately be a millionaire now that I'd sold this *Legends of the Dark Knight* story, because it was back in the days when guys like Rob Liefeld had earned $20 million for the first twelve months he'd done at Image. So I just assumed that the minute you walked into the American market, you could suddenly buy a solid gold house. I thought, I'll never have to work again, and was subsequently crushed when the comics market collapsed around me. But as ever with these things, once your foot's in the door, it becomes a little easier to sell your next proposal.

What followed that first *Legends of the Dark Knight* story?

Actually, loads and loads of rejected proposals. The minute I sold the Batman story, everybody said, 'That's it, you're in.' But it was the very same month that the market seemed to collapse — and I hope and pray I had nothing to do with this. DC shed around thirty percent of its titles that year, and so did Marvel. And the following year they shed another fifty percent. It was a very hard time to be breaking in. The mid-'90s was a nightmarish time for everyone, but especially for new people.

You collaborated with Grant Morrison on books like *Swamp Thing*, *Aztek* and *The Flash* throughout the nineties. How did that partnership begin?

I was just out of school and I went to interview Grant for a fanzine called *Fantasy Advertiser*, which sounds like a porn magazine — I used to be embarrassed carrying it home. At the time, he was doing *Animal Man* and *Doom Patrol* and *Arkham Asylum* at DC, and it was fascinating to me. This was a guy who'd grown up ten or fifteen miles from me, and he was working at DC, living the dream. And I loved the work he was doing! Although he was ten years older than me, we became friends pretty fast, and he was a tremendous influence on how I learned to write comics. The same thing happened with Neil Gaiman and Alan Moore, in the sense that Alan Moore actually just sat down and said to Neil, 'This is how you structure a comic. This is how you write a script. This is what should be in the top left-hand side of a page.' A similar thing happened with me and Grant. He was great for advice too, like how to deal with certain editors and who to avoid at certain companies. He understood the deadline pressures you could be under. It's quite a unique job. There's not many people in the world who do this thing. So it was great experience. I can't imagine having worked full-time in the industry without having Grant as a sounding board throughout the entire 1990s. I barely wrote anything during all those years without calling him up and saying, 'Does this sound okay or does it sound shit?' Every morning! He was enormously patient, whereas I'd have just told me to fuck off. [*Laughs*]

How did your co-writing duties get broken up with Morrison? And how was it different to, say, writing *Ultimate Fantastic Four* with Brian Michael Bendis recently?

The way Grant and I tended to work was we'd chat about the story in great depth, and then disappear off and write individual issues ourselves. It was less like co-writing than most people probably think. We were talking about our respective books a lot anyway, so it seemed like a natural thing to do. For me, it was a little bit more like the old Hollywood studio system. What they used to do was get an established writer and team him up with a rookie in a sort of Batman and Robin relationship. And that was the way it worked for me. Grant certainly learned almost nothing from any collaboration with me, whereas I learned an enormous amount from him. In the case of *Swamp Thing*, the only reason he co-wrote the first four issues was so I'd actually get the gig and get some regular work. It never actually felt like two established writers putting their heads together and coming up with something great. I was always very much the sidekick as I was growing and learning. He really knew what he was doing and I didn't.

Bendis is only about a year older than me, whereas Grant's the previous generation. Grant had been in the industry twice as long as me, and I'd always defer to him, whereas I'd never defer to Bendis. He's small and he's bald, you know? [*Laughs*] *FF* was just fun. Practically, it was difficult because we both lived eight hours apart, time-wise. But we actually worked surprisingly well together, considering we both have incredibly different styles. My style is much more plot-driven and visually orientated. I'll try and think of something that looks interesting and develop that into a story. I come to this whole process a bit more as an artist than a writer, whereas Bendis is completely the opposite and thinks very much in terms of dialogue and character, almost like a playwright. It could have been a marriage made in hell, but fortunately it worked out quite well. He did all the hard work, though. A plot, after all, is

Grant Morrison

Judging by the explosive and challenging nature of Mark Millar's current comics output, he clearly couldn't have had a mentor better suited to his talents than Grant Morrison. Morrison, who tapped into big sales with his reinvention of *JLA* in the '90s and *New X-Men* in the 21st Century, first tapped into the consciousness of hardcore comics fans with mindblowing cult books such as *Doom Patrol*, *The Invisibles* and *Animal Man*. A fellow Scot, Morrison made a name for himself writing stories such as *Zenith* for *2000 AD* and *Doctor Who* for Marvel UK before crossing over into the American market, a path that Millar, too, would follow. After cutting his teeth in the pages of the *Judge Dredd Megazine* and *2000 AD* with stories like *Missionary Man* and *Red Razors*, Millar was ready to step up to the next level, and it was Morrison who helped him do it. The pair collaborated on runs of *Swamp Thing*, *Skrull Kill Krew*, *Aztek: the Ultimate Man*, *Vampirella* and *The Flash* throughout the mid-1990s. By decade's end, Millar was firmly established as a pre-eminent writer of American superhero comics, a path that might just have taken much longer without all those Morrison co-credits.

just a few pages, whereas a script is close to twenty. They just asked me along to attract the chicks. [*Laughs*]

In your early stories, were you already thinking about subtext and any message you wanted to get across?

No, I think whenever you try and write something with a message, it becomes really laborious and unpleasant to read. If you actually come at it with the attitude, 'Well, I really want to show what happened with the American Indians so I'm going to write this Superman story about it,' it just becomes a chore, and the readers feel that they're back in school, you know? So wherever stories come from, I just let them come out, and if a subtext emerges, it's entirely by accident. I don't even think about using themes in my stories. They just naturally emerge. Normally, other people spot them before I do. I think that's true of most writers. You let the story write itself, and the theme or the message just comes to the forefront of whatever the reader gets from it.

That said, are you ever consciously trying to be controversial?

A lot of interviewers say to me, 'Oh, you're just being deliberately shocking or controversial.' But the honest truth is, I'm only interested in things that can make me raise my eyebrows. I'm not going to go and see a movie if somebody tells me, 'This is all about a Scandinavian poet who's in love with this woman in the next village.' That just doesn't interest me. I need to hear a great high concept. Somebody needs to tell me something in one line that's going to fascinate me. Comics have a very limited number of words and pictures to work with, so I think if you can actually arrange them in such a way that you're immediately grabbed from the first page, then you've succeeded. *Marshal Law*, a Pat Mills and Kevin O'Neill comic from about fifteen years ago, was always wonderful at doing just that. They had the best splash I've ever seen. I can remember it precisely: it was a guy who looked like Superman sitting on a toilet and shooting up with some kind of super-heroin. And he's found a vein and he's pulling on a cord between his teeth, and the caption just says, 'I'm a bit worried about Buck...' The sheer minimalism of that page, using those words against such a shocking image, just stuck in my head. It made me *want* to turn the page and read the next thing. It wasn't like, 'Oh, I'm so glad they offended me.' It was just that they interested me and immediately pulled me into their world, you know?

It's like, the idea of gay superheroes is just more interesting to me than straight superheroes, because I've seen straight superheroes before but I don't know what gay ones would be like. Rather than write a story that I've read a million times before, I'd rather write something new. And there's nothing more fun than playing around with these characters that everyone in the world understands. For instance, Superman as a Communist [in Millar's *Red Son*] is a very, very simple idea and something that I think would interest, to some extent, the mainstream. More than, 'Here's another story about Superman fighting the Parasite.' I like to play around with the archetypes, because there are so few mediums that have archetypes as interesting, as primary coloured, as the ones we've got. And they're always the ones that are more fun to fuck with.

Page Eight

1/ Wolverine rampage continues as he guts guys, takes heads off, kicks people's faces through ancient gravestones and so on, his attackers trying and failing to slash, knife, stick or choke the guy with chains.

CAPTION	: ICHIRO. THE KID.
CAPTION	: Flying halfway around the world in COACH just to save a few bucks—
CAPTION	: JACKASS playing Tetris—
CAPTION	: Laughing up some bad ADAM SANDLER flick—

2/ The fight continues, Wolverine really cutting loose here and going absolutely nuts with a big, sudden take-down of two of these attackers. We're maybe down to the final six of the original twelve by this point.

CAPTION	: --the whole way HERE.
CAPTION	: I'LL show 'em where they can stick their TRAP.

3/ Pull back and we see the fight from some distance away, one of our big villains watching the completely over the top proceedings from the safe distance of a tree. He's squatting up here among the branches quite supernaturally with a little gang of ninjas. I've doodled this looking much like a litter of big cats on various branches up a tree and they all have their backs to us here, all stretched out as these ninja guys invariably are.

DEAD NINJA	: (Japanese translation to follow)
TRANSLATION	: Logan is overpowering them, Master. Should we strike now before it's too late?

4/ Front shot of these guys, perhaps partially shaded, and we get a better look at them from a distance here as they watch the off-panel fight, watching Wolverine getting tired out. The big baddie here isn't dressed in a ninja outfit. He's a big, grey-skinned Asian guy wearing a smart suit and sunglasses to hide the eyes that must never be seen. He's called The Gorgon and one look from his eyes kills you instantly. Naturally, the "Gorgon" idea ties into his Hydra masters. His skin gives us the impression that he's a corpse reanimated and he might well be. He has an enormous, charismatic presence and we know he's going to be quite a foe to beat in issue twelve as he faces Wolverine. There's a light-ness to his footsteps too. He's barely touching these branches and we'll see why in a moment.

THE GORGON	: (Japanese translation to follow)
TRANSLATION	: No, I want to see what the Wolverine can DO. Let them TIRE HIM OUT a little.

Are editors often telling you, 'No, you can't do that'?

I generally know the limitations whenever I'm coming onto a project, one that's already established. If you're working in the DC or Marvel Universes or for *2000 AD*, you know that there are certain words that you can't say and there are certain parts of the human body you can't show. So generally I haven't really run into editorial problems too often, which may surprise people. After all, I worked on *Superman Adventures*, the all-ages Superman comic, for about nineteen issues, and I understood the parameters I was working within there. I tailored my stories to suit that book, and I never encountered any problems. It was only when a company would change its mind — they'd say they wanted something and then later say, 'Oh, sorry, that's a bit risky' — that I would encounter problems.

That's pretty much what happened with *The Authority*, a book that was kind of under the radar at DC because it was a WildStorm book and it was being put together thousands of miles away in California. They didn't really notice the kind of stuff that was happening in those pages. But the minute issue #13 ended up in the *Sunday Times*, and the word 'gay' was used to describe these two guys who looked like Superman and Batman, suddenly everybody noticed it. They suddenly realised this book had the words 'shit' and 'ass' in it and the superheroes were taking drugs and having sex with each other and they went apeshit. Whenever a company is a little unclear on what they want, then the writer and the artist are in a very dangerous situation. The execs might want the 'cool' that a certain type of comic can bring, but they actually don't want the dangerous ingredients, because it might get them into trouble as a corporation. That's understandable. I really don't blame DC for what happened with *Authority*, but you have to establish ground rules so writers and artists know what they can and can't do.

What was the story behind the *Authority* controversy?

My career didn't really start until the year 2000. I'd done a lot of dicking around in the '90s. Comics funded my lifestyle; I was able to buy booze and pay the rent and live a good life, but I'd never done anything particularly interesting. But I saw *Authority* as an opportunity. It was one of those things where the stars aligned. Frank [Quitely] and I said, 'Let's just do something like nobody's ever really done before. Let's start where other superhero comics draw the line.' We thought that was the only way we could possibly stand out in a market that had big-name books like *JLA* and *The Avengers*. Nobody had heard of Jack Hawksmoor… or the Midnighter. So we had to make people notice them.

Because it was characters nobody had heard of outside of the hardcore fan base, nobody at WildStorm gave a shit about what we were doing at the proposal stage. We did some crazy stuff in the first two issues that we'd never seen before, and the response was great. But the second it became a big news story and was all over the European press — we even did an interview on Israeli television! — then suddenly everyone started looking very carefully at what the WildStorm office was doing. To WildStorm's eternal credit, they were fantastic with us. They really were a firewall against the traditionalists in the organisation. Some people at the company really, really, really hated *Authority*, because it was the absolute antithesis of the kind of book they liked doing. They just told me, 'Look, we don't understand what people like about this book.'

The eventual edits were actually fairly minimal: a few little art changes here and there, a couple of words changed to pacify people. But as time went on, I think everybody just got weary with the fact that every issue took such a long time to get approved. You had your editor reading it, and everyone in management reading it. And this was happening every month!

How did all this affect the artist, Frank Quitely?

It was particularly aggravating for Frank. You always want to feel supported. When we lost Frank [to Marvel], it suddenly became a very unpleasant book to be involved in; suddenly there was just me, trying to hold the fort. The final issue went through about five drafts, where it was watered down and watered down to the point where I never even opened my complimentary copy box when it came out. What had started off as the most pleasant project I'd ever been involved in and the most interesting, had degenerated into the most nightmarish project I'd ever been involved in, before or since. I'm very, very proud of the first nine or ten issues. I think they're some of the best things I've ever done, and I'm really happy with them, but by the end it had completely collapsed. It was just a mess.

You moved over to Marvel after *Authority*. How different did you find the approach over there?

I never really felt in tune with what was going on around me at DC, despite having a more natural affinity with their characters. In hindsight, I think it was because DC was part of a corporate structure that doesn't like to rock the boat. So to them I was this guy who was like, 'Hey! Look at this! Here's guys who look like Superman and Batman and they're shagging each other!' I think with hindsight I was probably DC's worst nightmare as a creator. I'm sure they were delighted to see me go, almost as delighted as I was to leave.

Moving over to Marvel was brilliant, because what you had there was the most shameless self-promoter in charge of the company, in the shape of [Editor-in-Chief] Joe Quesada, whom I love. Instantly there was a real rapport between Joe, [former Marvel president] Bill Jemas and myself. We just really got on well. We were all marching in the same direction. I think that was the first time that had ever happened to me professionally. It was a wonderfully liberating time. You hear so many dreadful things about Bill. The fans have slaughtered him and creators who've been fired are coming out of the woodwork and slagging him off. But Bill was brilliant. He was the president of the company and yet he'd be constantly available to freelancers — you could call him up on his cell phone morning, noon or night, you could drop him emails. I learned a massive amount from Bill. He and Joe have very good mainstream tastes. Comics, in the '90s, became very insular. Bill and Joe opened it up again. They wanted to get out there in *Time* magazine and they wanted to get in the *New Yorker*. They wanted to see their names and their characters everywhere. It was exactly what comics needed at exactly the right time.

After DC, I was actually thinking of quitting comics. I'd sold a television show to [UK TV station] Channel Four. Marvel came along at just the right time and re-ignited my passion for the industry after the shit-kicking I'd taken across town.

Is writing more rewarding — or just more fun — when you have more restrictions or fewer restrictions?

Actually, both set-ups can be very rewarding. There is nothing better than being able to cut loose and do anything you want. But sometimes it's quite fun to have a little discipline as well, and be told — up front — that there are certain things you can't do. I like the idea of writing a comic that I can show to nephews and nieces, and one day to my daughter when she's old enough. I like the idea of people being able to read comics at the same age I was when I started reading them. Especially when you're doing Marvel and DC characters, you should try to reach as wide an audience as possible. I'm enjoying writing the Marvel Knights *Spider-Man* and *The Ultimates*, for example, as much as I enjoyed writing *The Authority*, despite the fact that there are more limitations on these big, all-ages characters. They each have their own rewards.

What triggered your creator-owned MillarWorld line of books?

The Authority

Out of the ashes of WildStorm's *Stormwatch*, the UK team of writer Warren Ellis and artist Bryan Hitch created *The Authority*. The mission statement: think big, think 'widescreen'. The Authority was a team of superheroes so powerful that they answered to no government or organisation, an absolute guardian force to protect the Earth and its people from any threat on any scale. Hovering above the world on the Carrier, an extra-dimensional spaceship the size of a city, and dispensing justice as they saw fit, the Authority naturally bumped into resentment and opposition from those over whom the team lorded. Former Stormwatch 'Black' team members Jenny Sparks, Shen Li-Min (a.k.a. Swift) and Jack Hawksmoor added science and magic to their number in the form of the Engineer and the Doctor, respectively, plus brute force courtesy of the godlike, solar-powered Apollo and his partner (yes, *that* kind of partner), the ultraviolent Midnighter. Ellis' run on the book ended with the Authority taking on none other than God, and when he took over with issue #13, Mark Millar began exploring the ramifications of a superteam unafraid to play God themselves. 'Think big,' indeed — no superhero comic was ever this fearless, before or since.

Page Ten

1/ Cut to an establishing shot of Ryker's Island.

CAPTION   : My Aunt May is seventy-two years old. She pops twelve pills a day
                         and has suffered three heart attacks in the last seven years.
CAPTION   : OF COURSE she's dead, common sense whispers in my ear. The
                         stress ALONE should have finished whatever that kidnapper started,
                         but I have to keep going. I can't just GIVE UP.

2/ Cut to interior and we're outside Osborn's cell again. Osborn is in here doing a jigsaw, his
back to Spider-Man. Spidey lowers down again on his web, upside down, and also with his
back to us. We don't see what the jigsaw is until much later.

SPIDER-MAN   : I know you know I'm DANGLING here, Osborn, so you can stop
                         trying to annoy me.

3/ Closer shot of Norman as he continues with his jigsaw, replying without missing a beat.
We should have some appropriate books lying around here too for this scene and some
photographs pinned to the wall. Let's consult on this later.

NORMAN   : Annoying you is the only pleasure I've got LEFT in life, Parker.

4/ Pull back and we see Spidey hanging here again before Norman and this otherwise empty
cell. There's nobody else around.

NORMAN   : What do you want anyway, boy? Can't you see I've got places to go
                         and people to see? I hope this isn't anything to do with dear, old Aunt
                         May again? She's not STILL MISSING, is she?
SPIDER-MAN   : Don't push your luck, scumbag. I don't know why, but I'm actually
                         gonna give you the benefit of the doubt and assume you WEREN'T
                         behind all this kidnap stuff.

5/ Norman continues with his jigsaw and Spidey explains.

NORMAN   : So why drop-by?
SPIDER-MAN   : To see if you can shed a little light on what happened to her. I've gone
                         over the details a million times and still came up with nothing, but
                         maybe there's something I'm missing here.
SPIDER-MAN   : Maybe I'm just too normal to see what this guy's up to, but you're the
                         King of the Kooks, right? Maybe YOU can figure it out why he hasn't
                         been back in touch.

Above: *Sample page from Mark Millar's script for* Spider-Man #6. *Courtesy of Mark Millar/Marvel Comics. Used
with permission.* Spider-Man ™ *&* © 2004 Marvel Characters, Inc.

I think after two years of doing books like *The Ultimates* and *Ultimate X-Men*, there definitely was a little part of me that just wanted to go crazy again. Forming my own line of books was a great way of reviving my creative juices and I'd recommend it to anyone. I also found I was getting a little bored over time. By the end of the second year of my Marvel contract, I was starting to think it would be great to cut loose and just do something nuts again. I'd also never really created any characters of my own. I just wanted to see if I could do it. Everyone always recommended it. They said, 'There's nothing like doing your own stuff.' And I really didn't appreciate that until I was actually doing it. From a creative point of view, it's wonderful. And from a financial point of view, it's been fantastic too, because obviously when you own something it can be exploited in a number of mediums. I won't get any benefit from an *X-Men* movie coming out, but I will from the *Wanted* movie.

But I did miss writing the Marvel characters. One thing I've realised is there's no good or bad kind of book to be working on. The Marvel characters satisfy one side of your brain, and your creator-owned stuff satisfies the other. So the trick really is to find some kind of balance. That holistic approach really works in terms of your career, too. I'm under no illusion about my worth here — the only reason the creator-owned stuff's been a big success is because I'm the guy who does all those top-five books at Marvel. If I'd tried to launch these exact same books five years ago, I'd have been dead in the water and you'd be interviewing somebody else in my place. Nobody would have even noticed them. My plan is definitely to do the creator-owned stuff in a big burst for six months, then go do some company-owned characters for two years, then come back once the reputation's big enough again and do another six months of characters nobody's ever heard of before and hopefully turn them into something like I've done with *Wanted* and *Chosen* and so on.

Do you ever run into deadline trouble where you have to rein in the amount of monthly books you do?

I never really run into any deadline problems, because I've always been aware that I shouldn't take on more than around two books a month. Three monthlies for me would be insane. I know some people can do it, but there's almost no examples I can give of anyone who's doing more than two books a month where I don't feel some book somewhere isn't suffering for it. Alan Moore never really did more than forty-eight pages a month in his whole career, especially in the '80s when I think his stuff was at its best. Neil Gaiman never did more than one book a month. I'm really careful not to take on too much.

I'm just a great believer in 'Good stuff takes time.' The artists I work with tend to be very, very slow artists. But they also tend to be, in my opinion, the best artists. They're the best guys in the industry. Sure, some pencillers can do three pages a day, but they're not very good. You might be able to understand the story, but that's not enough. I want it to look like the best thing I've ever seen. Guys like Bryan Hitch, they might only be able to do two or three pages a week, but those two or three pages will be better than anyone else's pages. John Romita

Jr., of course, is the clear exception to this rule. He's pencilled issues of *Amazing Spider-Man* over a weekend and produced better stuff than other guys have done in their entire careers. He's the Holy Grail as far as other artists are concerned. He's a legend. And he's Catholic, so I like him a lot. He's probably my favourite artist, and the chance to work with him is what sealed the *Wolverine* deal for me.

What's a typical writing day like for you?

I've always tried to mix with normal people and live a normal life, because I've heard horror stories of people who sleep all day, write comics all night, have a heart attack, die or have a nervous breakdown or whatever. That kind of lifestyle's good if you're Batman, but I think if you actually want to function in the normal world you should try to keep it close to a 9 to 5… especially since I got married and my daughter was born, I thought it was important to be like everybody else's dad. Anyway, in a typical day I get up around 7 o'clock, see my daughter off to school, and then I'll sit and do emails. Email is the curse of the 21st Century. Everyone got email thinking it was going to make us more productive, but it's made us massively less productive. Every day now starts with ninety minutes of replying to emails and checking stuff out online. It's awful, and I'm sure it's some defect in my character, but I actually can't start working until I've spent a good half-hour reading all the message-boards. I'm genuinely embarrassed about this neediness in my character. [*Laughs*] A few good reviews can totally brighten up your work schedule for the morning, and a few bad ones can crucify you for the day.

MillarWorld

After making his name with big mainstream characters like Superman and the X-Men, Mark Millar thought he'd carve out a little corner of the comics world he could truly call his own. The result was an unprecedented publishing strategy: a family of four titles, loosely linked under the MillarWorld banner, which launched simultaneously at four different comics companies. The most successful of these was *Wanted* from Top Cow, a six-issue mini-series about a loser recruited to follow in his father's footsteps as a superpowered hitman. *The Unfunnies* was a four-issue cartoon animal book with a decidedly adult bent to it, and was printed by Avatar Press. Image Comics were slated to publish *Run!*, a one-shot about super-speed, while Dark Horse took on the printing duties for three issues of *Chosen*, a tale about the second coming of Jesus Christ set in the modern day. While Millar's original plan was to alternate building his own library of titles with runs on the big-company titles he made his name on, so that the latter could prop up the former, there might be no need: *Wanted* drew so much attention that it landed a movie deal almost before the ink had dried on the top-selling issue #1.

Page Sixteen

1/ Closer shot of Fury as he consults his notes, leaning against a pew. All these people are doing a clean-up and a search around him throughout this whole scene, body-parts being lifted away and so on. Some seriously bad shit had been going on in this place.

NICK FURY   : Yeah, but we DID and what we found inside was pretty INTERESTING. Smoked-out a plot to take down Captain America, Tony Stark, Charlie Xavier, Reed Richards...

NICK FURY   : All in all, they were going for SIXTEEN key figures in the super-human community. And you know who topped the list?

SHIELD AGENT   : Tell me.

2/ Close shot on Nick looking serious.

NICK FURY   : Mister Wolverine HIMSELF.

3/ The SHEILD agent looks very interested and Nick explains as he takes what looks like a more high-tech version of a palm-pilot from his pocket.

SHIELD AGENT   : Well, I guess that explains what JAPAN was all about. Any idea who took him down? Logan's not exactly an easy mark...

NICK FURY   : From what we've been able to gather, the assassin in charge of these strikes calls himself THE GORGON.

NICK FURY   : Apparently, he's a mutant from Kyoto, taken down by the local cops eighteen months ago and resurrected by THE HAND some three weeks later.

4/ Big close-up and we get a good shot of an electronic SHIELD file here featuring The Gorgon from our opening scene. Obviously, this picture was taken when he was alive.

NICK FURY   : The Gorgon's a NINJA-MASTER, class-2 SUPERHUMAN STRENGTH and, stupid as it sounds, has a mutant power that lets him kill anyone he makes EYE-CONTACT with.

NICK FURY   : Word is he belonged to some Brotherhood SPLINTER-GROUP called The Dawn of the White Light and all indications are they've formed some kinda pact with the Hydra GRAND-MASTERS.

5/ Nick and the agent head for the exit.

SHIELD AGENT   : That all you've got?

NICK FURY   : So far. Hydra enforce a new language on their assassins every sixty-six days at the moment so linguists estimate another WEEK before they completely crack these emails.

1/ Cut to exterior as they head out the big church doors and we see all the tape everywhere stopping everyone from getting near the scene.

NICK FURY   : Think you got time to come back and help us out with this one?

SHIELD AGENT   : For something this big I'll MAKE the time.

2/ Close shot on the agent.

SHIELD AGENT   : This smell as bad to YOU as it does to ME?

3/ Reaction shot from Nick looking slightly worried. This is where we find out the identity of the agent he's planning to use here.

I'd say I do about eighty percent of my work before 2 o'clock, then I usually go and meet a friend for lunch. I never drink at lunchtime, because during the day it just hits me like a brick. If I'm drunk, I'd just come back and sit and watch TV rather than do any work. So I have a soft drink with lunch. Then I come back and work through the afternoon to maybe 6 o'clock. This is also when I switch the phone back on and do any important calls, put my five year-old to bed, then just have a normal evening. I don't even pick up a comic at nighttime — I do all that stuff during the day. A typical weeknight is just sitting around watching a DVD with my wife or having friends around. It's much quieter than the years before my daughter was born. At weekends we tend to cut loose a bit and I always, always get together with my old crew at least two nights a week to catch up. Fridays are sacred in terms of pubs and clubs. None of my friends read comics or even know what I'm working on, so Fridays are always a great release after a hard week.

How do you start to shape your stories once you have an idea?

This is maybe where me being a frustrated artist comes in, but I'll actually just sit and start drawing. If somebody says to me, for example, 'Would you like to start a new Spider-Man book?' — which Marvel actually said to me last year — I'll just sit and start drawing pictures of Spider-Man and jotting down little ideas for scenes. I've got a strange method that would look psychopathic to anyone else, but it's always worked for me. I'll start drawing pictures of Spider-Man and start writing lines of dialogue and it all eventually starts coming together. It's just these little ideas about what the character means to me and what's important about them, or some little scene that can eventually become this high concept for the series. What I'll do then is collate these ideas I've written down and email them to the editor or the publisher and say, 'Look, can I run with this?'

Once I've had approval on that stage, the drawings start coming thicker and faster. I sit and work out little disconnected scenes. I could maybe be writing an important scene in part six of a story at the same time as I'm writing the ending to part one. I just kind of know instinctively what should and shouldn't be in the issue and I get down all the really important ones before trying to fill in the blanks and find a way to link them all together. *Spider-Man*, for example, started with the ending to issue three and I loosely wrote the scene where he's been rushed in an ambulance to a hospital and the doctors are tearing off his mask to operate. That, to me, was the scene I wanted in the book and I worked backwards from there to make that scene work and find out how he got himself into that situation.

The actual typing up at the computer is just a way of linking a lot of these scenes together. It's almost like the story itself already exists, if that doesn't sound too odd. Stephen King's got a brilliant way of describing this. He said that being a writer is very much like being an archaeologist, in the sense that the story's out there, but it's covered in dust. And you've just got your little brush, and you're brushing away at it until you eventually uncover the whole thing and see what it is. That's what it's like for me. It's almost like you're channeling the story. You're sitting there, seeing a little bit more of it all the time, and eventually it all links up. The stories themselves come reasonably naturally in this sense. I never really follow anything other than instinct with them. It doesn't always work out, and I don't find it easy, either. I think I find it much more difficult than some people because it tends to take me twice as long. My output isn't huge, but I still work maybe fifty to sixty hours a week and I'm constantly tweaking what I've written and driving my editors crazy.

Do your personal politics have any bearing on the things that you're writing now?

Oh, gigantically. I came from a very political background. Growing up in this part of the world, you can't help but be political. My theory is that people are political because they need to be. People in the States generally aren't as interested in politics compared to people in the UK, because I think the standard of living in the States is probably a little better. Nobody really feels it's time to go out and march in the streets, because things are actually pretty good over the course of their lifetimes. But in the UK, things have been difficult in certain periods. The west of Scotland has been the poorest part of Europe for my entire life. There was massive unemployment throughout my teen years. That does radicalise you in a way that if you grew up in a middle class household you're probably not familiar with. You've got nothing to complain about besides girl troubles and zits. I've noticed that American writers tend not to be political, but very interesting in other ways.

I think that's one of the things that British writers really bring to the American market, a more political slant on their stories and perhaps a healthy cynicism for people in uniforms. I don't mean any disrespect to Americans, but the stars and stripes are very prevalent in the culture and this amazed me when I first started visiting the country. There's also a high regard for public servants like cops and soldiers we just don't have over here. It's very much a badge-worshipping culture and this extends to superheroes. The difference is, of course, that we in Europe regard anyone who puts on a uniform and tells you what to do with suspicion. For me, politics is enormously important. It's my hobby in my spare time. I work with politicians here. I draft speeches for them and I clean up speeches they've done themselves. I'm very interested in a career in politics, maybe, at some stage when I'm older and fully grown-up. Most people who've been reading this book probably have a real job in the real world but read comics in their spare time. Because these fictional realities are where I spend ten hours a day, reality has essentially become my hobby. I'm reading an account of the Clinton years by George Stephanopolous right now whereas most people I know are reading fiction as a form of escape. You might be daydreaming about being Superman or Batman, but I'm sitting here daydreaming about pushing a Private Member's Bill for a fairer welfare system through Parliament. [*Laughs*]

*　　　　*　　　　*

PETER MILLIGAN

Peter Milligan broke into comics the same way any number of aspiring British writers did — in the pages of the weekly *2000 AD* anthology. But unlike so many of those writers Milligan has spent the bulk of his career avoiding the spotlight of mainstream titles, choosing instead to follow his witty, warped muse through a résumé filled with eclectic titles. From *Strange Days* at Eclipse to a series of one-shots and mini-series at Vertigo (plus a colossal seventy-issue run on *Shade, the Changing Man*), Milligan seemed to be enjoying a career of relative obscurity. That all changed when he agreed to pen *X-Force* for Marvel in 2001. The book featured art by *Madman*'s Mike Allred and Milligan's fantastically riveting — and violent — take on modern celebrity culture. It was a huge success, eventually landing Milligan on *Entertainment Weekly*'s yearly 'It' list. Publicity of another sort found Milligan and the now re-titled *X-Statix* in 2003 when a proposed tale resurrecting the late Princess Diana landed Marvel in hot water with the British royal family. Now off *X-Statix* and onto *X-Men*, Milligan seems to have found a way to toe the company line whilst continuing to play by his own rules — a situation which is neither black nor white, just like Milligan's stories themselves.

What's the first comic book you can remember reading?

Probably unlike most of the people in my business, I wasn't a big comic book fan as a kid. I didn't hate them, I just didn't love them as much. What I do remember, as a kid, is drawing Superman.

How did you first get involved in the comics industry?

I was interested in art; I was interested in reading. It seemed like a particularly good way of marrying those two interests. I looked at these two friends of mine [Brendan McCarthy and Brett Ewins] who were on the inside, primarily doing stuff at *2000 AD*, and then started on the long route of submitting ideas to the guys at *2000 AD*.

What were the first scripts *2000 AD* accepted from you?

Probably some *Future Shocks*. Thankfully, I've forgotten my first one. I think that's a good thing all around. [*Laughs*]

Did you always have your eye on writing US comics?

Well, I guess we were kind of doing American comics even though we were doing them in England. Even though they were slightly different from American comics, they weren't as different as they were from, say, European comics.

What was it like seeing your work in print for the first time?

Good. Even now, it hasn't changed — there's always a mixture of disappointment and thrill, because things are never quite as you want them to be. Truffaut, the French film director, had a lovely anecdote, where he said one minute before the beginning of shooting any film, every director hopes he's gonna shoot the best film that's ever been directed. One minute after the start of directing, he knows he's fucked it up. I would say I adhere to the François Truffaut school of thought on that. However much a thrill it is, I think if you're any kind of writer or artist, you always look at how you could have done it differently or better.

Which comics writers influenced you early on?

As a man who largely comes from outside the comics discipline, I wasn't particularly influenced by any comic book writer. Obviously, people like Alan Moore and certain other people who came before me opened doors, but overall I'd say my influences in writing and art came from outside of comics. I was more interested in some of the Irish writers and literature in general. And that's certainly no bad thing. I think it helps you to be a little less shut into this comic book world if you can come to it with influences that aren't just about superheroes. I

Place of birth:
  London, UK
Date of birth:
  24 June 1961
Home base:
  London, UK
First published work:
  Future Shocks in *2000 AD*. 'Probably.'
Education:
  University of London
Career highlights:
  Bad Company, Enigma, Human Target, The Minx, Shade, the Changing Man, Strange Days, X-Statix, X-Men

think that stands equally true for artists as well — I think the really good artists are the ones who learned to draw not necessarily just by copying their favourite superhero characters, but who can actually *draw*, who can draw anatomy and have an interest in art.

How do your comic scripts generally begin to take form?

I like to build up the themes I want to touch on in the story. It might start off with, say, a piece of dialogue between two people. Take a scene between a paedophile priest and a guy who was abused as a child, you might have in your head, where finally this person meets the person who's destroyed his life and he has the opportunity to say everything and do everything he always wanted to do. From there you might slowly start to build it.

I often say to people outside of comics — in the film industry, say — that the comic book is a voracious beast. They really just consume ideas. They eat them up so quickly, you have to generate an awful lot. So I suppose the truthful answer to the question is, if you're going to generate lots of interesting ideas and dramatize those ideas, you have to have more than one strategy. When I'm doing a monthly comic book, I always have more than one strategy. Say I start from what I've just alluded to, a scene in my head featuring a guy who finally has the chance to come face-to-face with this person who's abused him. From there, you build up. You might do a bit of research into the psychology of kids and how they cope with that sort of abuse, or you might open the papers one day and read a small

Shade, the Changing Man

When Peter Milligan's *X-Force* caught like wildfire, the mainstream readers enjoying the book might have known of Milligan merely as 'that Vertigo guy' — if they knew of him at all. Milligan's biggest comics credit prior to *X-Force* and *Human Target* was *Shade, the Changing Man*, a wild and woolly trip of a book about Rac Shade, a dimension-hopping alien from a world called Meta, who arrives on Earth as a fugitive fleeing punishment for a crime he didn't commit. The character was originally invented by *Spider-Man* co-creator Steve Ditko in 1977, but had lain dormant for over a decade. From 1990 Milligan retold Shade's story in his own inimitable way for a full seventy issues. Milligan's other American comics work actually started with the futuristic gangster comic *Skreemer* for DC, which actually predated Vertigo. His subsequent work for the company was limited to mostly brief runs on titles such as *Enigma*, which ran eight issues and challenged readers with its themes of identity and sexuality and its loopy, cyclical narrative; *The Minx*, about a monkey shot into space and returning as a monkey god (among *many* things — we're simplifying a bit); and *The Extremist*, a sex-charged thriller set against the backdrop of San Francisco. Those readers who found Milligan's work were riveted; the challenge was often finding it in the first place!

article about some drug scandal in baseball. 'Baseball, that's as American as apple pie. That could be an interesting story to explore.' So you might then start with really big, major themes, like drug abuse, sex, gambling and baseball, but then the trick is to personalise it. I would try to think about a couple of major characters who could best dramatize all these really big themes I want. In that way, you'd start from the top and then dig down.

I've found that what's really important is that somewhere along the line you have to find something that's good and small and true. There's this great quote by James Joyce, one of my... I guess heroes, if I have heroes. He said, 'In the particular lies the universal.' It's a great quote to remember when you want to do a story about drugs and gambling and the idea of this almost secular religion called baseball and how it can be brought low by human foibles. I think that's a great idea for a story — but that's not the story, that's the idea for a story. What you then have to do is find the 'particular' in there that's going to make it human.

There's more than one way in which to approach a story. If it's a graphic novel, a stand-alone book, you might leave it alone for a long time and allow it to slowly fester and grow in the Petri dishes of your imagination. And slowly it'll mature and become something worth writing. With a monthly comic book, you have to force the issue a bit more, so you have to have more than one strategy of getting to the story you want to write. When you've worked out the story, you have to have these characters and themes that you're interested in enough to really go for it and catch the lion. Otherwise you're just writing by rote and it gets dull for you. And when it gets dull for the writer, it's not long before it gets dull for everyone.

I really like the freshness and the immediacy of a monthly comic book. It's half creative writing and half journalism in some ways. You're up against the clock all the time and sometimes you haven't got the time to make things absolutely perfect. You have to come up with good ideas but they have to be inhabited by real characters that you care about, which I think is the key thing. Otherwise you're just left with soapboxes and causes and major themes, which can be very dry and not interesting unless it's somehow energised and personalised by real characters.

When the themes are nailed down and you have characters in mind, how do you begin writing the first draft of the actual script?

Sometimes I dive in on the first page because I want to get the characters talking. But I've found that once I've gotten to the end, I've worked out where everything should be and I have to go back and either rewrite or entirely ditch the early couple of pages. So it might be that I'll write the first scene or two, to get that opening that's hopefully going to grab the reader by the neck and lay it all out, and then perhaps sketch out on bits of paper the major scenes. Because once you've got those bricks in place, you can start scribbling some of the bits of dialogue from different characters you feel are bringing out the theme of the episode. If it's a three or four-part story, you want to carry on an over-arcing story of what's going on, but at the same time there's got to be something internal in that one episode, so when somebody reads it, they feel satisfied they've had something relatively complete from that one comic, even if that comic is a part of a bigger story.

I do find that the more you work out the scenes and then the plot, the structure becomes very fixed and it often frees up your characters to talk like real human beings. I think that if you don't do enough plotting, you're often relying too heavily on your characters to direct the plot or talk about the plot. I think that's when you can get characters talking 'on the nose' or being expository. But if you've worked out the plot so that the plot is telling the story, the characters have the liberty to walk around the plot and be human beings and be the things that are bringing it to life, rather than telling it.

How long does it take you to write an average issue?

I never write an average issue. [*Laughs*] Sometimes it depends on which characters I'm writing. The two comic books I'm writing at the moment are part two of a *Human Target* storyline called 'Crossing the Border' — which involves under-age prostitution and sex slaves linked in with the smuggling of illegal aliens across the border from Mexico into America, and how they're subsequently thrown into this really horrendous and chilling world of child sex abuse — and part two of a *Venom/Carnage* storyline, where I'm introducing the child of Carnage and grandchild of Venom. Important though the *Venom/Carnage* story is, when you're writing a story about child sex abuse and sex slaves and the heaviest stuff that you can possibly imagine, you do feel it's incumbent upon you to think hard about what you write. There's an inherent responsibility in the story. I'm not saying I don't care about Venom or Carnage, but the *Venom/Carnage* storyline would probably be a lot quicker to write because you can have some fun with it, you can mess around. But when you're writing a story about Christopher Chance, the Human Target, who's trying to look for this girl who's gone missing and who, even as he speaks, might be being abused by paedophiles, those pages and those scenes are more considered sometimes.

When I've got good form and it's really going well, I can write an issue in a few days. But generally, when I've got a deadline, I like to have at least a week. Ideally, a couple of weeks. I think that my comics tend to be quite deep, or tend to have quite a lot of meat to them. I could do it in a day if I had to bash off something quickly, and I think that I'm proficient enough and good enough for the dialogue still to be witty and for the story itself to kind of hold together. But what it would lack is the considered depth, the stuff that maybe you aren't seeing at first glance, the stuff that lies below. That stuff takes the time and the hard work.

As you said, your work tends to run kind of deep. How important is it for you to have those extra layers going on under the surface? Are you ever in the position where what you're writing is *all* surface and no subtext?

Obviously it's only me saying that. Other people might say it's the most shallow stuff they've ever read! But I think that sometimes it's got to be story-led. Getting back to this *Venom/Carnage* thing, Axel Alonso, the editor, said, 'Pete, do you want to do this? It might be a bit of fun. Do a four-part *Venom/Carnage*. All I want is a lot of fights. Maybe Spider-Man can make a guest appearance, but just don't worry about it. Do something really light with a lot of fights — just a B-movie.' I said, 'That sounds really great.' But I then introduce this son of Carnage and grandson of Venom, so I created the character who would be the host body [for the alien symbiote]. He was this cop who was about to become a father for the first time. It's funny, sometimes you start off writing this really 'surface' thing and then you create this other aspect of the story, which was this cop having his first son, and then you're drawing parallels between the human child about to be born and this insane alien symbiote creature that's been born. Almost against your will, you start to draw parallels. 'Let's dig a little bit deeper there...' Sometimes you start off writing a popcorn, candyfloss story but then you think, why not make it a little more interesting? And before you know it, it's turned into something different — and usually something more interesting.

When you were approached to write *X-Force*, which later became *X-Statix*, were you afraid you'd be writing something without all that interesting depth?

Initially, yeah, and that I'd be signing up for something where I'd cease to have much creative elbow room, and then get trammelled into hideous, nightmarish, labyrinthine continuity problems until almost becoming a robot. That was my worst-scenario fear. I said all this to Axel Alonso, the editor who approached me to take on the book. I was worried, and that's why I initially

Human Target

Christopher Chance is either incredibly brave or incredibly foolish. He makes his living by impersonating those marked for death, putting himself in harm's way in order to flush out assassins and murderers. It sounds reckless, but it works — Chance is still alive and kicking on comics pages after three decades as the Human Target. Created by Len Wein and Carmine Infantino, the Human Target debuted in *Action Comics* #419 in a backup story, and, aside from a few appearances in *Detective Comics*, populated backup stories in *Action* for most of his career. Apart from a 1991 one-shot timed to coincide with a *Human Target* TV series on the ABC broadcast network (that starred rocker Rick Springfield, of all people, in the title role), Chance was mostly out of the spotlight and out of the crosshairs. That finally changed in 1999, when Peter Milligan and artist Edvin Biukovic collaborated on a four-issue *Human Target* mini-series for DC/Vertigo. Milligan dug deeper into Chance's psyche than the writers before him — just what made a bloke like Chance take all those crazy risks, and what sense of self does a man have when he's forever assuming other people's identities? Thirty-one years after Chance's first appearance, *Human Target* finally became a regular monthly series in 2003.

XSTATIX 26   1

PAGE ONE
1
CHAOS. We're in a palatial room, some opulent mansion, fill
of smoke and flying debris, dead SOLDIERS on the ground.
They look like the guys Xforce fought at the end of episode
one.

Venus holding Dead Girl…who appears to be falling apart.

CAP   ONE LAST PAY-DAY…

VENUS   DEAD GIRL! I THINK SHE'S…DEAD!

2
Myles, ducking from some bullets as Venus tries to lay the
disintegrating Dead Girl on the ground.

MYLES   AND I THOUGHT I WAS THE BRAINS OF THIS OUTFIT.

VENUS   I MEAN…REALLY DEAD. DISINTEGRATING. I'M SO
           SCARED.

3
Guy looks shell-shocked. On Tike, grinning.

CAP   WE'RE ALL SCARED.

GUY   TH-THIS IS SUPPOSED TO BE A WALK IN THE PARK.

TIKE   HAVE I HEARD THAT BEFORE?

4
Close on Guy…

CAP   THEY DON'T TELL THE FANS THAT.

CAP   HOW SCARED WE GET.

5
Tikes pulls aside some heavy drapes blocking a large
window. His eyes widen when he sees what's outside.

CAP   HOW HUMAN WE ARE.

TIKE   OKAY, X-STERS. ANYONE WID A WEAK CONSTITUTION
           BETTER LOOK THE OTHER WAY.

Above: *First page of Peter Milligan's script for the final issue of* X-Statix. *Courtesy of Peter Milligan/Marvel Comics.*
Used with permission. X-Statix ™ & © 2004 Marvel Characters, Inc.

said no. But Axel and I went out and had a few beers one night and we talked about it. He did a lot to reassure me. It was pretty much the same with *Human Target*. When Axel first approached me with *Human Target*, I'd never read this thing, and he sent me some black-and-white Xeroxes of some of the previous comics. I thought it was an amusing little dated piece of nonsense. Completely light and for what it was, harmless and fun. So anyway, he came up to London and I said, 'I don't want to do it,' and I remember talking to my then-girl-friend, now-wife, saying, 'I'm not going to do *Human Target,* but if I were to do it, this is how I'd do it...' And it's funny, that little 'if I were to do it,' it's amazing what happens. You know, '*X-Force* is great for what it is, but it really isn't a Pete Milligan kind of thing, but yeah, if I *was* to do it...' You then find your own way into what makes it different. Of course with *X-Force*, the amazing thing was Axel said, 'Oh, fuck that stuff. If we wanna do it, we don't do continuity, we do whatever we want to do. And if there are aspects to the X-Universe that are going to make it dull or not as interesting for us, let's ignore them.' I think the more modern culture at Marvel makes that possible.

You're ending *X-Statix*. Why?

I'm discontinuing the series for a while. It's kind of mutual consent, really. I was thinking of coming off it last year after the Lady Diana storyline had to be changed a bit. [*X-Force*] started as a joke, and I think it's always good to come out of those things before the joke runs too dry. But it's been a good run.

Have you told all the stories you want to tell with *X-Statix*?

I think so, yeah. Also I think we're ending on a real high at the moment: this storyline with X-Statix vs. the Avengers, this insane storyline with its ironic nod at the old Avengers vs. Defenders books — that obviously I've never read but Axel assured me were this major cultural thing of the past. It's this insane series of fights, with Captain America vs. the Anarchist. So we're ending on a real high. And a real heavy, kind of sad ending.

What makes a good editor for you?

Sometimes you want an editor that's good at getting out of the way, but also a good editor is one that gets *in* the way. Particularly with me — here I am, sitting in my study in London, England; I have almost no connection with any comic book person over here. I don't know any of the artists. I know Mike Allred, but I don't see him. I'm living over here and I'm writing about this other culture, America usually. Occasionally it's nice to have that link. To me, it helps, because I'm writing some strange stuff. So I think there are times when you want your editor to point you in the right direction, or to throw some ideas your way, or to back you up: 'Yeah, that's great stuff, what you're doing here.'

Is it hard for you to live in London and write about America?

It's a cliché to say that we're the fifty-first State, but you do feel pretty connected

— if not by an umbilical cord, then certainly by some kind of connective tissue that manages to stretch across the Atlantic. Part of it is language, part of it is history; part of it is television. The danger is that there's more potential in my position to fall back on stereotype and cliché, not having the day-to-day, dirt-under-the-nails kind of knowledge of America.

Your initial opposition to writing *X-Force* was the X-Universe continuity. But now you're writing *X-Men*, won't you have to deal with that same continuity?

I know, it's strange, isn't it? I seem to contradict myself. Partly I feel, after writing this *X-Statix* stuff, which is almost like the flipside of the mirror to the X-Men, I think it'd be quite amusing and interesting to write the more mainstream side. The X-Men are kind of the X-Statix's grown-up, more serious brothers. It's the other side of the story I've painted in *X-Statix*. So I think it'd be interesting to visit that. Also, just by writing *X-Statix* for a while, you do pick up what's going on more. So now the whole continuity thing is proving less of a horror to me.

Are you worried about maintaining the status quo on *X-Men*?

Obviously it has to be recognisable as the same book and the same characters. But at the same time, when I go in there, I want to put my scent down, as it were, and make it mine. And partly you do that by chucking things around a little bit and making a little noise. How I'm seeing it is as the flip side of *X-Statix*, taking elements of these clichéd, almost iconic characters now, but actually finding new aspects about

X-Force

The origins of *X-Statix* actually date back to 1983; Marvel's *Uncanny X-Men* was flying high, and adding a second X-title seemed like a natural fit. The result was *New Mutants*, a younger generation of heroes who learned to control their powers — as well as learning to protect a world that hated and feared them — while attending Professor Xavier's academy. A hundred issues later, however, the comics world had changed, and something grittier and more visually dynamic was the order of the day. Enter superstar artist Rob Liefeld, who transformed the title into *X-Force*, a proactive mutant strike team who took the fight to the enemy. Initially, sales and reader excitement were tremendous. But by the time Peter Milligan inherited the title with issue #116, *X-Force* was aimless and hadn't been a must-read book in years. That all changed with Milligan and artist Mike Allred's run, a scathing look at modern media and celebrity culture which completely ignored the current X-Men continuity. Thirteen issues later, *X-Force* transformed into *X-Statix*, for reasons never really disclosed. However, to confuse the issue even further, Liefeld was announced as being back on *X-Force* yet again in 2004 with a new mini-series, just as *X-Statix* drew to a close.

MY GENERATION/ONE   8

PAGE FIVE
1
SIMILAR SHOT. VERY CLOSE ON THOSE SAME EYES SO THEY FILL
THE PANEL (though we will learn next panel that this is a
transition shot)

CAP   WHAT HAPPENED TO THE YEARS?

2
WE PULL BACK and see Rocky. But a different Rocky. A 60
year old Rocky. His hair is a shorter more modern version
of his old style. A few whisks of grey at the temples but
not doing bad for his age. Same with his face. Still slim.
Older, more wrinkles, but still looks good. Probably had a
few nips and tucks. Probably won't see too much of this in
this panel but we're in the grounds of some mansion at
Rocky's 60th birthday party. A huge lavish affair. Waiters
and waitresses dressed as though at the court of
Versailles. The good and the great in attendance. A million
light years from the sweaty Marquee club.

CAP   *SIXTY.*

3
We pull back more and see more of the party. TRIXIE –
Rocky's trophy blonde 35 year old wife, knock out figure
shown off by some daring and expensive designer dress –
comes up with two glasses of champagne.

CAP   I MET TRIXIE, MY SECOND WIFE. AT A ROCK CHARITY
           EVENT ON BEHALF OF THE INDIGENOUS PEOPLES OF THE
           ARCTIC.

TRIXIE   YOU DON'T HAVE A DRINK.

ROCKY   I'VE ALREADY HAD TWO SCHOONERS.

TRIXIE   BE A DEVIL, GO ON.

4
WE COULD PULL BACK HERE so we see more of the house, the
party, the people. Trixie and Rocky small in middle ground.

TRIXIE   I BUMPED INTO TONY BLAIR IN THE BILLIARDS ROOM.
           ASKED HIM ABOUT THE KNIGHTHOOD.

ROCKY   TRIXIE!

TRIXIE   ALL THE OTHERS HAVE GOT ONE. IT ISN'T FAIR.

ROCKY   WHAT DID YOU SAY?

5
A LITTLE INSERT Close-up on Trixie, grinning, dirty.

TRIXIE   THAT I'D GIVE HIM THE BLOW JOB OF HIS LIFE IF HE
           MADE YOU A SIR.

Above: *Script page from* Vertigo Pop: London *#1, by Peter Milligan. Courtesy of Peter Milligan.*

them and about their interrelationships. With *X-Men* the interrelationships intrigue me more than what wacky supervillain they might be battling this week.

One interesting thing about some of these comic characters is you can approach them as a Greek dramatist might have approached the legends that he wrote about. When the audience came in, they kind of recognised this character as Oedipus, and they knew what was going on. They presumed if it was Euripides or Aristophanes or any of these guys, they would get a different version of these characters seen through the prism of the writer's interests, prejudices and so on. I think some of these great comic book characters are like that. With a new writer you're going to get a different slant, you're going to get a different idea. The characters are going to be the same, but told from a different angle.

How do you envision your version of *X-Men*?

At the moment I'm assembling the team I'm going to write. But there are certain things that I find interesting up front. For example, the sexual chemistry between Gambit and Rogue and how in reality that might work itself out, and in the shapeshifting characters you have that whole nebulous sort of Shakespearean world of shifting meanings. This very big, kingly stuff is going on, i.e. battling villains and sometimes themselves, but then you have that very personal stuff. That's what I'm interested in. How much are these people mutants and how much are they human? Exploring the tension between those different parts of these characters, I think that's probably the area I'm going to want to dig around and mine.

The content allowed in Vertigo books is obviously very different to the content allowed in mainstream Marvel books. Do you prefer to write with no restraints, or are having certain restraints challenging to you?

I'm hoping with *X-Men* it'll be challenging in a good way, in a creative way. I'll have to find creative ways of exploring the themes I've just talked about. I'm hoping that the moral constraints and the artistic constraints will, in a sense, make it interesting for me. But clearly, because they've asked me to do it, they know certain boundaries are going to be pushed a little bit more than maybe other people might have pushed them. But sure, there's going to be compromise. I'll probably try to push it and be told to pull stuff back, and then the creativity will come in with how we pull things back but still make it powerful and how we say things by *not* saying things. It'll be an interesting ride... for a while, you know. It might be that we very quickly get sick of each other and I don't do it anymore. But it'll still be interesting to find out. In many ways, *X-Statix* only really worked because it was a Marvel book... here were these mutant types that were a bit like the X-Men running around and doing this other stuff. I think that the tension between what they were doing and the fact that they were doing it within the pages of a Marvel book — albeit a Marvel book with a bit more largesse than most of the Marvel X-Men books, but still a Marvel book — I think in many ways that's what gave it its edge. If *X-Statix* had been a Vertigo book, it wouldn't have had that same edge or that same tension.

XSTATIX 26   9

PAGE EIGHT
1
On Venus, grinning but tough…

VENUS   WE'VE DONE THE HARD WORK. WE'VE BATTLED THE
            AVENGERS, FOUGHT THAT POP STAR WHO LOOKED LIKE
            LADY DIANA WITH A WIG…

VENUS   WE'VE RISKED OUR NECKS ALL OVER THE WORLD. WE
            DESERVE ONE LAST BIG SPLASH. THEN WE WALK AWAY.

2
Her pov Guy…

GUY   IS THAT POSSIBLE? CAN WE JUST WALK AWAY FROM ALL
            THIS?

GUY   ZEITGEIST COULDN'T. NOR COULD EDIE. NOR COULD SO
            MANY BEFORE US…

3
Single Venus, holding her champagne up to the sky.

VENUS   THAT'S WHY WE'RE SPECIAL. WE GET FAMOUS. GET
            RICH. BEAT UP THE BAD GUYS AND WALK AWAY.

Venus   WE'RE THE ONES WHO BREAK THE MOULD.

4
Guy takes her hands, both looking back at the party.

GUY   I HOPE YOU'R RIGHT. LET'S GET BACK TO BASE AND
            CALL IN THE OTHERS.

VENUS   BUT THE PARTY'S STILL GOING STRONG.

5
They're porting out.

GUY   THERE'LL BE OTHER PARTIES.

VENUS   I SURE HOPE SO.

Above: *Another page from Peter Milligan's script for* X-Statix #26. *Courtesy of Peter Milligan/Marvel Comics. Used with permission. X-Statix ™ & © 2004 Marvel Characters, Inc.*

Can you give us an example of things you've wanted to write in the past that weren't approved for print?

Well, the obvious one that didn't quite come out was the Lady Diana story. We had to change that at the last minute and make her hair black and change her to Henrietta and make her a dead pop star rather than a dead princess. That was an example, I think, of people getting cold feet and perhaps the publicity working too well. Because we got fantastic advance publicity, mainly in the guise of the British tabloid newspapers screaming 'Disgrace!' and 'Disgusting!' in the way in which they do. All of which I think was fantastic grist for the mill, fantastic publicity. And then I think certain people got scared, and what made me laugh about that whole episode was that certain people at Marvel, maybe for reasons that I don't understand, got very worried about what the British royal family thought. There were rumblings in the British royal family about how disgusting they thought it was. I thought it was funny that the decision to cancel it or change it happened shortly after your American Independence Day. I thought that was some deep irony. You know, 'God, you're free from us! What do you care what the British royal family thinks?'

When you were writing the Diana story, did you think it was going to attract that sort of attention?

Oh yeah, I thought it might raise eyebrows and I thought it might be a bit controversial. It certainly caught fire more than I thought it would. Maybe we, all of us, handled the advance publicity a bit wrongly, and leaked what it was going to be too soon. Because in reality, what we did in the comic wasn't particularly *anti*-Princess Diana. I think perhaps if we'd let the comic come out and speak for itself... but then of course, that wouldn't have helped the sales. But I was aware that it was a bit controversial. I mean, she's still an iconic figure. Then again, this is an American comic. It's not *America's* princess. I was amazed by Diana's continued ability to cause controversy. Marvel sometimes wants to clean up their act a little a bit. They'd go through periods, while I was writing *X-Statix*, where I was asked to take out certain cursing and religious things like 'Oh, God!' and 'Jesus Christ!' They go through little periods like that. And then they seem to not worry about it for a while. So they blow hot and cold.

There also tends to be a bit of self-editing in these situations. You don't want to work on stuff that you know isn't going to see the light of day. Obviously with Diana, I reckoned wrongly. But I thought the Diana storyline was *just* this side of principle. And it seemed to be going fine. And then there was a day or two where everything seemed to catch fire. For a while it seemed like the book might get nixed because of it. With the story I'm writing at the moment for *Human Target*, which deals partly in sex slaves and underaged girls being dragged into this very murky and horrible world, you have to be very careful. You don't want to pull punches, in that you want to say it like it is, because obviously it's a real thing that's happening and if you're going to write about it you owe it to people to make them aware of the horribleness of what's going on. At the same time, you don't want to even come close to writing something that might give some pervert somewhere a little cheap thrill. There is a responsibility both ways. Karen [Berger, Vertigo editor] asked me last time to take out a particularly gruesome line one guy says to another about what he wants him to do to this underage girl to break her in. The meaning is implied, but it's still sick. There might be some bastard somewhere sitting there jerking off reading it, and you don't want to give these people any excuse.

You've said that you don't read many comic books. Is that a choice you've made to keep other books from influencing your work, or is it because you don't enjoy reading them?

No, I do enjoy them. Sometimes I pick up a bunch and I read them, and I like them. I think it's just to try and keep myself fresh and try to keep myself so I don't feel as though my entire waking moments are filled up with comic books: either writing, talking about or reading. It's just to try and keep as much of me out of this comics world. I still have the slight idea that I'm a bit of an intruder, which I quite like. I just feel that so far, it's working this way. I don't want to get up to my eyeballs in all this other stuff. What I do is try to be selective. I'm doing *Black Cat,* so I might tell Axel, 'I want to read *these* things, which might be useful in the writing of *this*.' Certain comics that I might read tend to be linked to certain things I might be writing. With the comps I get, I don't just throw them away. I separate the ones I think might be interesting to read at some time, and I might read some of them. But I'm wary about either liking stuff so much that it starts to filter into how I do things, or being really disappointed in stuff and therefore being disappointed in the medium that I'm working so much in.

Does it worry you that you're going to write something as continuity-heavy as *X-Men* when you haven't read all those back issues?

Not really. There's two reasons I don't worry about it. For one, I think the readers have to realise that with new writers, and as you move on in years, things change. These characters have to be alive *now.* They're not museum pieces. And two, I think that's why you hope you have an editor who is eagle-eyed enough to pick up on that stuff. I am very honest when I'm writing stuff for Marvel. I'm writing a *Black Cat* mini-series, which I hope is going to be great. But I don't know too much about her. So I wrote some ideas for this mini-series, and Axel — who doesn't know too much about this stuff either — has run it past people who picked up certain continuity problems and certain historical glitches. So it's best to get directed by them, I think. Which then allows you to be free and tell vital stories about living characters. Otherwise, you just get so hamstrung and so scared, you let these characters get frozen. So I don't worry about it, I just go ahead and write it, and it's up to other people either to catch it before it goes out and say, 'This wouldn't happen,' or just to say, 'Well, that's tough. It happened fifteen years ago, but it was a different writer, a different time.' I think that most people who read this stuff know that.

*　　　　　　*　　　　　　*

GREG RUCKA

One gets the sense that not much intimidates Greg Rucka. Forget the fact that prior to writing, Rucka made his living racing around in an ambulance as an emergency medical technician or working as a security guard, among a variety of other colourful occupations — those were just the warm-ups. As the author of a series of well-reviewed crime novels featuring the character of bodyguard Atticus Kodiak, Rucka had no reason to venture into the uncertain, unsteady world of comic books; yet venture he did, with the 1998 Oni Press title *Whiteout*. The mini-series was instantly considered something of a minor classic, even winning an Eisner Award. Mission accomplished. But Rucka wasn't finished; next he'd take on some of the biggest characters in comics, starting with Batman (just as the Dark Knight was entering the ambitious crossover event 'No Man's Land') and eventually Wolverine and Wonder Woman. Today, Rucka continues to hold down one of the most prolific monthly schedules in the comics industry while still managing to squeeze out a new novel every now and then. Most writers would shrink away in fear from such an undertaking. But most writers aren't Greg Rucka.

You were actually a successful novelist prior to your comics career. When did you first try your hand at writing comic scripts?

I'd written a comic script in college for a friend of mine. He was quite a talented artist. I came up with the idea, and I wrote like four scripts for this comic. He drew half of the first issue and said, 'The hell with it — I can't do this.' I was actually a little burned by that, because I'd invested in the project. It's hard to write something and not give a damn about it — even for those writers who are notorious for phoning things in. My first novel was published in 1996, and at that point this same friend was working for DC. He gave the book to people in the office, one of which was Patty Jeres. I would continue to see those DC people, in particular Patty, at San Diego, and every year I'd say to them, 'I'd love to do comics. I've written these novels. I'm a writer! Really!' And the editors would say, 'Go away, kid, you bother me.' Over and over and over again.

About the same time my third novel was coming out, I was down at San Diego and Patty introduced me to Bob Schreck. He and Joe Nozemack were just starting Oni Press, so I gave them copies of my first two books said, 'Look, I've written these, and I have an idea for a comic.' Bob sort of looked at me askance and said, 'You don't want to do these as a comic?' meaning the books, and I gave him the right answer. I said, 'Hell no, that would be ridiculous. These are novels, and that's not what a comic is.' He said, 'So what's the idea?' and I replied, 'It's about this US Deputy Marshall who's stationed in Antarctica, and there's a murder and she has to solve it.' They read the books and got back to me and said, 'Let's do it.' So I started writing. And that was how I got in. I did *Whiteout*. And in doing *Whiteout* I sort of showed that I had some chops at it.

I saw Patty again as *Whiteout* was just getting ready to come out. Patty asked me if I had any interest in writing Batman — there'd been a major bloodletting in the DC Bat-offices. Almost all the writers had been let go. So my response was, 'Of course I want to write Batman. I'd love to write Batman. That'd be fantastic.' Because, let's face it, Batman is the ultimate private investigator, and here I was writing this series of novels about PIs. So Patty talked to [*Batman* editor] Denny O'Neil and it turned out that Denny had read my first novel and quite liked it. That led to Denny and I meeting, which led to him saying, 'Okay, try a story,' which led to me writing a script and Denny liking it, which led to me getting more work. If Oni was the first step on the ladder, then Denny was the ladder falling over into a big pile of comics. [*Laughs*] I haven't been able to extricate myself since.

What kind of work schedule do you keep?

Place of birth:
San Francisco, California, USA
Date of birth:
29 November 1969
Home base:
Portland, Oregon, USA
First published work:
Whiteout
Education:
Vassar College; University of
Southern California
Career Highlights:
Adventures of Superman,
Detective Comics, Elektra,
Gotham Central, Queen & Country,
Whiteout, Whiteout: Melt, Wolverine,
Wonder Woman.

The ideal writing day has me up fairly early, by seven, seven-thirty, and sitting down to write, if at all possible, by a quarter to nine. And then I can go for about four to five hours before my brain says, 'That's enough of that, take a break.' And I'll take an hour, hour and a half and read, or have lunch and watch something that I've videotaped — I tend to watch a lot of reference or research material. Then I'll go back to work for about two hours before I have to go pick up my son. We'll have dinner, and then we have the evening together. Once the kids go down to sleep, I go back to work. And I do that until I'm exhausted and have to sleep myself.

How long does it take you to write an average issue of a comic book?

No such thing as an average comic book for me. I've had issues that I've written in, honest to God, three hours, that have come out to 44-pages of full script. And I've thought, 'This is junk.' But I send it off to an editor and they say, 'No, I love it!' Then the issue comes out and people say, 'This is fantastic!' I've had issues that I've spent five or ten days labouring over, and send it in going, 'I like this one,' and the editor says, 'I do too,' and the issue comes out and everybody says, 'Burn him!' It's not consistent. It depends on what I'm writing and which character I'm writing about. There are some days where you get the bear and some days the bear gets you. [*Laughs*] *Queen & Country* is the comic book that's most consistent in terms of time. It takes between two and four days to write a *Queen & Country* script. *Wonder Woman* right now can be anywhere from a day and a half to ten days. Same for *Superman*. Some issues of *Wolverine* have been like that too.

The Novels

Before gaining the keys to the comic book kingdom, Greg Rucka polished his storytelling skills as a successful crime novelist. His best known works follow the adventures of Atticus Kodiak, a professional bodyguard who debuted in Rucka's first book, *Keeper*, and has so far starred in a total of five novels. Although 'bodyguard' calls to mind a slab of hired beef, Kodiak is a layered, vulnerable hero, and Rucka's exploration of the business of personal security goes far beyond the stereotype of the thick-necked oaf. In *Keeper*, Kodiak protects a doctor at an abortion clinic who's marked for death by a group of pro-life extremists. The follow-up, *Finder*, found Kodiak pulling bouncer duty at a sex club before getting pulled back into the bodyguard game. In *Smoker*, Kodiak takes on Big Tobacco when he's enlisted to protect the star witness in a civil trial. Kodiak even gets mixed up with Britain's royal family in the fifth novel, *Critical Space*. Rucka finally stepped away from the world of Atticus Kodiak with *A Fistful of Rain*, which introduced a young rock star named Miriam 'Mim' Bracca who's targetted for blackmail and murder. One thing's for sure: you can't ever accuse Rucka of re-hashing the same old story.

Have you figured out a maximum number of titles you can carry in a month?

I hit a point where I realised that five was too much. So I guess the number is four. My ideal scenario is to get to a place where I'm writing not issue-by-issue but arc-by-arc. That way I could devote three weeks to writing six issues of a *Wonder Woman* arc, and once they're finished, sit down and spend a month writing the next huge *Queen & Country* arc. I'm also interested in trying it as an experiment, just to see how it would affect the story and the writing itself. But my opportunity to do that right now is nonexistent because I'm in the hole. I'm perpetually in the hole. Because I'm not carrying four books, I'm carrying five.

How are you with deadlines?

I used to be great about them. But then I had kids. And it bugs me, because I used to pride myself on, if I told an editor, 'You will have the script by tomorrow noon,' they would have it by tomorrow noon. And one of the first things you discover once you have children is they don't care. [*Laughs*] They really don't give a rat's ass whether you have a deadline or not. Nor can they be convinced to. And then they bring home germs and things like that. On a Monday, you can tell an editor in good faith that you'll have the next issue of *Superman* by Wednesday, and by Tuesday you discover that your son is throwing up. And you know what? You didn't get any writing done on Tuesday and that's that.

Do you ever have a problem with writer's block?

Yeah, though I don't tend to call it that. I've yet to experience true writer's block. There are days when I sit down and I go, 'Jesus Christ, I have no idea what I'm going to do.' Or worse, I know what I'm going to do and I can't make the words do it. But… I've never had a string of days where I just couldn't do it no matter how hard I tried.

How often are you in a position where the deadline dictates that you turn in a story before you're completely happy with it?

More often than I'd like. But the flip side is, I'm never going to be happy with it. There's a phrase, I don't know who it's attributed to, that goes: 'Stories are never finished. They're only abandoned.' I've got some things that I've been working on for *years*. They're coming on ten years now, because they're still not right yet. But at some point you have to pull the cord. When there's an issue of deadline and production and getting it to the artist and so on, then it becomes easier to draw a line under it for me. But very rarely do I put something in and go, 'It's done. It doesn't need anything else.' My gut always wants an opportunity to rework it.

Do your personal beliefs or political views enter into your stories? Your first *Wolverine* arc was about crooked gun dealers, for instance — where do the germs for such stories come from?

I tend to write from a number of different places. I write from anger. I write from

Page 8

ONE:
Angle, past DIANA, her LASSO shimmering in her RIGHT HAND, held out to her side, low and ready.

HALE, to the side, is scrabbling back off the couch in horror, as the CALE ILLUSION completes its horrific dissolve.

The reveal here, of course, is DOCTOR PSYCHO, standing on CALE'S DESK. He looks pretty happy, actually. Sure, it sucks that Diana's just blown the gig, but hey, he was about to get a Senator to make love to a couch, and he's done God only knows how much damage to C.A.P. already. Win some, lose some.

His only real concern is getting out of this without getting caught, and he's got a plan for that, too.

So all in all, we're looking at a fairly sinister, self-confident, and, of course, evil DOCTOR PSYCHO.

1 PSYCHO:	…it was **fun** while it **lasted**.
2 PSYCHO/linked:	Good thing Princess Pretty-Girl arrived when she **did**, huh, Senator?

TWO:
CU on PSYCHO, his grin is so malevolent. Not to be too crude, but both he and the Senator know they'd have gone all the way… which would have meant that Hale was fucking the couch.

3 PSYCHO: Who **knows** how **far** you might have **gone**.

Page 9

ONE:
Angle, past PSYCHO standing on the DESK, hands behind his BACK, as DIANA starts to move closer, feeding the LASSO out into her other hand. She's entirely focused on PSYCHO—her mistake for the issue, by the way.

HALE has backed off the couch, horrified, and ANDERSON is moving to join him.

1 ANDERSON:	Where's **Ronnie**? What have you **done** to her, you sick
2 PSYCHO:	She's **around** here **somewhere**. You should pick your **friends** better, Leslie.
3 PSYCHO/linked:	Ronnie's not the **saint** you **think** she is.
4 DIANA:	Enough. You'll **answer** the question, Doctor

TWO:
On PSYCHO, his grin getting BIGGER, as he brings his HANDS up .

5 PSYCHO:	No, I don't think I **will**.
6 PSYCHO/linked:	You might see right **through** me…

curiosity. And I write from excitement or interest. Right now, we're doing a Medusa arc in *Wonder Woman,* and I'm a fan of Greek mythology and ancient Greek culture. Consequently, this is a very exciting arc for me, both in terms of the research and being able to play with the mythology. Oh, and being able to use those three and a half years of Greek I took in high school. That's an example of me writing from excitement.

By comparison, you look at something like *Queen & Country: Operation Morningstar,* which was the second arc of that series, and that was written out of pure rage. I started the story a year *before* 9/11, but I was already spitting blood. I was so angry at what the Taliban were doing in general, and then I was a hundred thousand times more furious about their treatment of women. I am very curious and interested in gender politics and sexual politics. It's there in my work, so this won't come as a surprise to anyone who studies my writing. So I wrote *Operation Morningstar* out of white-hot fury. I wanted to say, 'These people are *bastards.* You can dress it up however you like but what they're doing isn't Islam — it's just *evil.* It's not just wrong, it's *evil!* You don't execute women *because they're women!'* So there you get a story born out of anger.

And then a good example of curiosity would be a mini-series I did for Marvel about three years ago called *Black Widow: Pale Little Spider.* It came out under the MAX line, so it was like 'Ooh, titillating!' But what it was about was a murder in the bondage scene in Moscow. Moscow has a notorious S&M scene, and I was curious about the trust issues at work in that. I've never been into the scene, but I've always looked at it from the outside and been fascinated by why people play these roles. When you read literature about people who are into bondage, one of the things you keep coming back to is this issue of trust and then the freedom that comes from surrendering. And the power relationships, the whole issues of 'topping from below' [whereby a 'submissive' attempts to be in charge of a 'dominant' through some form of manipulation] and so on. And I was like, 'You know, that fits perfectly into this whole paradigm of, [*adopts Russian accent*] we take this person and we make her into super secret agent!' That's a dominance game. That's a bondage game. Where you control every aspect of a person. So that arc became me trying to understand how that worked.

Once you have an idea, what then?

I look at the story and then I immediately look at the character and I go, 'What is the character's story in this? What is the character's arc?' Stories are primarily about character. I am of a group of writers who believes that the plot is not the most important thing. The character is the most important thing. Especially in a soap opera, and that's what comics are. They're soaps. People come back to them over and over again because they love the characters. Every now and then they get really excited about the story, but the reason they care about the story is because of the *characters.* It's not because they go, 'Oh, that's fascinating, what *would* happen if a giant meteor were hurtling toward Earth?' Rather they go, 'Wow, what does it mean to Superman when he's going to have to stop a giant meteor hurtling to Earth while Lois is trying to deliver somebody's baby in the back of a trapped submarine?' So the idea comes and then the character question is raised. How does the story affect the character?

Ideally, in the best plots, what happens is that the plot is paralleling and directly triggering a character's actions. The character should drive plot, not the other way around. Certain things happen on a timetable. For instance, you can say, 'I put the bomb underneath the car, and it's gonna go off when our hero turns the key in the ignition.' That's time-sensitive. That's an 'if-then' construct. And okay, that's a fine plot point. But that, in and of itself, does nothing for the character. The question then, is, 'How does the character interact with that situation?' Now you ask yourself, 'Logan [Wolverine] has found himself in this situation and he can't do the things he normally does. So, what does he do next?' That really moves the plot forwards. He can't stab 'em in the eye, so he goes home and has a beer. And while he's having a beer, he engages in some self-loathing, and talks to somebody and they have this conversation where he learns something. So he goes back to the location to try and right the wrong, but discovers he's too late. And now that he's too late... see what I mean?

Mostly with comics, all this plot/character interaction is held in my head. But if it's a multi-issue arc, more than three issues, I will actually break it down in notes first. I write very detailed synopses. This is also how I write novels, incidentally. Most finished novels come out to between a hundred and a hundred and twenty thousand words. Just the synopses for most of my novels are about thirty thousand words!

How much flexibility do you have when it comes to the way artists interpret your scripts?

I don't view my full script as something that the artist has to be slavishly devoted to. I am a writer, and I'm a good writer. I'm good enough that I can make a living at it, so clearly there are enough people out there willing to spend money to validate that assertion. There are things I have trained and studied and learned and practiced; I know how to plot and to pace and I know how to write dialogue and character. I can give you a theme and I can write a story that's emotionally resonant and will leave you, hopefully, if everything works well, *feeling* something at the end. Those are the things I can do. I cannot draw. And even if I could draw, I cannot draw as well as, say, [*Felon* and *Adventures of Superman* artist] Matthew Clark or [*Queen & Country* artist] Jason Alexander or [*Queen & Country* artist] Mike Hawthorne. And it would be the height of ego for me to turn around and say, 'You have to draw it as I wrote it.' The purpose of the full script is for me to put in everything possible so they understand the story we're trying to tell together. Very rarely in a script will I say, 'It *has* to look *this way*.'

How much control do you want to keep over the actual panel-by-panel pacing? Can your artists add or cut panels as they see fit?

I have real problems with deletions if they haven't been run past me. Insertions bother me less. This is going to sound very self-serving or defensive, but I've truly encountered this. The fact is there are some very lazy artists out there, artists who are more concerned with drawing a page that they'll be able to sell at a convention later than they are with drawing a page that will actually forward the story. So I get nervous about deletions, because for a lot of the weaker artists out there, they think fewer panels on a page means it's an easier page. You talk to a really good artist and they'll tell you that is not the case. They will tell you that they would gladly take a multi-panel page over a splash page. I find that an interesting litmus test.

Do you have any control if pages come back and you aren't happy with them?

It depends. I have honestly had instances where the pages that came in were so wrong that I called the editor up, nearly in tears, saying, 'This is *so* not the story!' And was told, 'Well, we can't do anything. There's just no time.' Then there have been other instances where the editor has turned around and spoken to the artist and the artist has then held the page hostage. Honestly, they do this. They'll just say, 'I'm not going to redraw it.' They get it back and they don't return it, and then when they return it, it's the exact same thing. I've had pages come in that were so not what I wanted... and the artist wouldn't redraw them, so the inker had to do the repair work. Conversely, I have had editors and artists who when asked to change something go, 'Sure, no problem.'

Do you have any weaknesses as a comics writer that you feel a good editor can help you with?

Whiteout

Rucka's comics debut was a wholly original take on the whodunit, and therefore a perfect fit for the wholly original publishing plan of Oni Press. *Whiteout*'s Federal Deputy Marshal Carrie Stetko has been banished to the very ends of the Earth — the frozen continent of Antarctica, and its lonely outpost of McMurdo Station. When a dead body turns up, Stetko has an entire continent to comb in order to find the men who last saw the victim, and it's not long before Stetko is narrowly avoiding becoming the next dead body herself. The sequel, *Whiteout: Melt*, ups the ante by involving Russian nukes and international intrigue. *Melt* won a 1999 Eisner Award, confirming what readers had already discovered: Rucka was a storyteller worth watching. His publisher, Oni Press, had been founded just two years earlier by Joe Nozemack and Bob Schreck on the promise of spurning the mainstream comics ideal and pursuing high-quality stories off the beaten path. The company also printed the first comics work by filmmaker Kevin Smith, as well as Judd Winick's *The Adventures of Barry Ween, Boy Genius*, Paul Dini's *Jingle Belle* and a whole host of superhero-free, groundbreaking fare. Further serendipity: both Rucka and Oni make their homes in Portland, Oregon.

Greg Rucka

Pages 20 and 21

ONE:
Angle, exterior London, late afternoon. We're near the houses of Parliament, at the foot of Lambeth Bridge (and yeah, this is a specific reference—I'll get you photos if you need it).

WALLACE and CHACE are walking side by side, each smoking. They're at the top of a flight of stone steps at the Parliament side of the bridge, about to descend. The THAMES flows past on our right, their left.

It is still raining.

1 WALLACE: You were at school with Rachel Beck, weren't you?

2 CHACE: Ray? We shared a couple of classes. Languages, mostly. French and German. Why?

3 WALLACE: You meet her father?

TWO:
Angle as CHACE and WALLACE descend the steps. CHACE is glancing at WALLACE. WALLACE is drawing on his cigarette. CHACE is curious.

4 CHACE: Once. He took a group of us down to London one weekend. Dropped a good fifteen THOUSAND pounds on us. Food, wine, chauffeurs.
5 CHACE/linked: Even wrangled us private FITTINGS at RIGBY and PELLER.

THREE:
Angle, as WALLACE leans against the stone railing, looking at the Thames. CHACE has stopped, focused on him.

6 CHACE: I'm asking AGAIN, Tom. Why?

7 WALLACE: Nothing SINISTER. Colin Beck was mentioned in the Routines from Paris this morning.
8 WALLACE/linked: Mark Stephenson thinks the DGSE may have him under surveillance.

|continued|

There's a term they use in the role-playing game community: I'm a plumber. I want to plumb the character. I want to get into all the nooks and crannies and understand them. But that can easily get self-indulgent. It's a very narrow line, and it's a line that I try to remain constantly aware of, but constant awareness does not necessarily equate to successful evasion. A good editor will snap me out of that. We got heat because our first five or six issues of *Wonder Woman* were very quiet, very slow. I didn't have her punch anybody. And the criticism was, 'Nothing is happening.' Which I took great umbrage at, because what they were really saying was, 'She's not fighting anybody.' And those are two very different things. I hate violence for the sake of violence, but on the other hand I think dramatic violence is one of the most effective tools in a writer's toolbox. Consequently, fight scenes have to be used judiciously and properly. A fight for the sake of a fight is nothing but a way for a writer to fill pages. Sure, you can have fights for fun, you can make the fight exciting, you can make it over-the-top... but that's not what I'm saying. Here's an example: if it's Batman stopping a mugging, well, we've seen that *eight thousand* times, so unless this mugging is significantly different, all you're doing is filling four pages with Batman punching people. I think that's insulting to the reader.

On *Wonder Woman*, the guy behind the scenes is Ivan Cohen, and he's a very good editor. Specifically, he's a very good communicator, and he is constantly cautioning me, 'We need something to *happen*. We need to see Diana in costume, and we need to remember that she has super powers!' These are valid points, but you also need to establish the world around Diana first. Once we have all these pieces in place, once those scenes are set, *then* we can blow things up. Then we'll have a valid set of reasons for her to throw a punch. Like everything else, violence is an aspect of character. I used to do stage combat in the theatre, and when I was learning it the guy who taught me was fond of saying, 'If you do the fight right, it's the story in a microcosm.' In other words. what you do in a fight can reveal more about a character than anything they've said. Wolverine, for instance, fights a very different way to Superman. So... does your hero bite the bad guy? That says something. Does the hero kick them when they're down? Likewise. Does your hero slap? Punch? Overall, I consider a good editor keeps me honest, keeps me from being lazy, catches me when I go wrong, and steers me back on course when I stray too far into self-indulgence.

How do you approach writing characters as iconic as Batman, Wolverine or Wonder Woman?

In all of them, I try to go to the core of the character. Which itself is different for everybody who approaches them. Mark Waid is a fan of Batman saying 'chum', for instance. The idea of Batman saying 'chum' makes me break out in hives. That's not *my* Batman. I can remember sitting down to write the end of 'No Man's Land' with Devin Grayson, when she and I were actually writing those issues together. There was this one line, where Batman is giving Nightwing instructions about a bomb. Nightwing says something like, 'It's a bomb!' and Batman's original line was, 'Get it.' And Devin and I looked at one another and said, 'No. No, no, no.' The line we decided on was 'Go.' Because that's Batman to us, that's the core of the character. Never two words if one will do. Everything is as efficient as possible. Everything is committed. It's a zealot's passion. He doesn't waste time. So every time I go to one of the big iconic characters, I first have to ask, 'What is the heart of the character for me? What is that iconic piece?' In some characters it's easier to spot than others.

You've been quoted as saying Frank Miller's *Daredevil* was a big influence. Was that in your mind when you started writing *Elektra*?

Yeah... I get misquoted on *Elektra* a lot. Especially about that. Even to the point where somebody told me that Miller was angry at me about something I'd said. That really kind of worked me up, because I have nothing but respect for that guy's work. *Especially* those pieces. I'm writing comics because of *Batman: Year One* and *Daredevil: Born Again.* Everybody goes to *Watchmen*; I go to those two Frank Miller pieces. The Elektra character has a fundamental problem because I actually believe she's *done.* Frank knew what he was doing. He created the character and he ran her all the way through her arc. And then he brought her back in a very inventive, very bold book without, I think, the intention of her turning into the cash cow that she inevitably became. So she was nightmarishly difficult to write because, honest to God, Frank had done everything with her that could be done. Brian Michael Bendis and I had a talk about it when I took over the book from him. He said, '*Ohh-hhh,* this is hard.' [*Elektra* editor] Stuart Moore and I went round and round until we finally settled on a story we could tell about her that we thought hadn't been told. It was a redemptive story of

No Man's Land

After a powerful earthquake rocks Gotham City, the burg goes from merely crime-plagued and corrupt to downright unlivable. The city is such a hellhole, in fact, that the United States government takes the radical step of cutting it off from the rest of the country. Bridges leading into town are destroyed, the rivers become floating minefields, and nobody is allowed in or out. Naturally, all Batman's insane foes get loose and start carving up the city into their own deadly territories. At first, Batman is nowhere to be found, and new heroes must emerge. Of course, you can take the Bat out of Gotham City but you can't take Gotham City out of the Bat — and soon the Dark Knight is taking back his turf with a vengeance. This 1999 mega-crossover spanning several consecutive months linked all the core Bat-books and a number of companion titles including *Robin* and *Nightwing* into one big sprawling epic, and Rucka was right in the middle of it. In addition to pitching in on the *No Man's Land* comic storytelling, Rucka also penned the companion novel, which further fleshed out Batman's role in one of the most pivotal events of the hero's long career.

Greg Rucka   *Wonder Woman #205*
                                              Page 40 of 40

Page 22

ONE:
Splash, reveal, yes, the moment we've all been waiting for.

In FG, CIRCE, blindfolded, is half in profile, her head turned, chin up, listening to
MEDOUSA. Thinking of how a blind person turns their head when they're speaking to
someone, listening to someone. She's still grinning.

EURYALE and STHENO are both standing, and they're overjoyed. They're sister has
returned after three thousand years.

And MEDOUSA stands, looking down at CIRCE, the HAIR SERPENTS all alive,
looking around, moving, each of them independent, each of them curious and happy.

MEDOUSA is naked, of course, but has WRAPPED herself in the BLACK TARP. And
she is beautiful beyond words. Her GOLDEN WINGS rise up above her shoulders,
folded back, her TALONS the same GOLD. Her skin is flawless, and mouth as if made to
be kissed.

But her EYES are nothing but SHINING BLACK ORBS, and there's a malevolence that
cascades from her in waves.

Her HANDS have pulled the TARP back from where she had draped it over her HEAD
as a cowl, so we get the full reveal.

1 MEDOUSA: ...**how** I might **kill** this...
2 MEDOUSA/linked: ...Wonder Woman....

        TITLE & CREDITS:
        Bitter Pills   Three of Three
        Script: Greg Rucka
        Pencils: Drew Johnson
        Inks: Ray Snyder
        Letters: Todd Klein
        Colors: Richard and Tanya Horie
        Edits: Ivan Cohen

        Wonder Woman created by William Moulton Marston

Above: *Final page from* Wonder Woman *#205. Courtesy of Greg Rucka.*

resurrection, where she has to confront her guilt. But even *that* story had been done. [*Laughs*] Frank had been there first. So that problem was there all the time. One of the things I had to do really early on was say categorically, 'This isn't Frank Miller's Elektra. It can't be! This is Greg Rucka's *version* of Elektra.'

Do you feel like you were successful with the book?

No, it feels like a failed experiment, for a variety of reasons. I think we got hurt by art changes on the book, and then the editor changed and consequently, whether intentionally or not, the plan that Stuart had worked on got subjected to another set of eyes and opinions. Good eyes — it was Joe Quesada — but he didn't agree with me on some fundamental issues about the character. I can give you a great example. For *Elektra* #10 we had this Greg Horn cover... showing Elektra in an easy chair, in what looks to be an abandoned apartment. She's sitting in front of a window and she's got a leg up on the windowsill, the sunlight is floating in, and her right arm is hanging over the side of the chair. And honest to God, it looks like she's airing out her pubes. That's not the original cover. The original cover has one significant addition. There's a syringe on the floor by her hand. And when you see that syringe, you realise that the silk around her arm is a tie-off silk, and what she's done is she's shot up heroin. I felt very strongly that when she's not working she doesn't know who she is. She doesn't know what to do with herself. That time in-between jobs will *kill* her if the jobs don't keep coming, because her assassin identity is all she is. Joe, Stuart and I went fifteen rounds on this, and Joe's final argument was this: 'Elektra can't shoot heroin because Elektra's a hero.' To which I said, '*She kills people for money.* Which is inherently anti-heroic!' But I was never going to win that argument, because there was a *Daredevil* movie coming out, and after that they had hopes for an *Elektra* movie, and she ain't shootin' up smack! So things like that seriously affected the book because I couldn't take it where I wanted to go. Sure, I can blame everybody but myself, but I'm going to blame myself as well. *Elektra* was real hard to write. I don't look back at those issues and go, 'Oh God, they're awful.' But I cannot help but look back at them and go, 'Wow, that was painful and not nearly as good as I wanted it to be.'

What company-owned character do you feel like you've done the *best* job with?

Huntress. The *Batman/Huntress: Cry for Blood* series I did with [artist] Rick Burchett. I'm very, very proud of those issues. That series did everything that I wanted it to do. It paid homage to the character in the ways I wanted it to pay homage. It reworked the character to a new-millennium sensibility that was justified. It had the element of tragedy that I think is critical to the character. It grounded the concept and made it less fantastic, which was one of the big problems I had with a lot of the stuff that had been done with her before; it was, for lack of a better word, so transparently 'comic-booky'. To this day, I'm very proud of that job.

What's your take on the current state of the comic book industry?

I remember somebody telling me that they were talking to Will Eisner, and they'd been bemoaning the state of the industry, and Eisner just said, 'I've seen it before. We'll come back.' And that statement mattered more to me, just secondhand than I think anything anybody else had said. I remember the early '90s. I remember being at San Diego and watching an obscenely long line waiting to get a book signed by Rob Liefeld. I started joking with my friends, saying that what I really wanted to do was have the balls to stand in that line for eight hours, get my cover of *Youngblood* or whatever it was signed, and then rip off the cover and run through the halls shouting, 'He signed it! He signed it!' I hated the whole issue of speculation*. For God's sake, I wrote it, please give me the courtesy of reading it! If you want the foil variant, fine, but *read* the damn thing!

I'm not willing the sound of the death knell on the industry. The thing is this: if comics were not an artistic medium, in and of themselves, I think we'd be in far more trouble. But they are an artistic medium. They are a form of art literature unlike anything else. And for that reason, if none other, they will endure. They're primal. There are stories you can tell in a comic you cannot tell any other way. You can't tell them on a stage and you can't tell them on a screen and you can't tell them in a novel or on radio. The best comic book stories are the ones you read as a comic and the only way they could have been told was as a comic. Those are the best. You look at something like *Watchmen*, and simply as a piece of comic book literature it is still, even now, the ultimate expression of what you can do within the medium. Just how you can intertwine narratives and juxtapose images in a way that film really can't do. I get real tired when people bastardise the medium in that way. Sure, it's a superhero comic but it doesn't mean it's not Art with a capital 'A'.

*   *   *

---

* *The speculator boom of the early '90s saw certain 'hot', 'rare' comics —* Youngblood #1 *being one example — attaining ridiculous prices at resale, despite print runs sometimes in the millions.*

DAVE SIM

He's been called the Godfather of the Small Press, and with good reason. In a time when ten-issue runs are considered lengthy stints, writer/artist Dave Sim has shown comic fans the true meaning of the term loyalty. Over twenty-five-plus years, Sim has clocked in a whopping 300 issues (over 6,000 pages) of his satirical aardvark-starring comic *Cerebus*. And he did it all without flashy covers, slick paper or hokey gimmicks. Quite the opposite, in fact. To Sim, it was always about the story and entertaining his readers. Originally created as a parody to tap into the *Howard the Duck* craze of the '70s, *Cerebus* evolved into much, much more. Sim (and background artist Gerhard) may've finally finished up the tale in 2004, but he's not quite ready to put the aardvark away for good. He's currently busy sorting through all his notes and artwork to pull together a *Cerebus* archive. And that shouldn't surprise anyone who knows Sim. This is the man who introduced 500-page 'phone book' paperbacks collecting each *Cerebus* story-arc, and even wrote a 'how to' primer for aspiring comic creators on self-publishing. Never short of ideas — or words — Sim has been perhaps the biggest fish in the small press pond.

You've spent about three decades in comics now. How did you first get your foot in the door?

Basically through fanzines, which were one of the few avenues open to people who were not living in New York City in the 1970s. I was just doing short strips and illustrations for anyone that would pay ten or fifteen bucks for them. The more published work you had to show other fanzine publishers, the more you could attract the attention of someone like Mike Friedrich. That was my big breakthrough point, when Mike accepted work for *Quack!* and *Star*Reach*.

He was the pioneer of what was called temporarily 'ground level' comics. There were 'underground' comics and 'over-ground' comics, so Mike decided we needed ground level comics. The idea was basically, let's steal the underground comics format — which was colour covers with black and white interiors — but let's do content that's closer to mainstream comics. I was doing a comic strip in Canada called 'The Beavers' and I ended up doing that for his funny animal title, which came out in the wake of *Howard the Duck*'s success.

Then it was more things like that. I pitched Mike on the idea of a funny animal series, having looked at *Quack!*, which was all funny animals at the time, including the work I was doing. It wasn't the same as *Howard the Duck* though — it wasn't working as well. I tried to figure out why it wasn't working as well and I realised that the thing that set *Howard* apart was the funny animal in the world of humans. And I thought, okay, I've figured this out but I'm not the brightest light on the Christmas tree. Somebody else is going to notice too, so I'd better hurry and do my funny animal in the world of humans and pitch it to see if that isn't the missing equation why *Quack!* isn't going over as big as *Howard the Duck*. And at that time, sales were down on *Quack!* and *Star*Reach*, so Mike was cutting back all over the place. He had the misfortune at that time of being the guy who turned down *Cerebus* and *Elfquest*.

So *Howard the Duck* was more the inspiration for *Cerebus* than *Conan* it seems. But if Mike Friedrich turned you down, why did you still go ahead with it?

The idea behind doing three issues of *Cerebus* originally was if I could put them out and either break even or not lose too much on them, coupled with the other things I'd been doing elsewhere, I'd have a package of six or seven comic books that I'd be able to send to Marvel, DC and Charlton.

Place of birth:
　　Hamilton, Ontario, Canada
Date of birth:
　　17 May 1956
Home base:
　　Kitchener, Ontario, Canada
First published work:
　　First scripted story was for Skywald
　　Publishing's *Psycho Winter Special*
　　in 1975, story called 'The Cry of
　　the White Wolf'
Education:
　　'I dropped out at grade eleven. I think we all figured out the same
　　thing. Whatever this school gig is about, this isn't gonna do
　　anything for me in the comic book field.'
Career Highlights:
　　Cerebus

After doing those three issues, what made you decide to keep going?

The fact that I *could* keep going. Stores were buying it on a non-returnable basis, which just completely streamlined publishing. It took ninety percent of the risk out because returns are always the biggest risk on it. I knew right away that with a $1 cover price and whatever retailers bought them at (probably fifty or sixty percent off), 2,000 copies was $800. And the printing bill had been about $400 or $500, so I'd just made $300. It wasn't enough to live on, but it was a profit. Then it was a matter of doing freelance work one month, as lucrative as I could get, and the other month writing and drawing *Cerebus*, which is what I wanted to do.

It was a case of don't do anything stupid. So I said to myself, easy does it, let's just keep this going. Don't change the format. Don't change the logo. Don't change the price. Make the design of the numbers the same on each of the covers. Make it look as much like a Marvel comic as you can with those numbers in the box. Just real basic things. Then as long as people are buying this, the most important thing was to stay on schedule. That was the other thing — anytime I was doing stuff with any of the independent publishers, it would take them six months or a year to get an issue out. You can't build an audience if you're putting something out every six months. If you say it's bimonthly, make it bimonthly. I was the only one putting dates on the cover. I put February on there to make sure that I got my ass in gear and got it out in February.

You're truly a rarity in comics. Sticking with a title for a long run is far from

Howard the Duck

Trapped in a world he never made, Howard the Duck may seem like one big joke to today's comic book fans, but he was all the rage when he debuted back in the '70s. The brainchild of comics writer Steve Gerber, the foul-mouthed, cigar-chomping duck made his first appearance in Marvel's *Fear* #19 back in 1973 when he slipped through a dimensional gateway of sorts and met up with the Man-Thing. Stuck on Earth, Howard put up with us lowly humans, rather than the funny animals from his homeworld. Originally created as a joke, Howard became so popular that he received his own title set in the Marvel Universe a few years later. With his sexy human girlfriend Beverly, Howard ran around the Marvel Universe crossing paths with such characters as Spider-Man and the Defenders. Quickly turning into the social satire comic of its time, Howard was the Groucho Marx of the Marvel Universe. His cult-status even landed him a live-action motion picture in 1986 with *Star Wars* creator George Lucas executive producing. (Unfortunately, it's now known as one of the worst films of all time.) Marvel recently gave Howard another kick-start with a mini-series in its more adult MAX imprint, proving that this duck has certainly swum the test of time.

common these days, but 300 issues in a row is unheard of. Did you honestly think you'd make it to the end?

I hoped I would. I definitely tried to minimize everything that might get in the way of me getting there. I was one of those people that always thought lightning only strikes once. Charles Schultz got *Peanuts*. He did other strips and other work, but I don't think he ever doubted for a minute when he saw the reaction to *Peanuts*. He knew, 'Okay, I've got it. I've got it this time, don't let go of it.'

At what point did you realise you wanted to do *Cerebus* for 300 issues?

That was after the second year. I think issue #12 or #13 had come out and I thought, okay, I can keep going. How long am I going to keep going? I didn't want to be in the situation that Hal Foster had ended up in when he finally retired from *Prince Valiant*. I read later interviews with him where he said that the last couple of years the strips were lousy. That was a really unhappy confession. I never wanted to be in a situation of saying, 'I've got my thing. I did it for however long I did it and the last ten issues were crap.' So basically I just said, 'Where can I guarantee that they won't be crap?'

I figured you could still be working at peak efficiency in your fifties, so I thought I'd cut myself some slack and just do it until I was in my late forties. I picked what I thought would be a really impressive number and then sort of calculated mentally where that would take me to. And I did the math wrong — I thought it was March 2003. [*Laughs*] It was three or four years later that I finally did the math again correctly and found out there was another year. That was kind of a drag.

Did you ever consider bringing *Cerebus* to another publisher so they could handle the boring paperwork?

Yeah, actually I was just unearthing the *Cerebus* archive material, and I ran across about eight or nine letters between me and DC. Can we bring *Cerebus* to DC? And the final answer was no on my part. It was definitely the control issue. I looked at what was going on at the time with the *Teenage Mutant Ninja Turtles* and said, 'No, I think the Turtles went from being one kind of thing when it was just [TMNT creators] Kevin Eastman and Peter Laird and their funky comic book to when it became this commercial property.' And the commercial property definitely outweighed it. It just tipped the balances so the 'real world' Turtles were far more well known than the self-published comic Turtles.

Too much work went into *Cerebus*. My heart and soul is in the comic book field. What is in the comic book field seems very vulnerable to me. The movie Hulk and the TV Hulk are more widely known than Jack Kirby's Hulk. And to me, that's wrong. With *Cerebus*, I decided this is going to be the comic book equivalent of a Russian novel — you know, 6,000 pages and every kind of theme that I can possibly address — and hope that it is this monumental work. I want to say this is a comic book; it's not a blueprint for an animated cartoon or a good idea for lunch buckets or any of the rest of it. This is exactly what it is. And I hope that a few more guys come along and say the same thing. As I've said to a number of people, if I could be guaranteed that a movie never got made, I'd be happy to sign a deal in Hollywood.

Do you have any regrets now that you're finished?

No, not really. That had to be ruled out mentally very early on. If you're doing 6,000 pages, at what point do you start doubling back and fixing things? I do get weird ideas like stealing Greg Capullo away from Todd McFarlane and getting him to do *Ultimate Cerebus*. Start over at #1 and tell the story over again, but make it look like an Image comic. And then just sit back and take seventy percent of his money.

You were a big comics fan as a kid. Did you ever think you'd become a comics writer?

Yeah, I definitely always wanted to write. I was a much better writer than an artist, but I think I always preferred being an artist. I definitely wanted to be Neal Adams instead of Denny O'Neil. It was far more glamorous and far more satisfying. As an artist, you can sit at the end of the day with your page up on the wall and go, 'I did that.' When you're a writer, you sit and look at a stack of typed pages... and it's a stack of typed pages. It could be anybody's stack of typed pages. You can re-read it and look at what somebody did to it when it came in, but in the comic book field, to me it's always been second best.

What specific comics or creators have influenced your work the most?

Denny O'Neil was the biggest and most phenomenal thing that was happening when I was fourteen or fifteen years old — when *Green Lantern/Green Arrow* #76 came out, which was really the first 'relevance' comic. It was concerned with genuine societal issues. There was so much debate going on in society about what was right and what was wrong. Was Vietnam right or was Vietnam wrong? I think it was very disorienting for the adults, but for a kid it was striking at a far more genetic level because there was a realisation just from the way the adults were reacting to it that this was completely different. You realised that there had never been protests before. There had never been demonstrations like the Chicago Democratic Convention in '68. I can remember seeing the riots on television. You can tell by the way my parents were watching it that this was not just standard television stuff.

So Denny O'Neil actually bringing that relevance into comics was just staggering. You could see the people it was having an impact on. I was still pretty young at that point, but when Elliot S! Maggin did his Green Arrow story 'What Can One Man Do?' — which he did as a college paper and then sent it to DC and Neal Adams drew it — you could just see that bada-bing-bada-boom! Denny O'Neil just created Elliot S! Maggin. It was like, yeah, I think this is going to be something. This will be a place to write, not just a place to do superhero fantasy.

Are you totally finished with comics now?

I'm not really totally done with comics. I think I might be done writing and draw-

227 FEB PGS 8 9 10

OH–

(1) HI AGAIN! ♡♡

HI.
(2) LISTEN, WHY ARE YOU SO MAD AT ME

(3) I'M NOT MAD AT YOU

(4) YEAH? THEN WHY DID YOU LEAVE THE STAROOM SO SOON

(5) OH–AS I WAS JUST TELLING CEREBUS... I THOUGHT WE HAD A DATE HAHAH...

(6) YOU KNOW... JUST THE TWO OF US... WHEN I SAW THAT TONY WAS.

(7) HAH! I DON'T THINK IT HAD ANYTHING TO DO WITH OUR SO-CALLED "DATE"

(8) I THINK YOU'RE JEALOUS OF TONY.

(9) WOW

(10) THAT'S AMAZING THAT'S JUST WHAT YOU SAID SHE WOULD THINK

(11)

(12)

(13)

HHHH

(14) WOULD YOU LIKE A GLASS OF WHITE WINE?

(15) NO THANK YOU.

(16) ENOUGH CEREBUS HAS TO HH CHEATED

(17) CLEAN OUT THE WOODSTOVE RIGHT! THAT'LL CLEAN IT OUT THE WOODSTOVE

(18) TWO YOU JUST HAVE A NICE CHAT YOU WON'T EVEN KNOW CEREBUS IS HERE

Above: *Page from Dave Sim's sketchbook. Courtesy of Dave Sim.* Cerebus ™ & © 2004 Dave Sim.

ing them. Right now it's looking more like I will be the custodian of *Cerebus*. It seems the right thing to do.

Can you tell us about your writing technique?

I think it's probably pretty commonplace for writers who also draw their material to work on the board as much as possible. I don't think I had a formal notebook until probably the mid #20s of *Cerebus*. And then I had a notebook — which I called the albatross — which I carried with me everywhere. That was where I wrote dialogue, outlines, page 1, page 2, page 3, page 4, and tried to fill in next to them what happens on those pages. I'd write exchanges if I had a particularly funny exchange that I wanted to get very tight and little head sketches and little rough layouts of what I wanted the page to look like. But invariably, once I was sitting at the drawing board with the blank page ruled up and roughing in dialogue, sketching in where Cerebus was going to go — and about how big he was going to be and where his arm went and what was in the background — seeing it on the page, there's another personality halfway between the writer and the artist that takes over.

Left to his own devices, the writer would overwrite, just because he's the writer. He's in love with his own work. Once the artist is trying to establish what he's going to draw and how big he wants it to be, suddenly that dialogue balloon that was five sentences long becomes two sentences because the artist wants this head to be bigger. So there's that jockeying back and forth going on. The writer

Cerebus

The sword-wielding aardvark named Cerebus may have made his mark in comics with an extraordinary and unprecedented 300-issue run courtesy of the small press' loudest voice, Dave Sim, but it is Sim's outspokenness and often-controversial stances that have really pushed this black-and-white independent book to the forefront. Religion; politics; feminism: no topic was too large or too sacred for Sim to take on, and not just through his characters. With a number of essays in the back of his issues, Sim would often speak his mind... sometimes with huge consequences. With his 'Tangents' essay, however, Sim put out his final word on feminism. Besides sparking a flurry of feminist outrage (and a loss of readership), Sim's administrative assistant Carol West actually resigned after typing in a draft of the first two parts of the essay. But to his credit, Sim continued his outspoken ways and in 2004 finally completed his 300th and final issue of *Cerebus*, in which the little guy finally departed the mortal plane. Over the course of six thousand pages, the Earth-Pig certainly led an adventurous life, taking on numerous roles from pillager to Prime Minister to Pope. Now maybe he'll finally get some rest. Sim certainly will.

is trying to demonstrate how good he is with words and the artist sort of takes the writing and tries to use it just as pure communication. What's the least number of words to get this idea across?

Then there's the letterer as well. The part of you that is going to letter the pages has to decide, okay, where is the emphasis in the sentence, and how large should the lettering be? Is the guy shouting? Is he being very emphatic? Does his lettering look different from anybody else's lettering? And most of that is just picturing as vividly as you can in your mind, what is it that I'm trying to get across here? How should he look? What should he be saying? How should he be saying it? You're balancing all of those elements all at the same time and the actual writing is usually not as complicated as the writer is trying to make it at first. I have to work to get five perfect sentences here, and when you get them done and satisfactory to the writer in terms of communicating the idea, three of those sentences could be very well composed but they're not necessary. Anything you can cut, you cut.

You have to fill the role as editor too, right?

Yeah, except because it's a built-in editor, you don't have to be cutting it back mentally at the initial stage. You can overwrite on the page in light pencil and as soon as you look at it you can say either, 'That's exactly what I need,' or, 'It's overwritten.' Sometimes I would write it out on the page. I'd write five sentences and then go, 'This will be funnier if it's eight sentences.' That's the other thing, bringing in the comedian. Is this funny enough? Five sentences may be funny, but if the guy's really nervous, three extra sentences, even though they're redundant, are going to emphasize the humour. In which case, the writer wins the argument. The artist just has to make the head smaller. Funny supersedes the writer's interests and the artist's interests. Then there are other times where I would write three lines of dialogue that were funny. I'd work very hard to get the phrasing right, to get the maximum funniness in how it was said. And then when I roughed in the face, I'd get a perfect facial expression that the words were just going to distract from, so I'd erase the words and make the head bigger.

Everybody wins their argument because we're all on the same page. This isn't a writer's book or an artist's book or a letterer's book or an editor's book. Whoever's got the best idea, we're all just sitting here looking at the same page. If that panel isn't working, what's the problem? If the answer to what's the problem is, well it's not funny enough, then you bring in the comedian and go, 'Okay, well what's funny? What would make that funnier?' And you've got the comedian writer and the comedian artist. The comedian writer is going, 'Well, you can have him saying this, but that's not going to get you from here to here.' Then the comedian artist can go, 'Well, what if he was just looking like this?' And then you just get a mental image in your mind and if you laugh then you go, 'Yeah that'll be funny. Put it down in light pencil.' If you put it down in light pencil and you laugh even more and go, 'Wait a minute, what if the teeth are really showing, or what if one eye is closed and he's looking over his shoulder...' Just anything that'll make it funnier or anything that'll make it more dramatic if it's a dramatic part. That's all being negotiated in the light pencil stage.

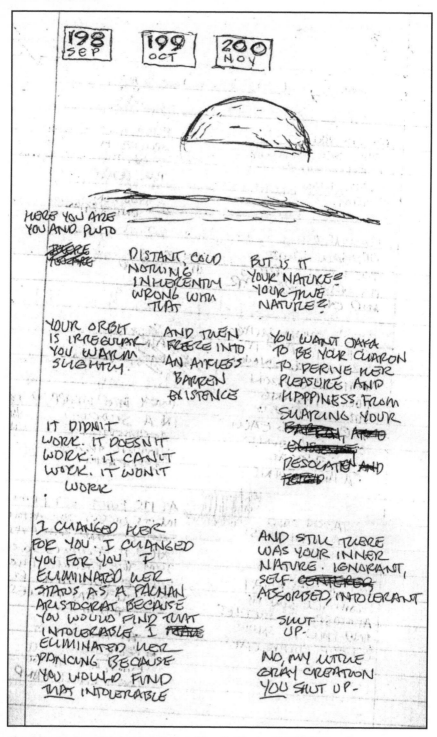

198 SEP 199 OCT 200 NOV

HERE YOU ARE
YOU AND PLUTO

THERE YOU ARE

DISTANT, COLD
NOTHING
INHERENTLY
WRONG WITH
THAT

BUT IS IT
YOUR NATURE?
YOUR TRUE
NATURE?

YOUR ORBIT
IS IRREGULAR
YOU WARM
SLIGHTLY.

AND THEN
FREEZE INTO
AN AIRLESS
BARREN
EXISTENCE

YOU WANT OAFA
TO BE YOUR CHARON
TO DERIVE HER
PLEASURE AND
HAPPINESS FROM
SHARING YOUR
BARREN, ATRO
EXISTENCE
DESOLATE AND
FRIGID

IT DIDN'T
WORK. IT DOESN'T
WORK. IT CAN'T
WORK. IT WON'T
WORK

I CHANGED HER
FOR YOU. I CHANGED
YOU FOR YOU. I
ELIMINATED HER
STATUS AS A PALNAN
ARISTOCRAT BECAUSE
YOU WOULD FIND THAT
INTOLERABLE. I FELVE
ELIMINATED HER
DANCING BECAUSE
YOU WOULD FIND
THAT INTOLERABLE

AND STILL THERE
WAS YOUR INNER
NATURE. IGNORANT,
SELF-CENTERED,
ABSORBED, INTOLERANT

SHUT
UP.

NO, MY LITTLE
GRAY CREATION
YOU SHUT UP-

That's why I've always pushed for the guys who are looking to do the whole package — the ones who want to be self-publishers — to do all of their thinking in light pencil. Don't start doing this super tight drawing of the face and then sit down and start writing the dialogue because you might find out you've got the perfect line of dialogue but that head's too big and you don't want to erase it because it's a gorgeous head. Work it all out before it's gorgeous. Always just use light enough pencil drawings and quick enough pencil drawings and quick enough lettering that you're happy enough just to erase it and replace it with something else.

It sounds like you have a very fast and loose style.

I'd say it's more flexible. You're trying to keep as much flexibility in deciding what the page is going to look like, how big everything is going to be, how many words are going to be on there, what the words are going to say. You want to keep that as flexible for as long as possible until you say, 'Yeah, this is the best that I can do this.' But make sure that a good chunk of the day is taken up with just designing the whole thing and keeping it as flexible as possible and keeping your options open. It is very, very different from the collaborative way of working.

So you never actually scripted out an entire issue in your notebook and then went to the boards?

That would just be an accident of getting on a roll. I would sit down to write the four pages so that I would have enough to draw and suddenly go, 'Oh, oh wait! And then he does this!'

With such a flexible approach, how do you know exactly how to pace the story so you don't run out of room too soon?

That's just experience. That's definitely one of the things where the bimonthly schedule and later the monthly schedule helped. Most of the best creativity you're going to get under the gun: I *have* to fill these pages. I have no idea what I'm going to do on these first four pages. Side-splittingly funny would be great. So just ask yourself, 'Anybody in here got a side-splittingly funny idea for the first four pages?' And the mere fact that you have to do it, there's just no ifs, ands or buts about it. You get some of your best work that way, just by putting yourself in the nutcracker. It's a matter of staying loose and staying funny and staying alert for what you can do to make this interesting. If you put yourself under the gun, you learn to be funny spontaneously. You learn how to pace the story just by instinct.

How about deadlines? What exactly did you do to keep on schedule?

It was a matter of priorities. If writing and drawing your comic book is priority number one in your life, you're not going to have a very conventional life. I can pretty much guarantee you that. On the other hand, the people who say, 'I can only do two comic books a year,' or, 'I started on a bimonthly schedule and I got two of them out but then...' it's a matter of what do you fill that '...' with? Look at what it is that distracted you and if that's going to distract you again, then you're probably not suited to doing this for a living; you probably should just have it as a hobby.

What about writer's block? Ever find yourself facing that uncomfortable beast?

That was never a problem for me. Writer's block wasn't the problem; holding back writer's flood was the issue. My problem was all of the different ideas that I had about politics and religion for 'High Society' and 'Church & State'. Once I started sitting down and writing them, all of these branches and tributaries would come off of it. I always had to restrict myself by saying, 'No, pick one of those ideas that will emphasize the point and that you can make entertaining and do in three or four pages, and then we have to move on to something else.' It's frustrating in a lot of ways because you're always restraining yourself. You're always reining yourself back in. That's difficult when one of the points of what you're doing is an expression of freedom. It's free but only because it's you that's restraining yourself instead of an editor.

How much of your personal life comes through in your writing? How much of Dave Sim is in that little aardvark?

In the story, quite a bit. I've always been a thinker. Extrapolating. Theorising. Speculating. It's always been a big part of who I was. And I've always been intrigued by opposing viewpoints. I was always as interested in the Republican viewpoint as I was in the Democratic viewpoint on issues. I would have my own opinions but very seldom a straight party line sort of situation. So it was reasonably easy for me to come up with — and I'll flatter myself — and develop pretty fully a post-industrial matriarchal society. Even though I thought that was a) a terribly bad idea and b) functionally impossible. It was a matter of, well, given that it's functionally impossible, how few corners do you have to cut? And how many points do you have to fudge in order to create a plausible or as close to plausible matriarchal society?

It was only much later on when I read the Bible and the Koran that my own viewpoints started locking in in a far more vivid and clarified way. Everything before that was just: isn't it interesting how all these different viewpoints contend? As soon as I developed the matriarchy — a society based on motherhood — the opposing political force would be daughters. So then I went barrelling off in the direction of developing a whole political philosophy for daughters, which ended up being pretty close to modern day feminism. What interested me was doing contending political viewpoints accurately, doing the dualities accurately, rather than saying, 'Well what is it that I believe?' What I believed didn't really enter into it. What I had to do was come up with enough interesting ideas that I could make entertaining and funny and engaging enough to maintain a readership for twenty-six years.

What tips would you give to today's aspiring writers trying to break into the industry?

It depends on what they're talking about by breaking into comics. The mainstream

⑫

⑬ IT JUST WASN'T
ENOUGH THAT
YOU LIKED IT.

⑭ I DIDN'T.
I DIDN'T
FUCKING
LIKE IT.

⑬ IT'S NEVER FUCKING
WATTAYACALL
ENOUGH THAT
YOU LIKE IT.

⑮ IZZAT
WATTAYACALL
OKAY
WITH YOU

⑯

⑰ SEE? IT
ISN'T IT'S
NEVER
FUCKING
WATTAYACALL
OKAY WITH
YOU.

⑱ IT'S LIKE ·· IT'S
LIKE YOU'RE
PART CLICK
OR SOMETHIN'

⑲ EVERYTHING'S
FINE AN' THEN
SOMEBODY
FUCKING
SAYS SOMETHING
OR SOMEBODY
FUCKING
DOES SOMETHING

⑳ AN' YOU'RE HURT
AN' YOU'RE MAD
AN' YOU'RE UNHAPPY
AN' YER OFFENDED

㉑ ALL AT THI'
SAME
FUCKING
TIME

㉒

⑫ DON'T YOU
EVER
GET WATTAYACALL
TIRED OF
THAT

DOESN'T THAT
WATTAYACALL
FUCKING TIRESOME

㉒ "MICK! MICK!
READ THIS --
READ THIS -- "

㉕ " NO FUCKING
MEMO! NO FUCKING
"HOWZIT GOING"

㉖ I'M CEREBUS THE
KING SHIT. FUCKING
READ THIS - FUCKING
NOW.

Above: *Page from Dave Sim's sketchbook. Courtesy of Dave Sim. Cerebus ™ & © 2004 Dave Sim.*

is a very different thing from my end of comics. In this end of comics, what you have to do is actually just produce comics. Again, start with a modest beginning. Try doing a ten-page story and see how long it takes you to do. And if you just write — you don't know how to draw — then you're going to have to find an artist to collaborate with. And that's going to become complicated at that point. But in either event, you have to figure out whether or not you have the aptitude to do it. The first thing you're going to find out is, is this even a remote possibility as a way to make a living, or is this always just going to be a hobby? If you sit down to do a twenty-page comic book story and it takes you a year and a half to do, the odds are it's always just going to be a hobby unless you can find a way to do it faster. Much, much, much faster. If you sit down and you can do a page a day or a page every three days, then that'll tell you something as well. At that point you have to again figure out if you have the aptitude.

Then it's a matter of whether the comics you're interested in doing and that you're capable of doing are interesting to enough people. Which is why you should just go and get them quick printed at Kinkos at first and pass them around; show them at comic book stores. See if the guy at your local comic store will let you put them out on the counter. If they just sit there gathering dust, well, that tells you something right there. You're capable of writing and drawing a comic, but nobody's interested in buying it. Or nobody's interested in buying that one; maybe you should try a different comic book. I would definitely recommend avoiding what everyone else is doing, which is something that a lot of guys have trouble getting their minds around. Don't just do another Image comic. We've

The Small Press

Sure, DC and Marvel make up the bulk of the comics industry, with their characters' shiny capes, big muscles and insane superpowers. But the real heart of the industry lies in the small press. Black-and-white interiors, idiosyncratic artwork and rarely a superhero to be seen. What the world of small press comics lacks in gloss and glamour, it more than makes up for with blood, sweat and tears. For decades, creators have been telling truly personal tales for the sheer art of it. *Cerebus* may be the best known of the bunch, but plenty of other creators have joined the good fight. The Hernandez Brothers' *Love & Rockets* series was full of character-driven stories primarily based on the lives of Maggie and Hopey in a fictional barrio of Los Angeles. Jeff Smith's *Bone* — the tale of three cousins lost in a mysterious valley full of talking bugs, fire-breathing dragons and the Lord of the Locusts — had a more mainstream bent, mostly due to its Disney-like art style and fantasy grounding. Set in the modern world, Terry Moore's *Strangers in Paradise* centres on a love triangle between two women and a man, shrouded in espionage. Those are but a few of the more notable small press titles over the years. But whatever your taste, the small press is sure to have something for you.

got Image doing Image comics. Don't just do another superhero or another paranormal team of mutants. On the Fantagraphics side, here's my dull, boring life with all of my irritating friends. If you've got something to add to that, that's fine. But we've got a lot of those. We don't have as many of those as we've got of superheroes, but I think we really do have enough of those at this point. Unless you've really got something to say. A lot of times that happens later on.

The really early stuff that I did as an amateur, there wasn't any content to it. I was just seeing if I could do it. Can I do a five-page superhero strip? Can I do a five-page detective strip? You don't really get to the point of thinking, do I have anything to say to anybody? At first it's just, can I do this? That's the first thing you have to figure out. Am I capable of doing this? Do I like doing this? I can't think of anything worse than using all of your extra hours that you're not at your day job writing and drawing comics if it turns out you hate doing it. Do something else in your spare time. To me, those are the most obvious questions that you have to answer for yourself.

But another big part of it is just fun. If you're genuinely having a really, really good time, that will communicate to the audience. And I think a lot of times it becomes apparent when people are reading your material that this is not fun. If it was fun, it would be selling better. Or interesting. It doesn't have to be all clowns and hats and horns. If you're genuinely interested in what you're doing, I think that communicates more than anything else. And a lot of times something that's very difficult for an amateur writer to know is, how interested am I in this? How interested am I in the material? Or do I just want to be a famous guy going to comic book conventions? If you're wrong about your own motives, then you're probably going to be wrong about your book. If you just want it so you can be famous the way Todd McFarlane was the time you saw him at a comic book convention and that's why you're doing the comic book, that's going to communicate to the audience and that's gonna turn them off.

You've seen comics grow, shrink, explode, implode, expand, you name it. What's your take on the industry today?

Yeah, as [Flaming Carrot creator] Bob Burden once said, 'I've been around the block so many times I feel like my turn blinker got stuck.' It's pretty much the same it's always been. The different parts of it expand and contract. I think that the people who have been around a long time have figured out that we're maybe not as interested in the explosive growth that we had in 1992 and 1993 as we thought we were. You get a lot of ugly stuff coming in once everybody starts smelling millions of dollars. I think that's rather happily gone by the wayside. So I think the superhero end of things will always, at least for the foreseeable future, be the largest part of comic books. It's what comic books are in North America, anyway. You just take that as a given.

*　　　　　*　　　　　*

KEVIN SMITH

Kevin Smith's career was intertwined with comic books long before he ever started writing them. After a semester's worth of film school, Smith dropped out and sold his comics collection to help finance his first film, *Clerks,* in 1994. His second movie, *Mallrats,* was filled with comic book references, and even featured Stan Lee offering sage advice to the main character. Next up was *Chasing Amy,* a film about — among other things — comics creators. After Smith began penning comics that expanded upon his movie universe (for Oni Press), it seemed like only a matter of time before he tackled established superheroes. His chance came when Joe Quesada, co-editor of Marvel's newly created Marvel Knights imprint, invited him to take a crack at *Daredevil.* Smith's interpretation of the Man Without Fear earned him critical praise, big sales, and a Harvey Award. He was later tasked with resurrecting the original Green Arrow, Oliver Queen, for DC, with similar success. Though his comics output of late has slowed to a virtual halt, Smith and superheroes will never be strangers: the one-time screenwriter for the proposed *Superman Lives* movie is now hard at work on a big-screen version of the Green Hornet.

Did you think about writing comics prior to your film career?

Writing comics was probably the first thing I thought of, prior to actually writing films. I grew up reading comics, but then fell out of it when I was in high school. Later, my friend Walter Flanagan re-introduced me to comics, and they'd kind of grown up in my absence, become a hell of a lot more readable and enjoyable. So I figured, 'Hey, this is something I would like to do.' But the comics industry seemed like a very close-knit community, one that was rather tough to break into, so I didn't pursue it. I felt like, 'Well, the chances of me getting a comics writing gig are probably *nil* and *none,* because I've got no previous writing experience.' So I abandoned that idea, and a couple years later I got into film. Because the movie career worked out, it opened the door for me to write comics.

While we were making *Chasing Amy,* I approached Bob Schreck, who was working at Dark Horse at the time, and gave him this pitch for a *Bluntman and Chronic* comic book that could tie into the movie. He dug it and took the idea to [publisher] Mike Richardson, who subsequently passed on it. So that went away, and the movie came out and was kind of successful, but there was no comic book tie-in. Between *Chasing Amy* and *Dogma*, Schreck decided to break off from Dark Horse and start his own company, called Oni Press. He remembered that I had wanted to write comics, and asked if it was something I still wanted to pursue. I said, 'Yeah, I'd be into it.' Meanwhile, over at Marvel, Joe Quesada had been given editorial control over a bunch of books, under an imprint called Marvel Knights. I knew Joe, he had done some opening-credit stuff for us on *Mallrats*; comic book covers that reflected the cast and characters in the movie. Joe said, 'Hey, they gave me *Daredevil* and I remember you're a big Daredevil fan. Do you want to write it?' And again I was like, 'Yeah, man, that sounds like a totally cool idea. I'd be up for that.' Around the same time, I was working on a Superman screenplay for Warner Bros., so I got to go up to the DC offices. While I was there, I met an editor named Darren Vincenzo who was overseeing *Green Arrow*. I said to him, 'Hey man, if you ever lose the writer who's on the book now,' — who I believe was Chuck Dixon — 'I'd be happy to write it, because I feel like we could probably put it in the top twenty, if not the top ten.' And he just gave me a bizarre, 'What are you talking about?' kind of look, because they were still largely *closed ranks* over there.

After I'd written the 'Jay and Silent Bob in Walt Flanagan's Dog' story in *Oni Double Feature*, and that got published and did kind of well, DC came back to me. Darren Vincenzo called me up and said, 'Hey, Chuck's moving off *Green Arrow*. Do you want to do it?' I was like, 'Yeah,' but at the same time Joe was hounding me about starting *Daredevil*. After much balking, I finally jumped into *Daredevil*, while concurrently writing some *Clerks* stuff for Oni. A couple years later, I finally got back to *Green Arrow* when Bob Schreck left Oni and took a DC editorial gig. And that's pretty much my comics tale. Later on I would go back to Marvel and start — and never

Place of birth:
   Red Bank, New Jersey, USA
Date of birth:
   2 August 1970
Home base:
   Red Bank, New Jersey, USA
First Published Work:
   Oni Double Feature #1
Education:
   Vancouver Film School
Career Highlights:
   Daredevil, Green Arrow,
   Bluntman and Chronic, Clerks,
   Spider-Man/Black Cat

finish — two series. One, *Daredevil: The Target,* was a four-issue mini-series, but of those only one was published and the script for issue #2 has just been sitting there. The other, *Spider-Man/Black Cat: The Evil That Men Do,* has also just sat there, unfinished, for the last two years at this point. I got to issue #3 and then got involved in *Jersey Girl* and never got back to finish it. Hopefully I'll be doing that soon.

Having previously written only movie scripts, what was it like writing your first comic book script?

It was a little more involved than writing a film script because when I write screenplays I don't tend to be as descriptive. They're basically dialogue-heavy, and the lack of description I chalk up to the fact that I'm going to be directing it. I *see* it as I'm writing it, so I don't really feel the need to write down everything. But with a comic book script, given that an artist is going to have to visualise it — and I can't draw for shit — I tend to be a lot more descriptive, detailing what's in each panel — what it looks like, what's happening — in addition to all the dialogue. I'd say I probably put more work into the comic book script than I do into the theatrical film script.

Being a dialogue-heavy screenwriter, was it difficult to move into the comics medium, which demands an economy of dialogue through the sheer lack of panel space?

Well, when I was writing the 'Walt Flanagan's Dog' script, nobody reined me in,

The Films

Throughout Kevin Smith's bold, bawdy oeuvre, he's managed to explore themes both complex (love, relationships, religion, bisexuality) and not so complex (ramifications of the giant poop monster on society). His first five films fall into what's called the 'View Askewniverse', a rough continuity linked together by recurring fan favourite characters Jay and Silent Bob. First up was Smith's $27,000 debut *Clerks* in 1994, which the filmmaker funded with credit cards and the sale of his comic book collection. It won awards at both the Sundance and Cannes film festivals, and suddenly Smith was on the map. The follow-up, 1995's (relatively) big-budget *Mallrats,* failed to live up to *Clerks* in the minds of critics and most fans. For 1997's *Chasing Amy,* Smith got back to his low-budget roots and crafted a tangled love story that topped even the acclaim of his debut. *Dogma,* two years later, generated an enormous amount of controversy with its frank and funny take on Christianity, and finally Smith ended his Askewniverse explorations with *Jay & Silent Bob Strike Back* in 2001. Minus Jay and Bob, Smith's *Jersey Girl* underperformed in 2004 thanks to negative buzz surrounding the real-life Ben Affleck-Jennifer Lopez romance. Next up: *The Green Hornet* and *Fletch Won.*

because they wanted me to do what I wanted to do. If there was too much dialogue, nobody said anything, and it was never really a problem. Later on, when I was working on *Daredevil*, Joe would sometimes break up my dialogue a little more over the panels as he drew, just so it laid out better. But I've never really been tagged for, 'Oh, you've gotta rein in some of that dialogue,' because, chiefly, dialogue is what I do.

What were some of the comic books that got you interested again after high school?

I had written this essay on Batman when I was a senior in high school, largely based on the *Batman* TV show and the Frederic Wertham book, *Seduction of the Innocent*. About a year later, when I first started hanging out with Walt Flanagan, I knew he was into comics so I gave him that paper to read. And he was just like, 'Oh, dude, this ain't Batman. You don't know from Batman anymore. I gotta get you something to read.' That 'something' turned out to be *Dark Knight Returns,* which I absolutely loved, and I was like, 'What's next?' Walt was like, 'You gotta get *Watchmen*,' so I picked up an issue of *Watchmen* and started reading it. After that, I got back into collecting seriously. The first week I started buying comic books, *Batman: The Cult,* the prestige-format mini-series by Jim Starlin and Bernie Wrightson, came out, which I loved. I then went back and got all the *Watchmen* issues I had missed, and things like Matt Wagner's *Mage,* John Ostrander's *GrimJack,* the Alan Moore *Swamp Thing* — and the Rick Veitch run that followed — and the Frank Miller *Daredevil* run. Those were the key books.

How extensive was your collection before you sold it to finance *Clerks*?

I did a price guide value of the whole collection, and it was $10,000 and change. It was pretty big. It was all mostly Modern Age stuff. I didn't go back and buy any Golden or Silver Age or anything like that. I only went back as far as 1985.

Since you were such a fan of Frank Miller's *Dark Knight Returns* and *Daredevil*, was it intimidating to write *Daredevil* yourself?

Very intimidating. In fact, I almost bowed out on the whole project based on exactly that intimidation factor: I was like, 'What on Earth am I going to do with this character that hasn't been done before, particularly in the hands of Frank Miller?' I remember calling up Joe to pass after stringing him and [Marvel Knights co-editor] Jimmy Palmiotti along for a while. I finally called him one night, pre-*Dogma*, before we went off to Pittsburgh to shoot the movie, and said, 'I'm not gonna be able to do this. I don't have it in me. I'm just not good enough, blah, blah, blah.' Joe was really disappointed, and a few minutes later I got a call from Jimmy, who pretty much bitched me out for not having enough balls… so they kind of played good cop/bad cop. I took my medicine, thought about it, and then called Joe back and said, 'Wait a minute, maybe there is something we can do here.' That night I started writing the first issue.

How did you begin to build that first *Daredevil* story?

It actually came from that exact moment I was hanging up the phone on Jimmy after he'd bitched me out. Somebody in the house was watching TV, I think it was a [Roger] Corman movie called *God Told Me To*, and something in that — about somebody giving this dude a kid and maintaining it was the Messiah — sparked the idea for the 'Guardian Devil' storyline. So it kind of stemmed from there, but only the seed of the idea, since 'Guardian Devil' doesn't really resemble that movie at all. Later on, as I was writing it, I basically said, 'If you can't beat 'em, join 'em,' and just wrote a story about how you can't really write any new stories; about how it had all been done before. So the storyline winds up being about Mysterio, and how he gets a very hackneyed idea to drive Daredevil insane because he can't beat Spider-Man. Mysterio had maybe had one fight with Daredevil early on — I think in an Ann Nocenti issue — and he'd come back to take on this B or C-list hero as some kind of swan song, because he was dying. Everything he does has been done before, like when he tries to follow the Kingpin's path — like in Frank Miller's 'Born Again' — and just sets about dismantling Matt Murdock's life.

Once you had the idea, how did you begin to script it?

Basically I just wrote from issue to issue. I never really had an outline and I didn't map the whole thing out. I just knew where it was beginning and knew where it was going to end. And then I just wrote until I filled up an issue. When I had twenty-two pages, I built myself a little cliffhanger for the end of the issue and then moved on to the next script.

What kind of editorial input did you get from Joe?

Like I said, I would write these massive word balloons, and Joe would be like, 'I can't put all these words in one panel and fit the art in too, so if you don't mind, I'm gonna move them around a little bit.' And every once in a while Joe would have a really good suggestion, story-wise, and we'd use that. Our biggest sticking point was the death of Karen Page, and how exactly she was going to die. We all came up with a collective solution — me, Joe and Jimmy. I had her being a shade more mercenary, I think, and they softened her up a little bit for the death sequence. I had her actually giving Bullseye the *real* baby, and then we changed it to her giving Bullseye the doll from the manger in the church, and that's why she got killed. But generally they let me go and do what I wanted. The beauty of that project was that Joe Quesada really directed that script. If you read the script, the dialogue's all there, but he turned it into something beautiful and operatic. He really made it *noir*-ish and really cinematic. He truly is the co-author of that book, moreso than any artist I've worked with, before or since. That run on the book is as much his as it is mine. Some dudes execute what you write, and some dudes elevate it. He really elevated it.

Do you have the artwork in mind when you're writing?

A little bit. But — weirdly — I'm just not that visually oriented, so I tend to only have a vague picture in my head about what the scene or page is going to look like. Thankfully, every time out, the artist has surprised me and brought something to the table where I'm like, 'Ooh, I didn't see that coming. That looks great.'

After *Daredevil,* how did the *Green Arrow* run take shape?

When Bob Schreck moved over to DC, he called me up and just said, 'Do you still want to do *Green Arrow*?' I said, 'Yeah,' and he replied, 'Well then, based on your history of lateness in comics...' So I had already acquired this reputation of being behind on my schedules. As you know, this industry prides itself on sticking to the schedule... in a really hyper-anal-retentive way. If that particular book's not out the day it's supposed to ship, boy, the fanbase bitches and moans. So Bob said, 'To make sure that we're not late, I'm not going to solicit until I get the first six scripts for the first six issues,' which was a smart plan. It kind of worked out, even though we wound up being late on that book later on, in the second half of the run. Anyway, I wrote an outline for *Green Arrow* and sent it to Bob, and he was like, 'This sounds good,' and then I went ahead and wrote those first six issues. We were off and running...

Did you have an idea ready to go when Bob called?

Pretty much. Basically I knew I just had to bring Ollie Queen back from the dead. His character had been killed off, and I had to bring him back in a somewhat plausible way, albeit in a very fantastic universe. I knew that was my main story point, and I knew where I was going with it. After that, it was just connecting the dots to make it all happen. That run is very early Alan Moore DC-influenced. I wanted to write a Green Arrow version of the *Swamp Thing* run that Alan Moore had done in the '80s. So you see a lot of his stuff in there. I can't do it justice, of course, because he's brilliant and I'm not, but a lot of his influence is in that run.

Marvel Knights

In 1998, Daredevil, the Man Without Fear, was the Man Without Sales. The character who had proved so riveting to readers of Frank Miller's 1980s run was no longer a draw, a B-lister with no heat and no excitement. That all changed when superstar penciller Joe Quesada and equally superstar inker Jimmy Palmiotti were named as editors of a new Marvel offshoot called Marvel Knights, a grim-and-gritty corner of the superhero world where stories could get as dark as they needed. Joining the Marvel Knights family were *Daredevil* and three other titles desperately in need of a little adrenaline shot: *The Punisher, Inhumans* and *Black Panther.* Quesada and Palmiotti took over art duties on *Daredevil,* and added to the buzz the title's new writer: filmmaker Kevin Smith. Sales soared, and suddenly Ol' Hornhead was cool again. The success of *Daredevil* and Marvel Knights had a lasting impact, not only for the character — which surely wouldn't have landed on movie screens in 2003 without its Marvel Knights rebirth — but for the creators involved as well. Smith later went on to write *Green Arrow,* while Quesada's proven mettle on Marvel Knights later landed him the desk of Marvel editor-in-chief.

Your first *Green Arrow* story arc involved the biggest characters in the DC Universe. How did you decide on your approach to writing Superman or Batman?

Thankfully, many great people had done those characters prior to me, and so the groundwork was already laid. Oliver Queen was, of course, the Oliver Queen from the Denny O'Neil run, circa the 'Hard-Travelling Heroes' era, and Batman was the one from the Grant Morrison *JLA* run. Superman… I don't know if I took him from any particular run, while Aquaman was just influenced by who he was in the DC Universe at that point. That's when he still had the hook on his hand and had stopped wearing the cool orange outfit. You're kind of strapped a little bit by how the characters are presented elsewhere in the Universe at any particular time. You can't present a Batman that's jokey and giggly and shit like that, because that's just not the Batman that's currently being written. The 'my little chum' Batman is not the Batman that exists in most of the books today. The freedom is in what you can put in their mouths, what you have them saying, but tonally you have to hone pretty closely to what's already there, what people are doing with the character at that moment.

What was your favourite Green Arrow story as a reader?

I guess it was probably *The Longbow Hunters*, that prestige-format mini-series by Mike Grell. I liked that quite a bit. Oddly, though, I don't really use much of the *Longbow Hunters* storyline in 'Quiver' at all.

What's the appeal of superheroes for you?

I get off on the idea of a person who's willing to put on a mask and go out and do the right thing. It appeals to the youth in me, I guess, and on a storytelling level it's always such a compelling notion: the idea of the vigilante, a person willing to take the law into their own hands. I also like the notion of people with infinite power, who could enslave a nation but instead choose to selflessly help it. The 'noble causes' storylines are definitely the stuff I get off on. That said, in films I don't really tell that story. Ever. I generally write about wise-asses who talk a lot and don't really do anything heroic. I guess my comic book writing is very much influenced by all the comic books I'd read from 1989 onwards, and my movie work is just… different.

It's weird; when I read some of the *Green Arrow* stuff I've written, or the *Daredevil* story, it just doesn't seem like it comes from the same guy that writes the movies. But maybe that's part of the appeal, because it's not something I necessarily identify myself with as a writer. It's more experimental. I fully grasp that I'm no great shakes as a comic book storyteller and I acknowledge that the reason we've had great sales on the books I've been involved with largely has to do with the fact that I have this day job which is more high-profile. But then I certainly never got into comics to win awards or anything like that, I just did it because I love reading comic books, and here I was being afforded the opportunity to write them as well. It's like being a kid in the toy store with that two-minute clock that allows you to pick out as many toys as you want. Or even the tired analogy of a kid in somebody else's sandbox.

When I read [Brian Michael] Bendis' stuff, I think, 'Now there's a guy who's a born comic book writer.' And it's not like he can just write comic books. I think he can pretty much write anything he wants. But he really gets the comics genre, and has clearly been immersed in it. It's his lifeblood. Me, I'm just more of a tourist who jumps in and gets to do what he wants, and does it for no other reason than that it's fun to do. It's a wish fulfillment from a younger age.

Are there any comic book titles or characters you'd still like to write?

You know, there aren't. Comics, at one point, kind of jumped the track for me and stopped being fun. They started being a job. I got so late on things, it became, 'Oh, there's this thing lurking out there that I've yet to finish,' and it lost the joy. I never did it for the money, so it never felt like a job at first, but now it's just become one more thing I have to finish that I owe somebody. It's kind of lost its lustre. And the more I read other writers, whose stuff I really dig, I'm like, 'You know, I did my time, I should just bow out gracefully.' I got really lucky with my two major-label runs on *Daredevil* and *Green Arrow*, inasmuch as they were really well-received and did great in sales terms, but I don't think that means I could or should stick around and keep doing it. Open it up, I say, let another guy have a shot, because otherwise it's that closed-ranks thing again.

Do you envision a time when you're no longer writing comics, period?

Yeah, definitely. As soon as I can finish off this *Daredevil: The Target* run and the

Green Arrow

The Battling Bowman has seen his share of changes since his debut in 1941. Green Arrow first featured in *More Fun Comics* #73 with sidekick Speedy already intact. Apart from the trick arrows and Robin Hood costume, the archer's entire shtick was lifted almost entirely from that of Batman; what with the secret identity as millionaire playboy Oliver Queen, the youthful ward who doubled as crimefighting sidekick, the arrow-shaped signal light above the city, the Arrowcar, the Arrowplane, etc., there was little original about the character (a fact Kevin Smith alluded to in a gleeful bit of dialogue between Batman and Green Arrow during his run on the book). However, having left the Golden Age behind, he was reworked by Denny O'Neil and Neal Adams in the late 1960s and early 1970s. A rabble-rousing liberal with a social agenda, Green Arrow was finally *about* something — Speedy even got hooked on smack! — and the 'Hard Travelling Heroes' era in which GA appeared in the pages of *Green Lantern* remains the definitive portrayal of the bowman. Ollie Queen bit the dust in 1995 and was replaced by his son, Connor Hawke, but Smith subsequently resurrected Queen as his first order of business when he took over as writer.

Spider-Man/Black Cat series, I think I should just be a comics reader for a while.

Will you ever come back to it?

Maybe. There's always the lure of working with Joe, because it was such a great partnership. But there are no characters that are screaming out for me to take on. I guess there are those where I'm like, 'Boy, I'd really like to give that a shot someday.' I've always been a huge Batman fan, but I think I wrote *my* Batman in *Green Arrow.* I've been offered *Detective Comics* and *Batman,* or the chance to create my own Batman book. I was going to do *The Brave and the Bold* as well at one point. But ultimately I just don't know what more I could do with the character that hasn't been done already. At a certain point, you're just spinning your wheels. The tone's been established and you can't really go away from that tone.

Very rarely does a character truly get re-invented. I love *Ultimate Spider-Man,* I think it's great, a really fantastic read. But at the end of the day, Bendis just writes Spider-Man the way Spider-Man's always been written, only the character has way better dialogue than he's ever had before. Ever since Frank Miller re-established the tone of Batman — or maybe *established* the tone of Batman — from *Dark Knight Returns* onwards, *that's* been Batman. People add new edges to it, like I really dug the way Grant Morrison would write him, as this surly supergenius, but there aren't too many more ways to skin that cat. *Daredevil,* when I was writing it, I just stuck pretty close to the tone that Miller and later Nocenti had established. And as much as I enjoy the *Daredevil* stories that Bendis is writing — and he's definitely telling different stories to Miller — it's still tonally the same book.

[DC Editor] Mike Carlin told me a long time ago that the trick to comics is understanding that there is no beginning, no end, just a middle. Essentially, they're soap operas. You've never seen the beginning of a soap opera and, unless it's cancelled, you'll never see the end. Basically, your job is to constantly tell Act II. Sure, they do alternate reality books like 'Elseworlds' and the 'Year One' stories, but ninety percent of the marketplace is Act II. And as a fan, I can say this: you really don't want creators to fuck around with the status quo too much. You don't want this or that writer to change too much of what you love or you're familiar with, because there's a reason you buy that book every month. You have an affinity for the character and the settings, and so creators had better not screw around with them too much. You do, and you risk pissing off the majority of the fanbase. But at the same time it's nice every once in a while to read something really new. I think people like Bendis have found a nice balance, which is to do *Ultimate Spider-Man,* where you're essentially telling variations on the same stories that have been told time and time again, from the first time Peter got his powers onwards. He's just telling better versions of those stories, with way better dialogue. It's not like you open up that book and suddenly Peter Parker is some kind of a vigilante spirochaete or something. If you're going to change anything, just change the writing, make it better than what's gone before. Make it more intriguing. Because these characters were set in motion thirty, forty, fifty, sixty years ago and there's a reason they've lasted that long: the recipe works.

Those unfinished mini-series don't seem to jibe with the work ethic you have in other areas of your life. Couldn't you just put them on your schedule and get them done? Or has writing comics really turned into drudgery for you?

It definitely became that way when I got beyond the pale in terms of lateness. I was preoccupied with something else, with making a film, and it got to this point of like, people bitching at you to finish it, and it's just this thing you haven't accomplished yet and your mindset is not there, your heart's not in it any more. So I'm waiting for a time where things have settled down, when I'm actually enthused to finish the story. Lately, in terms of comics, I've been very enthusiastic about reading other people's stuff, but not very enthusiastic about writing my own.

What are some of the books you're reading right now?

I love *Gotham Central*. I think that's a really great book. I didn't think it was a book I was ever gonna get into. When they first announced it, I was like, 'A book about the cops? Who gives a shit?' But it's really well written and quite engaging. *Ultimate Spider-Man* is a book I came to late, but really adore, *Powers* likewise. I'm pretty much a Bendis whore at this point. Those are the books I open up first when I get home. Morrison's *New X-Men* run I really enjoyed... I'll pretty much follow that guy anywhere. The same with Alan Moore, to a large degree, although I fell out of the America's Best Comics at a certain point. Garth Ennis' stuff I'm still a big fan of. The Punisher's not my favorite character in the world, but I'll still read that book.

How do you get along with comic book fans?

In person I've never not gotten along with a fan. I tend to do most of the *Wizard* shows and whatnot, and the fans are just insanely gracious. I'll do Q&As, — and granted they're not all comic book fans; some of them are fans of the movies — and I'll pack a room, standing room only, and not an angry fan in the bunch. But the anonymity of the Internet, of course, allows everybody to be the biggest jackass on the planet. So you get a lot of people who bitch at you about how terrible you are, shit that nobody would ever say to your face. I've yet to meet one of these people who say this shit on the Internet who would dare say it to me in person. And it's not like I'd be, 'Dude, I'll kick your ass,' but nobody's got any balls in real life. It's easy to have balls when you're hiding behind a cute made-up name. That aspect of fandom is kind of irritating.

How are the comic book fans you meet different from fans of your movies?

With a movie, somebody can tell you it sucks if they don't like it, or people can go on at great lengths about how much they do like it. But at the end of the day, it's subjective; it's mostly about how they view your flick. At the end of the day, it's your flick. It's not like you've adapted somebody else's flick. When you're writing for comics on the other hand, you can be compared to every person who's written a certain character before you or after you, and that leaves room for a lot more criticism, about whether you did it right or wrong, whether or not you screwed the pooch or elevated the book in some way. Your average newspaper or magazine movie critic can be pretty fucking harsh, but not nearly as harsh as some random comic book reader on the Internet. 'You've raped this character!' — I've seen shit like that on the Internet about stuff I've written. I took a lot of shit for killing off Karen Page, a character that nobody cared about until she was dead. Take me. I used to read *The Flash,* and then Geoff Johns — whose writing I really dig on *JSA* — took over and I just didn't dig his *Flash* stuff so much. I stopped buying *Flash,* but I didn't fucking find Geoff Johns and go, 'Listen, man. You've raped the fucking Flash.' I didn't feel that way. He was just writing a different kind of Flash. It's easy on the pocketbook to drop a title, but the people who continue to buy the book feel that they've bought a ticket to fucking hunt you down and bitch at you about how terrible you are. If it's bad, a) don't buy it anymore and b) don't talk about it. Because every knock is a boost, right? It's that old silly adage of, 'There's no such thing as bad publicity,' which after *Jersey Girl* I would strongly disagree with…

Are there any comic book writing clichés that bother you?

My pet peeve in comic book writing is when people have characters refer to other characters by their names. 'Well, *Captain America…*' 'Listen to me, *Falcon.*' There's always that initial thought, comma, character name, comma, continuation of the thought. Most of these characters have known each other forever. You don't really need to refer to their names at all. Stan Lee used to say, 'Every comic book is some kid's first.' Well, kids don't read comic books that much anymore. [*Laughs*] Largely, you're dealing with a marketplace that's very familiar with all these characters. So it never felt necessary to me to have Spider-Man refer to Daredevil as 'Daredevil'. If you've gotta do that, shorthand it. Call him 'DD', call him 'Spidey'. But going on with the proper names is just something that bugs the shit out of me in a comic book.

Is there anything you've written that you feel came up short?

Daredevil: The Target issue #1, probably. I just wasn't happy with it when it was done. It was really a project I shouldn't have started. That was just me being very territorial and kind of immature. Brian Bendis was talking about using Bullseye in a storyline, and Joe had promised me when we were working on 'Guardian Devil' that the next time that character appeared, I was gonna write him. We had to do some sort of payback for the whole death-of-Karen Page thing. I got proprietary and put my foot down and prevented Brian from using the character in his storyline. Joe said, 'If you're going to do that, you have to write the Daredevil-Bullseye story.' I said, 'All right,' and wrote one issue, and then wrote the second issue like a year, year and a half later. It was such an asshole move on my behalf. I should've just let Brian use the character. Eventually he got to use the character in another storyline he did. It's one of my big, big regrets. Not just in comic book writing, but in life in general. Such a lousy move on my behalf… and it's not even a very strong book.

What do you feel is the best comics work you've done?

I really loved the last two issues of the 'Guardian Devil' arc. One is Mysterio talking the whole time, and the issue after that is the aftermath. I really feel like I hit my stride at that point. On *Green Arrow*, I loved the Batman issue. I loved writing Ollie and Batman together. And I loved the 'Onomatopoeia' storyline that I wrote, because I liked that character and it was very pat. There was no explanation given, he was just a psycho. But I'm more partial to the *Clerks* stuff that I've written, like the first issue. Very talky, very fun, very sarcastic. Just twenty-two pages of wise-assery.

*   *   *

JILL THOMPSON

It's a rare thing to find a medium Jill Thompson hasn't yet
conquered. Best known for her creator-owned (and Eisner Award-
winning) *Scary Godmother* — a delightfully twisted take on fairy
tales, witches, vampires and a myriad of monsters — Thompson has
translated her clever all-ages tale into comics, children's books and a
computer-animated TV special. After making her mark on American
comics with *Scary Godmother* and as an artist on titles as diverse as
The Sandman, Wonder Woman and *The Invisibles*, the Chicago native
looked overseas for inspiration. Her 2003 graphic novel *Death: At
Death's Door* was a new take on Neil Gaiman's *Sandman* story arc
'Season of Mists'; Thompson rewrote and re-drew the story in the
style of *shojo manga* — a Japanese girls' comic. Remodelling a classic
tale by one of comics' modern masters in a style she'd never before
attempted could have been — and perhaps *should* have been — a
catastrophe. Instead, it was note-perfect and a bestseller. A second
volume is now in the works. Despite obstacles both cultural and
physical (as you'll read below), in the end it was just another
medium conquered for Jill Thompson.

What was your introduction to comics?

I guess I first became aware of newspaper comic strips, rather than comic books
themselves. *Peanuts* was my favourite. I was copying *Peanuts* all the time. At that
point, I remember telling my mom that when I grew up, I was going to draw
Snoopy. And she told me that the reason I get to see Snoopy is that somebody
already draws it, and maybe I should make up my own cartoon. So I promptly put
together a cartoon that was pretty much exactly like Snoopy and called it *B Dog*.
B Dog was a capital letter B with a Snoopy kind of ear on the back, a foot on the
bottom of the B, a nose and then an eye. I went on to make many, many, many
notebook paper comic strips based on the character. B Dog lived with two senior
citizens — I don't know why — and pretty much every adventure was B Dog
stealing the food of the grandpa guy. And the grandpa would end up in the very
last panel chasing B Dog and going, 'Grrrr, B Dog!' That amused me for a long
time. [*Laughs*]

What comic books followed *Peanuts*?

I guess I moved on to *Archie* comics. I remember this family two doors down from us were having a garage sale. Because they were moving across town, they were selling almost everything they had, and amongst all of their many possessions was a great big box of comics. It was like I had hit the mother lode. I was very young at this time — seven or eight — and I didn't understand that you could buy comics, at the drug store on the corner or wherever. I just assumed they were already in your house or someone brought them to you. But here were all of these comics, really old Archies from the '40s and '50s, which are still my favourite era of *Archie*. I got that lot for like a quarter or something. I took them home and was just completely amazed and entranced. At that point I knew exactly what I wanted to do when I grew up: I wanted to draw comics.

Was there ever a point in your life where you stopped reading comics?

No. That's why I can't answer the question when women ask, 'How do we get more women reading comics?' Because my experience is, I started and I never stopped. I'm not sure how to bring people back into it, because I never left.

What path did you take to become a professional artist?

Well, gosh. I've always wanted to draw comics. Throughout high school I knew that's what I was going to do. I would have these great career fantasies of walking into the Marvel offices with my portfolio and they would offer me all of my favourite comic books to draw because obviously I loved them so much and

Place of birth:
 Chicago, Illinois, USA
Date of birth:
 20 November 1966
Home base:
 Chicago, Illinois, USA
First published work:
 A four-page jam piece in a book
 called *Just Imagine Comix & Stories*,
 a black-and-white anthology
 featuring a character named
 Bananaman
Education:
 American Academy of Art,
 Chicago
Career highlights:
 Death: At Death's Door, *Scary Godmother*, *The Sandman*

I was the best. 'Here's *Spider-Man*! Here's *X-Men*... you can draw any book you want.' 'Oh, yay! And will Terry Austin ink me?' 'Of course, he's called *all day* asking if he can ink you!' 'Oh my God!' Everybody in my family was very supportive of what I wanted to do. At no time did anyone ever say, 'Why don't you want to do a real job?'

I remember one day my father brought home a number of what at the time I considered 'scary' comics, in with a box of Archies. It was like an issue of *Thor* and maybe *X-Men*, and one of the covers had a big John Buscema or Jack Kirby-ish guy who was beating the crap out of another guy. His teeth were all bared, and there was a monster, and they all got pushed into the bottom of the comic box. I didn't want to read those, all I was interested in was *Archie*. But I got through the whole box of Archies, and there was nothing else that I hadn't read. So I was left with no recourse but to read the scary comics. Of course, I was completely hooked. It was like crack. Soon after, we found a comic book store in the town next to us. In fact, it was Rick's One Stop Comics on Oak Park Avenue in Oak Park, Illinois. I don't know what Rick thought about a teenage girl walking in — because I was the only one! I don't remember ever seeing another girl in that store the whole time I shopped there! He had back issues, and from that moment on, that's where all my allowance went. I was more and more determined to draw comics.

I started going to conventions. My father would take me downtown to the convention on Sunday and sit in the car and listen to football games. At those conventions I started meeting artists like Bill Reinhold, Bill Willingham and others. They would look at my drawings and my portfolio, and Bill Reinhold recommended that I go to the American Academy of Art [in Chicago], because that's where he went. I didn't think that I needed to go to school to learn about comics, because I would just copy John Byrne or other guys that I liked, and that would be all that I needed. They said, 'That's okay, but you really should go to school.' So I did.

Did you envision being an artist who wrote her own stories?

Way back at that point in my life, I just wanted to collaborate with people. I wanted to be a penciller. I didn't have any designs on writing. But then I didn't really have any original ideas. All my ideas focused around writing stories for existing characters that I loved.

When did that finally change?

When I started working on *Scary Godmother.* I would always have a piece of an idea here or there, but nothing that I could ever follow through on. I remember a lot of people telling me, 'You should write your own stories,' but I didn't have any, I had nothin'! I would visualise characters or scenes or things I'd like to draw, but these were maybe two pages long and that would be it. The way it happened, I didn't sit down and plan to do *Scary Godmother*. Once the idea came about, it started writing itself.

And after that, you were able to start writing other stories?

Yeah, and yet they were still very difficult to do. I think the first thing I wrote for someone other than myself was a *Simpsons* story. I had to draw that whole story out before I could write it. I had an idea of what I wanted to do and I knew how many pages I was supposed to write, but I just couldn't sit down and write any kind of useful page description. I had to do layouts in my little notebook and then write in the dialogue, and then hone it once it went to the page. I completely drew the story, then sat down and wrote what I drew. But back then I couldn't envision any kind of panel description or anything unless I first drew it. And that's the way it worked with *Scary Godmother*, too.

Take us through the *Scary Godmother* process, from the initial idea to how you plot out the story.

It depends. I have an improv background, I used to do improv with a drama group, so I have always fallen back on a fairly simple assembly of the who, the what and the where. Sometimes I'll just take a load of random ideas, throw them in a hat and pull one out and try and write a story around whatever it is. I do a lot of stuff on the fly. When I start writing, I will have one intention, but sometimes by the end, just because of something a character has said or a facial expression I've drawn, I'll have thought of something completely different and the story will veer off a hundred and eighty degrees from what I'd originally planned. And then I'll take the remainder of stuff I didn't use and stick it away for something that I might end up using later.

Scary Godmother

Sometimes lighthearted, sometimes harrowing, but always entertaining, Jill Thompson's creator-owned *Scary Godmother* is a creepy-cool series unlike any other. As Thompson says, it's meant to appeal to all ages, a trick she manages by imbuing her clever, colorful characters with plenty of wit and whimsy without ever talking down to younger readers or alienating older comics fans. Scary Godmother is herself a pleasant contradiction — a gal trained in both the arts of the fairy godmother and of the witch, she's neither goody-goody nor bad seed, but instead an intriguing mixture of both. Beyond that, it's really the cast supporting Scary Godmother that makes the stories soar — from reluctant kid vampires to werewolves in bad polyester shirts to indescribably funky monsters from underneath the bed. They're a lot of fun, but they've also got an edge to them; the reader gets the sense that as delightful as these characters are to read about, one might not escape their actual company without a few bite marks and scratches to show for it. In fact, maybe that's why *Scary Godmother* is so addictive: it's not afraid to be as ghastly at the same time it's being a total gas.

Anyway, after I get my germ of the idea, I'll start writing and writing and writing, not in any structured format, but just a long paragraph of '...and then this happens and then this happens and then they go here and then this happens.' Sometimes there will be a dialogue between characters and I'll just write all that down. And then afterwards, I'll break it down and see what works. But I certainly don't write full scripts for myself when I write *Scary Godmother*. The only time I've actually written full script for myself is when I wrote the *Death* manga, because other people in the process needed to see that it worked in script form before I actually started drawing. That was actually very hard to do, and it felt like I had wasted a lot of my time... because I already knew in my head what I was going to do with the art. But if somebody needs to edit a project, they really need to see a physical script, because they can hardly just foresee what I'm going to do.

Scary Godmother publisher Robb Horan trusts that whatever I'm going to do, he's going to like, and he'll be entertained and interested by it. But DC, being more formal, need to know *exactly* what's going to happen before you do it. And sometimes that's hard, because often I don't know what's going to happen until I draw it, and when I draw it, it makes me think of something that's much better than the thing that I wanted to do in the first place.

Would you describe your approach to writing and storytelling as unorthodox?

Yes. I would say it's fairly unorthodox. I certainly couldn't recommend it to anyone other than myself. But there are things that I have learned throughout my writing career that are much more traditional and I would feel comfortable passing along as tips to anyone who's planning on breaking into the business. The most important thing for me is not to be overly wordy; you want to make sure that everything your characters say is important and progresses the story. I hate comics that are just 'blah, blah, blah,' and you're actually *reading* what's happening instead of *seeing* what's happening. I think that's a very bad use of the comics medium. I don't want to see a splash page with tons of captions around it telling me what I should be seeing. Mostly, people think that it should *all* be about the writing, especially for Vertigo readers. I don't think that's true, and I won't buy those comics.

Since your stories are prone to change while you're in the middle of drawing them, do you worry about the effect that might have on pacing and their overall structure?

I don't want it to sound like I'm just kind of sketching and drawing and suddenly I'm on page twenty-two and I go, 'Yay! I'm done!' I have an outline with the amount of pages that I'm dealing with. What major action happens on each page is clearly delineated for myself. If suddenly on page ten something happens that makes me think of a different idea, I'll go back and write out another outline with a new idea incorporated in it to make sure that my pacing and my flow work properly.

Are there stories you feel are inappropriate for the *Scary Godmother* universe?

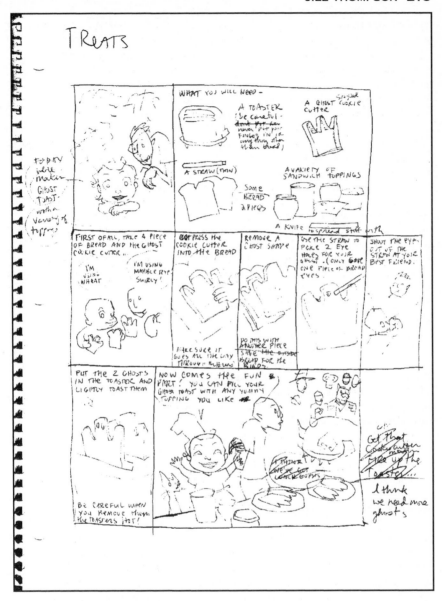

Above: *Sketchbook rough for the* Scary Godmother *story 'Treats', which appeared in* Sirius Gallery 2000. *Courtesy of Jill Thompson.* Scary Godmother ™ & © 2004 Jill Thompson.

Probably. Yeah, sure. The reason I do *Scary Godmother* is to tell stories that entertain me... and hopefully others. Any given story must be accessible for me in my thirties to read and enjoy, yet must also be suitable to hand to my seven year-old niece so she can read it. This was a balance that I felt was largely lacking in the comics industry. For instance, my dad used to read *Archie Comics* on the train on his way home from work. Then he'd hand them off to me, and at that time I was maybe eight or nine years old. My point is, we both got a kick out of them. They were G-rated, like *Bone* or *Akiko*. There's danger going on, there are issues happening, but it's completely appropriate to hand off to younger generations. It's not suggested for 'mature readers' and neither is it suggested for 'children only'. I also felt strongly there were things out there that were being written for children that I wouldn't give to my nieces because they were so dumbed down. It was so insulting. So I was largely trying to create something that I missed from my own youth. I was at the Las Vegas convention last October, and the amount of police officers that came up to me and told me they read *Scary Godmother* was very heartening! [*Laughs*] 'Yes, I'm on the vice squad, and I read *Scary Godmother* on my off time.' I couldn't believe so many cops read *Scary Godmother*! Who would ever have guessed that?

Since you were an *Archie* fan as a kid, what do you think of that title these days?

It became too politically correct for me. I haven't picked up an *Archie* comic in a long time. I mean, I'll look at them in the grocery store because they're right there at the checkout counter. But... when Moose couldn't be stupid, he was just 'dyslexic' and when Big Ethyl couldn't be called ugly... I mean, c'mon! Sure, it's terrible to call people such things, but most of those original stories revolved around some misunderstanding or somebody's extreme personality trait. Somehow, when they no longer had that, they were less interesting characters. They used to be fun. I certainly never felt that reading those comics back when I was a kid made me think that all athletes were stupid, or that it was good to be mean to girls that were less attractive than Betty or Veronica, or that all guys like Reggie were asses.

How did the *Death* manga, *At Death's Door*, come about?

DC pretty much told me what they were looking for, and asked me if I could do it. I said, 'I guess so. Sure, I could probably draw like that.' I love manga, but I'd just never taken a stab at drawing in that style before. I knew that there was so much symbolism and that manga artists use things in their storytelling format to convey emotion — things that we don't use. I tried to read as much Japanese manga as I could. Mostly translated, but a lot that wasn't, just to see if I could tell what was going on from the context clues I was given in the way it was illustrated. Like, what was the common theme when people were angry? Well, there was this crazy lightning bolt that went on in the background. There were times when their faces were eliminated, and it was either at times of shame or anger. If I could pick out a few major techniques and use them in mine, it would feel more authentic, rather than just someone who's drawing a character with big eyes or a scene taken from some anime.

There's so much wordless expression that goes on in manga. One moment between two characters, maybe with them apologising to each other because of some teenage misunderstanding, might go on for eight pages. You get that in so much of their storytelling, and I wanted to be able to do that convincingly in mine. Mind you, I was adapting something that had already been written, and something that was very, very dialogue heavy, so it was kind of the opposite of the medium into which I was trying to adapt it. It was a challenge. I had a huge task set out before me. For a start, I had to try and edit Neil Gaiman. Now if you read through Neil's *Sandman* arc 'Season of Mists', it's like, well, you don't know what to take out, because everything means something. I certainly liked it the way it is. I had to almost make the Cliffs Notes out of his work and then incorporate stuff that wouldn't change the story as it stood, and yet would make it more suitable to a different type of comic. In the end, I liked what I did. I think I did a good job. Neil liked it.

Once you started, how did you begin getting the story down on paper?

The most compelling factor was the fact that the minute I actually said I'd do it, I was suddenly under a deadline. [*Laughs*] I was like, 'Wait a minute!' What I had to do first was break down what I was going to include and what I was going to cut out from 'Season of Mists'. I wanted to incorporate what seemed to be the most important elements of teenage girls' manga: there's a love affair of some kind. There's a misunderstanding. There's a lot of humour. A lot of family turmoil. Overall, what I wanted to do was just focus on the decision that Dream

Sandman: Season of Mists

Neil Gaiman's *Sandman* books were inspired reads right from the first issue, but it was with the 'Season of Mists' storyline that the series really started firing on all cylinders — and it's from this arc that Jill Thompson drew her *Death: At Death's Door* manga. Thousands of years ago, Morpheus condemned his mortal love to Hell after she spurned his affections. Seeing the error of his ways, Morpheus risks his very existence in order to journey into the bowels of Hell and free his lover's soul. Morpheus is expecting Lucifer to put up a fight, but instead the clever devil takes a different tack: he simply closes down Hell, locks it up, and gives Morpheus the key. And because Hell is as necessary a part of the universe as Heaven itself Morpheus is now saddled with the great responsibility of choosing the netherworld's next keeper. It's a more challenging and bewildering task than it first appears, as every manner of god and wannabe power player from the four corners of all existence wants a shot. The arc was collected into the fourth *Sandman* trade paperback, and if you only read one of them — as if you could resist the rest — this is the one to get.

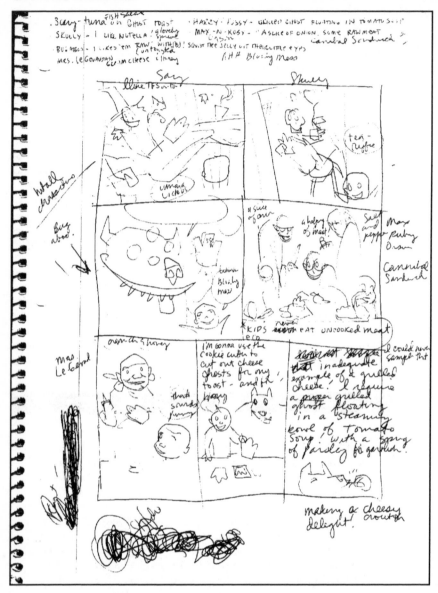

had to make of what to do with the key and how it affected his sister, and I had to break it up into a certain amount of chapters. It was nineteen ten-page segments with a splash in the front and a splash in the back. But rather than give it to DC in instalments, I wrote the whole thing and handed it in.

What was the approval process like?

They had to send it to Neil, because he has to okay everything to do with *Sandman* and The Endless. He had a couple of comments, both minor, that he added and that was it. I really love the characters in *Sandman* and I kind of understand how and why they do what they do. I wouldn't want to mess with that. I think the one thing people worried about was, 'Is she going to do something stupid with these characters?' What I was majorly worried that Neil would say, is, 'Death would never do that,' or, 'That's ridiculous.' I have a huge amount of respect for the characters he's created and I'd never try to do something completely out of character. I talked to Neil for a long time before I started on *At Death's Door* and a couple times throughout, just to make sure that I wasn't going to mess up.

Way back when, how did *Sandman* have an impact on you as a reader?

Before I actually worked on *Sandman,* I totally loved that book. I couldn't believe that I would ever get to work on it. At the time it was *the* comic for me to draw. It played to all my strengths as a penciller. But Neil does that when he writes for someone anyway. He usually has you draw one story, and then he sees where you excel. And the next time he writes for you, he writes to make sure the experience is to your benefit.

You're currently writing the second volume of the *Death* manga. Is it easier the second time around?

Actually, no. The process of writing the second manga has been so much more difficult for me. This time I'm not adapting something, so I have to write a completely new type of story. I'm running into this huge case of writer's block, because DC needs to see everything beforehand, and I really want to just hit the ground running. I want to start in with my idea and then finish it as I go along. I know that while I'm drawing I'm going to have that elusive brainstorm that I usually get in the middle of it, and I'm never going to know what it is until I get there. Instead, I've sat down at the computer trying to write what's going on and it's been very, very hard. This will probably be a big test for me.

Has the writing come easy for you on any projects?

I wrote this story for WildStorm that I collaborated on with my studiomate, Tony Akins. It was called *Masks: Too Hot for TV,* and it was pretty much [the reality TV show] *Cops,* but for superheroes. That's how it was presented to me. Of course, I live in the city of Chicago where we have some great... *and* often corrupt police officers. [*Laughs*] And if you know anything about watching *Cops,* or if you ever talk to any police officers, the cops always win. And I thought about Chicago cops versus the low-grade villains that you would find in any culture that would actually have superpowered people. You've got your guy who's slightly powered, and he's using his powers to go steal radios or run a prostitution ring, or sell crack. How would the cops react to that? That thing — I could've written a hundred pages of story, more.

It seems to me that I work better when I'm writing somebody else's characters. I think that's the way my school trained me. I didn't realise it until I worked on the manga, but the trade school that I went to — interestingly, [comics painter] Alex Ross also attended — wanted you to get a job in art. You were supposed to be able to walk into a rep or agency, and whatever job that they had available, you were supposed to be able to do it. All they wanted was for you to be consistently employed — which, of course, is something that I do enjoy being. So when someone calls me up like [DC's] Karen Berger and goes, 'Jill, we want a 192-page manga based on *Sandman*. Could you do that?' I was like, 'Sure I can,' even though at the time I had no idea if I could. Because that's what I was trained to do.

Are you ever in a position where you're pulling all-nighters in order to hit your deadlines?

I'm actually pretty good at hitting my deadlines, and anyway I'm too old for all-nighters. I just can't do them anymore! I got a horrendous case of tendonitis in the middle of the *Death* manga last year, and right now I'm unable physically to keep up the pace that I used to be able to do. I think I finally wore myself out. I

Death and The Endless

In the *Sandman* series, Death and her six siblings comprise The Endless — think of them as the Powers-That-Be behind the scenes who keep the universe running smoothly (or not). Each of The Endless represents an aspect of the human condition and also rules his or her own domain. Death's job is self-explanatory: when one's time comes, it's Death who's there to ease the transition between the 'here' and the 'hereafter.' Her brother, Dream, also known as Morpheus and a host of other titles, patrols the subconscious, his realm The Dreaming. Despair's occupation is to bring low the hearts of humankind, while her ambiguously sexed twin, Desire, instills single-minded longing in all it touches. Destiny is something of a mystery even among The Endless; he is the oldest sibling and, as his name implies, addresses inconstant fate. Delirium, on the other hand, is the youngest sibling; her realm is not quite insanity, but close enough. She was once known as Delight, but no longer. Finally there is Destruction, who went missing centuries ago and remains a sibling apart from the rest. Like any family, they have their squabbles, only the results of their clashes affect all of humanity.

Above: *One more page from Jill Thompson's sketchbook, again for the* Scary Godmother *tale 'Treats'. Courtesy of Jill Thompson.* Scary Godmother ™ *& © 2004 Jill Thompson.*

heard recently that [penciller] George Perez has tendonitis, and I thought, he should have had it fifteen years ago, the amount of detailed work he turns out. I'm very disciplined, though. When I have a book to do, I have to get a page a day done. Writing is easier; sometimes you can write a whole issue in an afternoon. I can never do more than a page a day drawing. I have in the past. I've forced myself to do it. I think on *Sandman* there was one time I did four pages in a day. But back then I could work for twenty-two hours straight.

What's your schedule like normally?

I keep to a very consistent workday for six days a week, sometimes seven. But then I always have. I'm a very good morning person. I like to be done with work by 8 o'clock at night. Usually it's 6 o'clock, because I like to go and do some physical activity at that point. I used to have things that I'd bring home with me, little things that I could work on. There would be times, after eating dinner or something like that, I'd spend on those. Now, though, not so much, because of the arm. And I want to *keep* drawing, so that's why I have to listen to what my body's telling me right now. [*Laughs*] And what my acupuncturist tells me, and what the hand surgeon is telling me. The last thing I want to do is have somebody chop about in there.

Did you ever identify what it was that caused you such problems physically on the first *Death* manga?

All the way through the first book I was trying to figure out what was different about the manga page a day as opposed to a normal [comics] page a day. I think it came down to the fact I was actively drawing in a style that was not natural to me. I had to really keep focused on it, because if I lost concentration, I would suddenly have a *Scary Godmother*-looking Death instead of a manga-looking Death. Or I'd revert back to my *Sandman* type of style. So to make sure that I was always drawing in a manga-type style, I think there was something going on in my hand, either tensing up or just a lack of looseness that was bad for me. It's the only thing that I'd ever done differently and the tendonitis is the result. Now I have pain whatever I draw. It's there when I do details. It's even there when I write in cursive style. When I'm painting and I'm doing the detailed linework for watercolours I have to stop every now and then and take a break.

When drawing someone else's stories, what kind of scripts are helpful for you as an artist? Do you prefer very detailed descriptions or loose outlines?

There's a fine line between writing something that's richly detailed and evokes an image for your penciller and something that's so unnecessarily dense it hinders them. I've had experience of both. The latter is just awful. I do think, though, that dialogue is really important when you write for someone else, just because as well as a sense of what's supposed to happen in the story the artist can get a feeling of body language and the facial expressions. If someone can write really good, succinct, conversational dialogue, that's so helpful to an artist.

More so than physical descriptions?

Physical description has to be rich too, but if it's so overly detailed you feel like you have no leeway, it becomes almost *draining*. I've worked on a book like that, where I got a headache from trying to read the script. And even after reading these hugely detailed panel descriptions or scene descriptions, I would have absolutely no idea what to draw. That was like a multiple-aspirin job. When I started talking with [*Aquaman* and *H-E-R-O* author] Will Pfeifer about writing, we discussed exactly this problem. Like, if you want to describe Superman walking into your average college kid's dorm, you can maybe add in a couple of cultural references or something that evokes the mood without necessarily saying, 'There are several flannel shirts on the floor, covered by a pizza box — and name the pizza place, which has to be on there — and several pornography mags are rolled up in the corner.' You get the idea? And if you have an actual give-and-take with your writer, as an artist, you can call up and say, 'Is he *this* type of guy?' And if the writer says yes, then you know what to draw. But if you get so much description, to me that's almost like being chained to the script. It's like there's no collaborative effort at all.

Is your husband [*100 Bullets* writer Brian Azzarello] a helpful sounding board when you're having creative struggles?

Yeah, he is. Because what I write is simple to him. And he can just solve my problems during dinner. It's like, 'You should do this,' without even thinking about it. And I'm like, 'Oh, why didn't I see it that way?' I think sometimes you're just too close to it.

Have you two ever talked about collaborating on a project?

We've always said we don't want to work together, largely because of the conflict that it would inevitably bring. Right now, we always have something to talk about at the end of the day, but if we're working on the same exact thing… well, you get the idea. I think it's nice that we don't work together, healthy.

*   *   *

BRIAN K. VAUGHAN

Big ideas are nothing new for Brian Vaughan. The writer of such high-concept series as Marvel's *Runaways* and Vertigo's *Y: The Last Man* knows a great idea when it hits him. Heck, that's probably why Vaughan catapulted himself from a mere footnote in writer Devin Grayson's chapter of the first *Writers on Comics Scriptwriting* into a full-fledged chapter this go round. While he didn't turn many heads with his early work on Vertigo's ailing *Swamp Thing*, it was Vaughan's creator-owned *Y* — the tale of Yorick, literally the last man on Earth after a strange disease wipes out every other living male mammal on the planet — that garnered him critical acclaim. High praise also followed him on *Runaways*, the story of a group of superpowered kids who unknowingly discover their parents are evil supervillains. Toss in a run on *Mystique* here, a *Spider-Man/Doctor Octopus* mini-series there, and *Ex Machina*, his new creator-owned series for WildStorm about a superhero who loses his mask to become mayor of NYC, and suddenly Vaughan's sneaking onto Top 10 Writers lists. Not bad for a kid who used to babysit dogs for a living.

Have you always been a big comics fan?

Initially I started out like most kids where you get comics when you're sick. When I was home and bedridden, my parents would stop by the drug store and pick up some comic books. It's weird to have the thing you love best associated with illness. When I got into comics originally, I thought they were activity books and you were supposed to cut out the panels and put them in a new order to tell your own stories. So I would sit around and cut up various comics, which is sad because I think my dad had old issues of *Amazing Fantasy* in the attic and I'd cut them up and put them together with *Battlestar Galactica*.

Did you want to be a comic book writer from day one?

I don't remember what the chronology was, but I think it was around seventh grade or so that someone got me the *Watchmen* graphic novel as a present. We were on a family road trip to visit the grandparents, and I read *Watchmen* in one sitting from beginning to end. As soon as I was done with that I just said, 'Well, that's what I'm going to do.' I'd always liked comics before that but with *Watchmen* I got into the whole world of it. I think it was the first time I recognised there was a voice behind them. I guess I'd always wanted to be a writer, but I had no idea how to break into comics or anything. I just knew it was going to be something in the field, whether it was as a screenwriter or a playwright or whatever.

What led to your first published work?

Well, it was a long and winding road, sort of like Joe Kelly's route into comics. We were both at NYU at the same time, and I was a double major in film and dramatic writing, which just doubles your odds of being unemployed. Joe had been the first guy to go through this thing called the Stanhattan Project. Two editors from Marvel — Mark Powers and James Felder — had set up this class to teach about comics. Joe was sort of the first-year success story, and I knew him as just the guy who used to wheel VCRs into the classroom. I figured if he could do it, I could do it. I was in the second and final wave of the Stanhattan Project.

At the time, Marvel had become a really incestuous place where interns would become assistant editors who would become editors who would then start writing the books. They really wanted to start looking anyplace else for writers. The guys liked what I was doing in the class, so they sort of threw me a bone. I think my first assignment was *Cable* #43. It was an issue that I had to dialogue, which was sort of back in the old school Marvel way. Sometimes one writer would plot a story and then if they ran out of time, another writer would dialogue the finished artwork. On this particular comic, I think the writer had started writing it and then probably got into a fight with the editor who finished writing some of the

Place of birth:
  Cleveland, Ohio, USA
Date of birth:
  17 July 1976
Home base:
  San Diego, California, USA
First published work:
  Cable #43 (dialogue only);
  Ka-Zar Annual '97 (full script)
Education:
  B.F.A. from New York University,
  Double Major in Film and
  Dramatic Writing
Career Highlights:
  *Ex Machina, Mystique, Runaways,
  Y: The Last Man*

story and the artist then got tired of waiting for pages and drew his own storyline. When I got the pages it was like a 'Choose Your Own Adventure' thing. You could just put the pages together in any order and try and make sense out of it.

So your experience cutting up all those comics as a kid came in handy.

Yeah, that was my auspicious beginning. From there, I think they liked how I was fast and living in the NYU dorm at the time. It certainly wasn't because I was good. I think I was nineteen when I did that first *Cable* story. The dorms were only a few blocks away from the Marvel offices, so I would just run over to Marvel — I didn't have a fax machine or anything and it was sort of before computers were fast enough to send anything bulky — and pick up pages and then a couple of hours later hand deliver the script back to them. It was more that I was fast and close. I did a bunch of other little assignments like a *Ka-Zar Annual* and pretty much grabbed work wherever I could. I got little assignments at both Marvel and DC. But I didn't get my first monthly book until *Swamp Thing* over at Vertigo.

How did you make the move over to Vertigo?

That was hard. Vertigo was where I'd always wanted to be, but it was almost like the Marvel credits I had under my belt hurt me more than they helped me. There's sort of a preconception that you're either a superhero writer or you're a Vertigo writer. So I had to break in all over again... almost. Devin [Grayson] was a big help. Devin and I sort of became friends since we were breaking in at the same time; we'd talk on the phone and complain to each other. I think they offered her *Swamp Thing* and she was already writing 150 different books and she was kind enough to say, 'I have this friend who's really a great writer. You should at least give him a shot.'

I was a huge Swamp Thing fan, but I think the thing that landed me the gig and probably destroyed the book was the fact that I loved Alan Moore so much that I didn't want to do an Alan Moore story. I really wanted to take the book in a totally different direction, just as Alan had when he took over the book, rather than just strip-mining his old stories. I wrote a really long detailed proposal and Vertigo liked it. Amazingly, I got the gig.

Were you doing any other jobs on the side to help support yourself?

I was maybe nineteen when I got my first cheque with Spider-Man on it. I had student loans, I'm eating ramen noodles and I'm sitting there staring spellbound at this cheque going, 'I can't cash this.' [*Laughs*] I was doing an assignment here or there but not enough to live on, and when I left NYU a friend of a friend of a family who lived in some opulent Central Park West apartment told me they were looking for essentially a live-in dog butler, so I took the job. I lived in tiny butler's quarters and took care of a dog for a while. Then I got a job working at St. Vincents, a psychiatric hospital, all grist for the mill once I started working for Vertigo. I had a lot of weird jobs — dog-walking and asylums to name but two — anything really that wasn't so time-consuming that I couldn't come home and write comics... but also that didn't make me want to shoot myself in the face.

What was it like seeing your first issue of *Cable* on the shelves?

Seeing it on the shelf was totally exciting; it was thrilling. And then to open it up was horrifying. I had met Neil Gaiman when I was a freshman and he was signing somewhere. It's funny, having spoken to other people who've met Neil and asked his advice, I've never actually heard the same advice twice. I think Neil's got some sort of superpower where he knows exactly what you need to hear. Neil said to me, 'My advice to you is to get published and get published fast because nothing will make you get better faster than seeing your horrible words in print and knowing that other people are reading what you have written.' And it's so true. When you're in film school, it's sort of a safe environment. You share your writing with other students but they're scared and needy themselves and they don't want to insult you because they don't want you to insult them. But when you see that comic come out and you know strangers are reading your words and you read just how bad they are, it really does inspire you to get better and to get better fast. Mind you, I don't know quite how Neil expected me to get published in the first place. It seems to be skipping a few steps just to say go and get published.

Maybe it's more how to become a better writer, rather than how to actually break in?

I guess so. Personally, I don't really have good advice to offer other than: write

---

Vertigo

Call it the bastard child of comics, the black sheep of the family or just a bunch of really cool freakin' comics. With over ten years of publishing behind it, Vertigo's always been the alternative bent to mainstream comics... as seen through the mainstream's eyes. In 1993, DC Comics decided to group all of its edgier, more mature comics under one umbrella of an imprint, Vertigo. Unlike the regular DC Universe, Vertigo isn't concerned with flashy costumes or high-powered superheroes. Instead it concentrates on telling deep, thought-provoking tales, no matter what the genre. Pick up a Vertigo book and you're pretty much guaranteed to be faced with black humour, drama and tragedy. Storytelling is what it's all about, whether you're looking at the tale of the Dream Lord Morpheus (as seen in the award-winning *Sandman*), the ticked-off Jesse Custer who's literally on a quest to find God after the big guy abandoned his post (*Preacher*), the muck-encrusted mockery of a man in search of more than his soul (*Swamp Thing*), or the magical mystical antics of that bastard John Constantine, who beat lung cancer and screwed over the devil all in a day's work (*Hellblazer*).

and live your life. I think the truth is that every writer has a million bad words in them, and you just sort of have to get them out of your system before the good ones can start to flow. There's a point in the middle of my career where I could almost feel I'd hit my millionth word. You can just see the pre-millionth word and the post-millionth word, and there's a huge difference between them. So just write a lot and read a lot and live a lot. Live a lot might be number one. I'm not one of those writers who thinks he can only write from experience but it does help.

That millionth word was probably around the time you started on _Y_. Did you realise the whole 'last man on Earth' idea was such a great concept when you came up with it?

Yeah, I think I did. It's certainly an idea that had been floating around in my head for a long time. I have a little anecdote about it: when I was in grade school, I fantasised that the little redheaded girl who sat across from me would fall in love with me if every other kid in the class would drop dead. I always wanted to subvert that idea in some capacity and the concept remained in the back of my mind. Even though _Swamp Thing_ was dying, the people at Vertigo were nice enough to say, 'We recognise _Swamp Thing_ didn't work out but we see something in your writing, so just bring us something that's you.' I didn't know how far I could take the 'last man on Earth' concept, but I sort of knew it was the ideal thing for me to pitch. It was the perfect Brian Vaughan story.

When I came up with _Y_, I thought I was the most brilliant guy of all time. But when the book came out people were like, 'Have you seen that 1924 film _The Last Man on Earth_?' or have you read the _Omega Man_ or 10,000 things that I had never read or seen which deal with similar things. You begin to realise that there are no new ideas, just new executions of old ideas. I do like novelty, though, so it is so nice to hit on something people see as refreshing. I also love a good high concept. It's so freeing if you can find something that's simple and striking and you can describe it in a sentence. There are a million ways to go from there, as opposed to a concept that's sort of murky or difficult to describe.

_Y_ features an almost all-female cast. _Runaways_ is a fair mix of guys and girls. And _Mystique_ features a strong female lead. Do you just feel more comfortable writing female characters?

I don't know. It's probably not a coincidence I'm writing so many. When I started working on _Y_, everyone was like, 'Won't it be difficult to work on a book where ninety-nine point nine percent of the cast is female?' But, strangely, when I was working on _Swamp Thing_, no one ever asked, 'Won't it be difficult to work on a book with talking plants?' Let's face it, talking plants are _much_ more difficult to write than women. I never really understand when people are like, 'Isn't it hard to write female characters?' I guess it is, but I suppose it's no harder to write male characters. I've got a lot of strong women in my life, which helps, but I like to think that even if that had not been the case, it's a writer's job to use her or his imagination and just try to stay true to the characters.

Brian K. Vaughan / **Y** #19 - SECOND DRAFT

Page Two

Page Two, Panel One
Push in closer on the three. Mann and 355 are frowning at the perplexed Yorick. They both look annoyed.

1) Yorick: Why are we--

2) Dr. Mann: Isn't it obvious?

3) Agent 355: Yeah, use your *brain*.

Page Two, Panel Two
This is just a shot of Yorick, stroking his chin, lost in thought. Maybe Ampersand is on his shoulder, frightened by something he notices off-panel.

4) Yorick: But if *we're*...?
5) Yorick: That means the *Wizard*--

6) Another Voice (from off): *GRRRRRRR*

Page Two, Panel Three
Pull out to the largest panel of the page. We're behind the Cowardly Lion in the foreground of this shot, framed so that we can't see her (or his?) actual face. The Lion is lumbering towards Yorick, who cowers in fear. 355 and Mann watch the lion dispassionately, completely indifferent.

7) Yorick: Ahh!

8) Agent 355: It's just the Cowardly Lion, Yorick.

9) Dr. Mann: You knew this was coming, didn't you? Remember what that girl said? Before she died?

Page Two, Panel Four
Cut back to the real world for this close-up of a drugged-up, half-awake Yorick, still in the dark room where we left him last issue (though that doesn't need to be apparent just yet).

10) Yorick (small, groggy): *Nnn... no... st'away... you can't come to Oz...*

11) Someone's Voice (from off): Forget about Oz, Yorick.

There's all sorts of varying degrees of man-hating in *Y*. Where did that come from?

I guess maybe some people think that I had some sort of agenda with *Y*, but that's not the case. Sure, feminism in all its various forms does intrigue me, but the thing I found most interesting from researching other stories where the men died and women were in charge was they'd immediately hold hands and go down to the United Nations and declare an end to war. But if you read serious feminist writers' work, and I read a lot, I realised that if you locked all the authors in a room they would have killed each other by the end of the day. There is no one universal thought on what feminism is or what the right way to advance the cause is. So I didn't want to put one or other view forward in *Y*. I wanted rather for it to be like each town we visit sort of represents a different way of thinking.

Funny thing, though. I moved to San Diego recently and I was looking for a comic book store. I took my girlfriend — who's now my fiancée — along and I guess I wanted to impress her. I wanted to take her into a store and do that humble sort of, 'Hey, I just wanted to introduce myself. My name's Brian Vaughan, I'm a comic book writer,' and then have them be dazzled by that. There was this woman behind the counter and I introduced myself and she said, 'Why do you hate women?' I told my girlfriend, 'That's the last time I'm taking you to a comic book store.'

What other characters would you most like to get your hands on?

I don't know. People ask me this and I feel like a jerk because there aren't too many. I did a Spider-Man thing recently for Marvel and that was a lot of fun. I've done Batman too. But as long as I've been writing comics I've been more concerned about doing new stuff. I think my best work is done on *Runaways* or *Y* or the mini-series called *The Hood* I did for Marvel. I was always thankful that when, say, Stan Lee started writing he didn't say, 'I have a Superman story I really want to do.' He said, 'I have this new concept.' So in answer to your question, I think I've already tackled all the characters who I had a love for as a kid and I'm now much more interested in creating new things.

As mentioned in the first *Writers on Comics Scriptwriting*, you're part of the young crop of new writers. What's your take on the industry now and how you guys fit into it?

I think the industry's great now. Well, I should say, the medium is great. I think the industry's in a lot of trouble because our audience is so tiny now, but I think it's sort of how cinema was in the 1970s, where everyone had left and moved on to television and studios had no idea how to bring the audience back in. So they just sort of found these young, reckless directors and they're like, 'Whatever. We don't know what works anymore, so just do whatever.' I think there are no real rules in comics these days. I don't think things have ever been as good across the board as they are right now. The underground stuff is incredible and even the mainstream superhero stuff is great. I think it's mainly because there are so few people reading and the editors aren't doing it to make money. They're just doing it for the sheer love of the medium.

I think that's usually the way it happens. When an industry is dying, the creativity is often at its peak. Because really the things that stand in the way of great art are mainly corporate concerns, like the audience is so huge we can't afford to lose any of them. There's a lot of interference, a lot of second-guessing your audience. But when your audience is really tiny and it's just a small, literate, dedicated band of readers looking for something new, I think you really can do anything. Take a comic like Bendis' *Daredevil.* I don't care if you hate superheroes, I think that's as good a crime story as you can find on television, in novels, anywhere. It's a really exciting time to work in comics.

Is it true you keep pretty odd working hours?

It is. I keep weird hours. Back when I lived in New York, my schedule would usually be I'd go to bed at around 10am and wake up at 4pm, at which time I'd deal with editors for about an hour. That's about as long as I can take — editors, no offense intended! I'd deal with general stuff then just spend the rest of the day sort of thinking about what I'm gonna write that night. I'd read or putter around or go do something. When my girlfriend came home from work I'd hang out with her until she went to bed around midnight and then I'd write until 8am or 10am. It's changed a little bit in California because now I have to be up by 1pm, since that's 4 o'clock in NY. But I'll still begin writing around midnight.

The Hood

If you suddenly found yourself with a mysterious blood red cloak and a pair of odd-looking boots that granted you the powers to turn invisible and walk on air, what would you do? Well, if you're an average guy, chances are you'd do pretty much what nineteen year-old Parker Robbins did: anything you wanted. That's the basic premise of Brian K. Vaughan's six-issue mini-series *The Hood* for Marvel's mature MAX line back in 2001. Robbins starts out as your basic everyday scumbag. He's cheating on his pregnant girlfriend, lying to his institutionalised mother and doing whatever he can as a low life street thug to make ends meet. In short, he's a small-time 'hood'. (Get it?) So when he discovers these newfound powers, he tosses his life of organized crime away... and enters the world of supervillainy as the Hood. Before long, he's caught the attention of the cops and a few other lower-tiered baddies like the Constrictor, Jack O' Lantern and the Shocker. And Vaughan himself quickly caught the attention of numerous comic fans as well with his realistic and uncensored approach to the Marvel Universe. These characters do more than curse, swear and bleed though; they actually make you think.

Page Eleven

Page Eleven, Panel One
Okay, instead of panels, this page is made up of four classic-style POLAROID PHOTOS (neatly arranged into two tiers of two). Actually, it's all the same photo, a "mental snapshot" from Yorick's past. At first, the photo is entirely white, but it will gradually develop over the course of the page.
Lettered onto the white space beneath the photo area is the following run-on sentence:

1) Text at bottom of Photo: I was a sophomore and a virgin but she was just a sophomore and we'd been friends since orientation but started hooking up with each other after

Page Eleven, Panel Two
The photo continues to develop. The washed-out white gives way to a few colors and vague shapes.

2) Text at bottom of Photo: she got dumped by one of my roommates and we promised not to fall in love but then we did on accident and she moved out of the dorms on

Page Eleven, Panel Three
The developing continues, and now the figure in the photo becomes more distinct.

3) Text at bottom of Photo: purpose and got her own shitty studio apartment in the East Village between a sushi restaurant and a pizza joint and I said she was completing the

Page Eleven, Panel Four
The photo is finally fully developed, and we can now see that it's a shot of Yorick's girlfriend Beth at age 19. The stunningly gorgeous blonde is now wearing sexy librarian glasses, and she's looking over the top of them up at us, very seductive. She's been unpacking boxes in her new studio apartment, and she's leaning over an open box of retro toys and other fun crap. Her shirt is open, and we get a flash of cleavage and a lacy black bra. I don't know if I'm being too subtle, Pia, but this needs to be the kind of image that will make every fanboy in the world fall in love. Either way, maybe we see an unmade bed in the background behind Beth.

4) Text at bottom of Photo: Axis because she's German and we were gonna wait until she was on the pill but then she gave me this LOOK that burned into my mind and then

Above: *An unusual layout request fom the script of* Y: The Last Man *#19. Courtesy of Brian K. Vaughan.*

I wouldn't call it exactly disciplined because I'm such a lazy person at heart, but I got into such a groove by forcing myself to write every day that I feel sort of uncomfortable and gross if I miss even a day. I write seven days a week. Even when I wasn't writing as much, I'd spend as much time sitting there. I was always working on something, even if it wasn't comics. I'd be writing a one-act play or a short story or something. But for comic scripts, it's about six pages a day. There's always some other work to do, but on average it takes me about a week to write a book.

Do you stick with one book each week or jump back and forth on titles?

I prefer to focus on one book at a time. I like to have a week where it's just *Runaways* and all I'm thinking about is *Runaways*. A few problems might pop up on another book, where maybe the artist will call with a question or something, but when it comes to the actual writing itself, I'll only work on one book at a time. A lot of people think that *Y* takes a long time to write and that I can sort of hack out a *Mystique* in a weekend or something. Often, *Mystique* is a lot harder to write than *Y*, because it's not necessarily what I'm good at. I think I'm pretty good at putting two characters in a room and having them fight about something, and I'm less good with motorcycles smashing through windows. But I like that challenge and that's part of the reason I wanted to do *Mystique* for at least a year, just to figure out how to write a differently paced, different kind of story.

How do you get into writing mode?

I have an office at home. Usually I go out in the middle of the night and just spend an hour walking around quietly, thinking about what I'm going to do. Then it's back to my office, which is as boring a room as you've ever seen. Just four white walls and nothing much else, because I'm *sooo* easily distracted. I can't even understand writers who can write with music on in the background. The truth is I plainly find writing really difficult and hard, and I need to focus.

I had a professor at NYU who used to always tell me he hated writing; it was his least favourite thing in the world. So I asked him why he was a writer if he hated it so much. And he said, 'I hate writing but I love having written. That's my favourite thing in the world.' And that's true of me too. I hate writing. I just think it's laborious and monotonous. Just the day-to-day drudgery of sitting at the keyboard and typing is really difficult for me. But when it's done, it's great. I do like the initial stage of coming up with the ideas, but sitting at that keyboard is just... well, to me anyone who has fun with that is nuts. For me, when I'm going on my long old-man walks and thinking about what the story's going to be or when I have a finished chunk of shit that I'm trying to sculpt into something pretty, that's where the fun is. But the transfer of ideas from head to screen or head to page is hard.

Do you prefer writing in full script?

I always have, since the very beginning. Even in the Stanhattan era. I think it was sort of the dying days of the old Marvel-style script back then, and they were like,

'You can do it plot-style but actually it's a dumb way to write.' I think originally Marvel plot-style was born out of a situation where you write like that if you're Stan Lee and you're writing eighty books a month and you have Jack Kirby finishing your scripts. I think artists these days appreciate getting as full a road map as possible. And I always give them permission to diverge from that, but I think their job is hard enough anyway. Writing is hard, but it's easy compared to drawing. So my scripts are very complete, very full.

Do you think visually when you're laying down your words?

I do. I'm not an artist; that's sort of an acquired skill. But I definitely see the page very clearly in my mind. I learned very early on that guys like Neil Gaiman do thumbnails of their scripts before they begin, and I started out doing that. But I would get the pages back from the artist and they would look absolutely nothing like the thumbnails that I had done — in fact, they looked a lot better! Nowadays, I try not to think too hard about it, because I want the artist to deal with that side of it and interpret it his or her way. I do try to think about how much information I'm going to put on a page. I am big on pacing, for me it's all about cliffhangers. Every issue ends with a cliffhanger. Every page ends with a cliffhanger. Even every panel sort of ends with a mini-cliffhanger to pull you onwards.

In terms of doing research for your work, haven't you gone to some rather unique extremes?

Well, yeah. I was writing a lot of crime stories when I was living in New York and I didn't really know anything about the police system. I'd heard about this auxiliary police programme in Manhattan where you could take a three-month course and learn all about police work. So I joined up for that, and maybe once a night you'd go out with a partner. You'd be uniformed but you didn't get to carry a gun or anything. You were supposed to be the eyes and ears of the police force; if you saw something you'd just call it in on your radio. I did that for writing research, sure, but also because writers generally live a very boring, lonely existence. You spend so much time inside a closed room you start to really ache for some kind of human interaction. In the early stages of *Y*, Yorick has a capuchin monkey, so I went out of my way on vacation to go to this monkey jungle place and try and see that specific kind of monkey, just to hear what it sounds like. So yeah, I do sort of go to ridiculous lengths. I'm currently living in San Diego, which is the most boring city on Earth, so I do a lot of Internet research and a lot of reading. Whenever I do crazy stuff, like join the auxiliary police, it's half about the writing and half just to make my life interesting.

What about Yorick's fascination with escape artists? Where did that come from?

I was always sort of interested in magic, particularly escapology. I even had a strait-jacket and learned how to get out of one. That wasn't originally going to be part of Yorick's character. Yorick is a lot like me a few years ago, but I like to think that I'm a better person now than he is currently. He's young, naïve, self-righteous and

Brian K. Vaughan / **RUNAWAYS** #1 - SECOND DRAFT / Twenty-seven Pages Total

Page Two

Page Two, Panel One
Pull out for this shot of Cap, Hulk and the Invisible Woman, as all three heroes suddenly "break character." Hulk is playfully reaching out to grab the Invisible Woman, but Cap is holding him back with one hand. The Invisible Woman is talking with Cap; she doesn't understand why he's stopped this fight.

1) Invisible Woman: What?

2) Captain America: First of all, you're not part of this mission. And second, you're, like... horrifically out of character.

3) Hulk: Hulk *smooch*!

Page Two, Panel Two
Push in on just Cap and Sue, as they confront each other.

4) Captain America: You're supposed to be the Invisible Woman, not Mrs. Skank-tastic.

5) Invisible Woman: You don't know what you're talking about, dude.
6) Invisible Woman: My older brother *interned* for the Fantastic Four last year. He said Sue Richards hits on anything that moves.

Page Two, Panel Three
Pull out to the largest panel of the page, as Daredevil and a miraculously "resurrected" Spider-Man join the others. Daredevil is lecturing Cap, while Spidey points at the Invisible Woman's sexy attire. Cap buries his face in his hand, clearly fed-up with this nonsense.

7) Daredevil: Just so you know, it's not cool to use "retarded" in a pejorative manner. My cousin's girlfriend is a retard.

8) Spider-Man: Hey, can you, um... send me that skin?

9) Captain America: All right, this campaign is obviously a bust, so--

Page Two, Panel Four
This is just a small shot of Cap, as he turns to address an off-panel voice.

10) Someone's Voice (from off): Alex Wilder, get off that thing *now*!

11) Captain America: Sorry, boys...

3/27

Above: *Another example of the inner life of Brian K. Vaughan's characters, this time in the script for* Runaways #1. *Courtesy of Brian K. Vaughan/Marvel Comics. Used with permission.* Runaways™ *and © 2004 Marvel Characters, Inc.*

thinks he knows everything but so clearly knows nothing. But at the same time, I thought he was funny, a likeable guy and sort of cool. But I remember pitching it to Karen Berger at Vertigo and Karen saying, 'I really like the pitch for *Y*, but the lead character is such a nerd.' It's funny, whenever anyone makes fun of Yorick I always take it very personally because I feel like they're attacking me. Anyway, rather than sort of finding something artificial to give Yorick to make him more interesting — like he's a professional gambler or a hitman or something — I decided to pull something that was even more nerdish from my own background and give it to him. And I think it's helped the book a lot. Escape is a big theme. Yorick in *Y*, more than any of my other characters, I draw from my own life.

What about your morals, religion or politics; do those ever come through in your work?

Yeah, a lot. It's hard for them not to, especially on a political book like *Ex Machina*. There's nothing more boring than a writer shoving his or her opinions down your throat, so I never sort of set out to do preachy comics that will teach you how to think correctly. I think most good writers like *asking* questions rather than answering them. I know so little about the world that I usually go into a comic trying to ask myself some questions and not necessarily trying to solve them. I just put it out there.

You're a natural at the high concept, big idea stuff that goes down well in Hollywood. Do you have any desire to go into film?

Y: The Last Man

Brian Vaughan's *Y: The Last Man* for Vertigo shows how every guy's fantasy can quickly become his worst nightmare. Back in the summer of 2002, an unknown plague wiped out every single sperm, foetus and fully developed mammal with a Y chromosome. In other words, every 'guy' bit the big one. The 'gendercide' instantly exterminated forty-eight percent of the global population or 29 billion men, with two notable exceptions: amateur escape artist Yorick Brown and his male helper monkey Ampersand. Unsure of why they were spared, Yorick must keep his identity hidden as he skulks about desperately trying to find his missing girlfriend, who was last seen in Australia. Too bad Yorick's an impulsive guy with a big mouth. He soon finds himself meeting a ton of different women, each with their own agenda — an Israeli Defence Forces combat soldier, a US congresswoman and one of the planet's premier bioengineers. Mix in some bloodthirsty Amazons, cloning, political intrigue, motorcycles, a mystic piece of jewelry and even a former supermodel who's turned to harvesting bodies and you've got yourself one brave new world. Who killed all the males and why is still a mystery that Yorick's hoping to unravel.

Well, I went to film school and I love movies and I would love maybe to do an independent movie someday, but for the most part, no. *Y* was optioned by New Line and it's gonna be a movie and the screenwriter who's writing it is nice enough to let me be involved, but Hollywood has all the disadvantages that comics don't. It's *sooo* much about money, and really it has to be. If you think about bringing just those first five issues of *Y* to the screen — like how huge the cast is, the effects for crashing planes and killing three billion men — it'll take a lot of money. Then you have to take into account, are we going to be able to recoup our money? Are enough people going to see this to justify its existence? There are so many stages of second-guessing and so much collaboration in movies, and that's just not the case with comics. Comics have very few people involved and you can just put it out there and hope that it works. I'd go to novels before I went to movies.

How do you deal with something like writer's block?

I just keep writing. That's what I've discovered. It seems to me that when people have writer's block, it's just that writing is plainly very hard. The only way to dig yourself out of that hole is to write yourself out of it. You just have to get to the point where you know that it doesn't have to be good, as long as you get something down on the page. When I'm just stuck there, I force myself to concentrate and just write crap. And I think if you can just shit out the worst stuff it'll get you going and the good stuff will start coming out. I think it's just about having discipline to force yourself to write even when you don't have anything in you.

Where would you like to see your career go from here?

I'd like to be solely working on characters that I had a hand in creating, and actually I'm getting pretty close to that now. It's not even so much about creator-owned. I mean, *Runaways* isn't a book that I own, but it is something that I helped create and it means a lot to me. I have nothing against superheroes or work-for-hire stuff, but it's not necessarily my strong point. Someone asked me recently where I wanted to be five years from now, and I was sort of surprised to hear myself say, 'Right where I am right now.' This is fine. This is great. To be working on *Y*, a successful creator-owned book, and sort of have my pick of the litter from Marvel. They've been very nice to me. I'm working on a kids' book like *Runaways* one week and a book with boobies and severed heads the next week. I get to write about whatever I want to write about any day of the week and I make a really nice living doing it. I can afford cable. And that's all you can ask for. This is just great. I'm having the time of my life.

*   *   *

BILL WILLINGHAM

Bill Willingham's not your average comic book writer. For a start, he's no overnight sensation. The veteran scribe certainly made a name for himself back in the '80s with Comico's *The Elementals*, a long-running superteam title featuring four heroes that return from the dead. Writing and pencilling the hit series, Willingham's timing couldn't have been more perfect. The big 'independents' movement was shaking up the industry, showing Marvel and DC that fans wanted more than just the standard superhero fare the Big Two had to offer. But then things started to go slightly awry. *Elementals* shipped sporadically and eventually Willingham appeared to give it up and pretty much step away from comics. Sure, there was an occasional mini-series or guest stint on a book here and there, but it wasn't until 2002 when his acclaimed and top-selling Vertigo series *Fables* began, that Willingham's name jumped back to the forefront of comics. Since then, his newfound success has spilled over to more mainstream work, and he's taken over as writer on *Robin*. As it turns out, though, he never really left comics in the first place. Instead, he just, 'made a lot of bad decisions, one after the other.'

Were you always a comic book fan?

I guess, like everyone, I went through phases. I read comics before I could read. We had a big sprawling family, so there were always plenty of older siblings to read to me. One of the things that happened back then was once we had read everything in the house we would throw all the comics in our wagon and go up and down the streets to trade. We would show up at someone's door and if there was a kid in there, we would go off in some corner, leaf through each other's stacks of comics and just trade one-for-one. It was common practice, and we would do it purely on the basis of, 'Have we read it yet?' So I read everything back then. I got out of comics in late high school, but then sort of realised in college that maybe it's not totally embarrassing to still be interested in these things, and got right back into it.

Even back then did you ever think you'd be writing comics one day?

Always. At least, as a kid I did. As a matter of fact, me and my neighbourhood friend Bruce Givan formed our own comic company, which we called B&B for Bruce and Bill — or Bill and Bruce depending on who you talk to. He created this character called Chameleon Man and I had Mantis Man, and we drew our own comics. As long as I can remember, I wanted to be in comics professionally.

You've drawn as well as written comics in your career. Were you originally more interested in the art?

Well, as a kid, I just didn't perceive a difference. You did comics and that entailed doing everything that you needed to do to make a comic book story. Then, later on, I began to realise that these things were broken down into different people doing different stages of the work. But I still didn't appreciate that there were occasionally people that were both drawing *and* writing. Anyway, I guess I liked drawing comics better, so I tried to break in on the strength of my art. I started writing as well simply out of the frustration, a case of, 'I like this story but I think I could have done it better.' But even when I was more focused on the art side of things, my main interest was in wanting to tell the story.

What was your first published work?

I started out doing an Elementals back-up story in a *Justice Machine Annual* that

Place of birth:
US Army hospital at Fort Belvoir, Virginia, USA
Date of birth:
22 December 1956
Home base:
Las Vegas, Nevada, USA
First published work:
'Valeria the Witch Queen' back-up in *Warp* #9 (illustrations);
Elementals preview story in *Justice Machine Annual* #1 (writing)
Education:
'I was deep into my third year of college (undergrad), before deciding it wasn't doing me any good (not to fault the college, mind you, but due entirely to my extreme lack of serious application, and the manifest distractions of a plethora of far-too pretty girls dotting the landscape).'
Career highlights:
Elementals, Fables, Pantheon, Proposition Player, Robin, The Sandman Presents: Taller Tales

was going to be published by Noble Comics, but they actually went under before it could see publication. Eventually, the Annual was picked up by Texas Comics. In the meantime, I had gotten work doing some back-up strips for First Comics on their *Warp* series. So I did the story for the *Justice Machine Annual* first, but my 'Valeria the Witch Queen' stories in *Warp* #9 and #10 actually came out before the *Justice Machine Annual* with the *Elementals* back-up. But both were published within months of each other

How did you feel when those first few issues finally saw print?

I was pretty pleased. I thought, look at this, I finally made it! But within a couple of months, I couldn't look at that stuff and see anything but grotesque mistakes. I am plainly not a big fan of my own artwork. There are things I like about doing both, in that if I'm going to write and draw a story, at least I don't have to jump through a lot of hoops to explain to the artist what I have in mind. I simply picture what I need to go on the page in my head and get drawing. But somehow I never quite managed to translate what I pictured to the actual artboard as well as I would have liked, certainly not as well as some other — rightfully acclaimed — comic book artists of this world could do it. I knew I was simply not in the same ballpark.

Your run on *Elementals* was pretty huge back in the '80s. It was certainly one of the most successful superhero stories put out by an independent company. How'd you come up with the idea?

I created *Elementals* largely by accident, back when I was living out of New York and trying to get work from Marvel and DC. I was getting plenty of encouragement from both companies but no actual work. This is when the independents were starting up: Pacific Comics, First Comics, Noble Comics and the like. I decided to do some samples and send them out to all of those companies, but unlike with Marvel and DC, I couldn't produce samples of their own characters; it was just far too much like hard work. So I just made up a generic superhero team to show that I could draw, without ever really thinking of it as an actual pitch. When Mike Gustovich — the founder of Noble Comics — subsequently called me out there for my first professional assignment, I assumed I would be working on their characters and their storylines. Instead he said, 'You're going to be doing the book you pitched to us. This *Elementals* thing.' That's when I realised that I had actually pitched a story idea, a whole new book.

After *Elementals*, you seemed to pretty much vanish from comics until you popped up at Vertigo a few years back. Where were you?

I am not sure it's vanishing so much as just making a lot of bad decisions, one after the other. The business relationship with Comico — who later published *Elementals* — was always kind of rocky, and at the same time I was learning to be a grownup and a businessman. The problem with the independents movement was that most people involved were just making it up as they went along. A lot of us plainly didn't know what we were doing, publishers included. At Comico, their heart was in the right place, but they didn't always know what the correct and proper thing to do was. Bad decisions were made, ones that completely undermined what had been set up in good faith. One of the few ways for an individual to enforce a contract is to sue — but to do that, you need the money, which I didn't have. So, the only lever I could think of using to force people to do what they had agreed to do was to just stop working. If the books stop coming out and money stops rolling in, that eventually gets their attention! But what I didn't realise was the damage that was doing to my reputation, because all the readers and editors at other companies were seeing was that *Elementals* wasn't coming out. So, yeah, I made some bad decisions and I was knocked around a little bit after the self-destruction of Comico.

After *Elementals*, I was broke for a long time because I got screwed on selling the rights. So anyway, I did not have the money in my account I thought I would have and I was supporting myself by travelling in my van from store to store, selling artwork. I was making my way out towards Seattle, and it was about that time I started on *Ironwood*.

***Ironwood* is the erotic adult comic you put out for Fantagraphics' Eros line. How'd you get involved in that of all things?**

That was another accidental series. [Artist] Steve Sullivan — who I had previously worked with at [roleplaying games company] TSR — had heard of this new group called Eros. They didn't know him from Adam but they found out he knew me. So they sort of did a deal with Steve along the lines of, 'Well

The Elementals

Earth, Wind and Fire weren't just a bunch of soul singers. Joined by Water, the natural quartet made up one of the most popular superhero teams to hit the independent comics scene in the 1980s: The Elementals. After an evil force growing on Earth threatened the multiverse's very existence, the lords of the Natural Order caused four young people to die, and then brought them back to life with the spirits of the four elements: the wind-controlling Vortex, the red-hot flame-forming Morningstar, the shapely water-wielding Fathom, and the rock-hard Monolith. With their past a bit murky, these four champions took on the two thousand-year-old evil that was the man named Saker. Created by Bill Willingham, *The Elementals* was a smash hit in the '80s thanks to its realistic approach. Gone were the days of pure black-and-white situations where you could tell heroes from villains just by looking at them. The Elementals faced some very real world problems, including death, murder, suicide and sex. Long-running subplots were a regular mainstay too, and loyal fans who stuck with the book were routinely rewarded with shock after shock, as heroes became villains, romance blossomed into death and the ultimate world war took centre stage.

if you can get Bill to do the covers...' So anyway, I was on the phone one day talking to them about whichever cover I was finishing up for Steve's book and at the end of the conversation they just asked me, 'So, what else are you going to do for us?' Just vamping, I started coming up with ideas over the phone, not realising once again I was committing myself to more work. Out of that conversation came *Ironwood*.

And following *Ironwood*, I started *Coventry* for Fantagraphics. That took off a little better, but then the 'distributors wars' hit. A comic distributor went under owing Fantagraphics lots and lots of money and they had to cut right back on the titles they were putting out. I started looking for other stuff to do. I did a few jobs here and there, like a Huntress two-parter for a DC anthology, but I didn't really start doing a regular gig again until Shelly Roeberg called me up out of the blue to see if I wanted to do some work writing for Vertigo. Shelly, an assistant editor at the tail end of Comico, was also the editor of *Elementals* for about five minutes. But it never occurred to me that after all those years she still had this fondness for having worked with me. She just called up and said write something for DC, specifically for Vertigo. I was dubious. DC had this reputation for just taking forever to decide on things. I told Shelly I just couldn't take eight years of meetings and still have any enthusiasm for the project when it was finally time to do it, and she made this bold promise, 'Thirty days after you propose something, I will give you a definite yes or no.' I think I proposed *Proposition Player* just to call her bluff, but she came through.

Y'know, as I'm recounting all this, I'm realising that everything I have done has been sort of accidental. *Elementals* was accidental; I didn't realise I was proposing an actual series at all. *Proposition Player* was largely to call Shelly's bluff, and *Ironwood* just came about because I happened to be on the phone talking to someone about doing some covers for something else altogether. And *Fables*, I didn't really know if it was a Vertigo type property at all; in fact, I plainly didn't think they would like it. I just happened be talking about *Fables* to Shelly when we were talking about something else. I mentioned this 'other' project that I was developing to maybe offer to Image or some company like that. And she said, 'No, no, no. You are offering that to us.' Now that I look back at my career, I realise that I have never made any actual decisions.

How about *Robin*? That's quite a departure for you, considering the Boy Wonder's such a straightforward mainstream character. Was that an accident too?

That was probably the first and most standard decision I guess I ever made in comics. *Fables* was underway; it looked like it was going to be a hit, and Michael Wright called me up and said, 'I'm the new editor on *Robin*, would you like to write it?' I thought about it, and my gut reaction was to just say no. But, before I called him up to decline the offer, I thought again, decided to see if I could think of enough reasons to say yes. I actually thought of quite a few, so I called Michael up and took the gig.

What specific comics over the years have influenced you as a writer?

The glib answer would be to say all of them, but specifically, let's see... In the superhero genre, I agree with those that say most of the really great stuff, the archetypal characters, were all created twenty to thirty years ago. Not a lot of great steps have been taken since, with one or two notable exceptions. I'd single out Hellboy as probably the only recently introduced character that has actually become an archetype. That character is just about perfect in every way, fully realised. Outside of the superhero genre, there's just all sorts of stuff I love and admire. The idea that someone takes it into his head to spend the rest of his life retelling the Trojan War in wonderful detail [in Eric Shanower's *Age of Bronze*] is just terrific, and then there are things like *Cerebus*. The 300th issue came out recently and the idea that Dave Sim set out to tell the life story of this crappy little shit-heel of a character through flashbacks and stuff, literally from beginning to end, is just astonishing. Overall, though, I think for me the idea has finally sunk in that comics is a medium, not a genre, so you can literally tell any kind of story you want to tell in there.

What title or character would you like to get your hands on?

Way back when, I would have killed a human being to do Wonder Woman, simply because I thought she was never handled that well. That was pre-John Byrne and George Perez and others, who sort of touched on some of the stuff I would have liked to have done. So that desire passed. Then there was a time when *Doctor Strange* would have been the perfect book for me. These kind of 'What if?' fantasy moments I have are based largely on the idea that when Frank Miller took over *Daredevil*, the reason this young punk kid got a shot at it was it was a dying book. There was really nothing more they could think of to do with it, and here's this little kid that keeps on saying, 'Put me in, coach, give me a shot, I can do something with this.' 'Okay, we were going to cancel it anyway, let's give him a shot.' With Wonder Woman or Doctor Strange, it was kind of the same: I could see something in those characters that'd never been handled well, so I wanted a shot at them. I would love an opportunity like that. Superman and Batman don't really interest me, simply because they are too big, too archetypal and too well covered. I don't know that I have in me that great Superman story that was never told. But I'm egotistical, like most writers. To sort of do what Miller did with *Daredevil*... who'd always been a 'B-list' character... I'd love a chance like that I suppose.

You're currently writing two monthly titles. How organised are you in terms of a daily working schedule?

I try to keep to a regular schedule. [*Laughs*] I am not a 9 to 5 organised type of person, but I do find that I've recognised certain patterns. Novelists always say, 'Writing is not fun. Having written is fun. Writing itself is torturous.' I actually like the process of writing, but it's one of those things where a little goes a long way. So I find myself getting into this mood where I just want to sit and write all the time, and I can get several scripts done over a period of days. So my scheduling is to sort of recognise when those moods are coming along and get as much done as I can. And then, when I am not in one of those kinds of phases, I get all the other work that's involved with writing done — the research, the looking things up, the planning. All that has to be done at some point, but I don't want it to interrupt the times when the actual writing is flowing, so that's where the organisation comes in.

How exactly do you conduct research for your books?

Two different ways. There's the specific and the general. For *Fables*, the general research is that I just give myself permission to read lots of fables and folklore stuff, and anything that catches my eye is just fair game. For example, issue #11 of *Fables* — the Jack in the Civil War story — came from just running across a book of the Appalachian Jack tales in a library, reading those and saying, 'Y'know, our Jack in *Fables*, this is him too. Because he's all those Jacks. Let's use one or two of these stories to come up with a Jack in the Civil War era thing.' So what I'm doing is looking for nuggets to pop up every once in a while that make me think, 'Oh, I can use this in an upcoming story.' Some of that is just mining for down the road. Okay, it's going to be several story arcs before I can get to this, but this is something I want to use eventually. That's the general research. And then the specific is, I've got a story coming up and I need to know about how the internal combustion engine works, or what have you. And most of that's done — at least initially — on the Internet now.

What kind of notes do you keep?

Bad ones! [*Laughs*] I'm one of those write-on-the-nearest-thing-handy-when-

---

TSR

Bill Willingham's held two regular jobs in his life: working as a proposition player in Las Vegas and punching the clock in the art department for TSR. It was at the latter where he brought the world of *Dungeons & Dragons* to life in comics — after a fashion. In the pages of *Epic Illustrated*, Willingham wrote and drew a series of ads drawn in sequential comics style for TSR's *Dungeons & Dragons* roleplaying game. And it wasn't easy, considering all the input and feedback from TSR's advertising department. 'They were very, *very* concerned over what you could and couldn't show in these ads,' said Willingham. 'That was during the time when *Dungeons & Dragons* was getting a lot of adverse publicity that it promoted Satanism. So they were very concerned about all the things that might've got them a bad reputation. You couldn't actually show violence taking place. There were a lot of scenes of the monster just leaping out and then the next time you see him, we'd just write, 'Later, after the monster was killed...' They didn't want us showing greed, so we couldn't show the heroes finding treasure or being happy that they found treasure. Things like that. They were mostly just hanging out in caves.'

something-occurs-to-me guys. I keep buying myself lots of tiny little notebooks that I swear I'm gonna keep with me always, and don't. The nearest I get to organised is this big drawer in my coffee table that has sort of become the semi-official place to store anything I write down, on whatever comes to hand, at least long enough to get it into whichever story it's bound for. I'm looking at it right now. I've got a water bill here that I've written a snatch of dialogue on. If I think of a good character or a turn of phrase that I want to use at some point, I write it down on whatever happens to be there, and then it goes into my drawer of notes. The nice thing about it is that once I use a note or whatever I do actually throw those things away. That way I always know what's in the drawer is material that is still available to be used. Right now, it's pretty stuffed, because most of what I've been thinking about lately is for far down the line. But I'm going to start taking some nice big digs into that drawer pretty quickly.

How long does it take to write an issue once you get into the mode?

Well, if you discount all of the prep work — which I don't think you should discount because that's a great part of it — the actual typing, revising and polishing takes maybe two days if it's really going well.

Do you write full-script style?

Yes, always. I can't do just the plot and then come up with words to fit what someone else has just drawn. That seems too much of a Frankenstein method to me. Here are a few parts lying around, see if you can pull them together in something resembling a story. My writing philosophy is, ask for more than you are going to get. So my scripts tend to be huge. A script for a twenty-two-page issue will come in at forty to fifty manuscript pages. Most of that is stage direction.

How closely do you work with your artists?

That is almost entirely up to them. I put my contact information on each and every script and if they can handle it without me, fine. With Mark Buckingham on *Fables*, for example, we like to get together and talk every once in a while. He's contributed some wonderfully evil ideas to the series that will be coming up. But if an artist wants to treat it just as a job, that's fine too. The funniest part of this job is when you get to look at the pages as they start to come in, and finally see how your script has been interpreted.

Robin and _Fables_ are pretty much polar opposites in terms of content, dialogue and just about everything else. Is it difficult to change your mindset when switching from one title to the other?

I think it's good to have polar opposites. Better that than two books that are similar enough so you might be stealing material from one book to another. There's no temptation to do that with *Robin* and *Fables*, and that suits me just fine. That said, switching back and forth can sometimes be a little difficult. See, you can't live with a script for as long as you do and still be objective about whether or not it's any good. What I would prefer to do is finish a script in its entirety and be so far ahead that I could put it in a drawer for two or three weeks and then take it out and view it with fresh eyes. Instead, the gauge I use is: when I'm done with a script, am I still enthusiastic about going on to the next issue? Finishing a *Fables* script, am I thinking, 'Oh, God. I've got to switch to *Robin*, but I really want to write more of this.' As long as that is sort of the feeling I get when I finish the script, then I think something must be working. Same thing when I finish a *Robin* script. I often want to continue right on to the next issue and not have to switch back to *Fables*. Of course, that reluctance to switch can also cause some anxiety, but I think in a creatively good way.

How much of your personal life comes through in your work?

In one sense, a lot, but in another sense, none at all. Take *Fables* #22, which has the Bigby character making a few snide remarks at the expense of the French at the end of the story. There were some adverse comments about that, like, 'Willingham hates the French.' But the one thing I want to stress is you cannot — especially with a huge ensemble cast book like *Fables* — say that any one character represents the author's beliefs. The whole idea of *Fables* is to come up with this wide and varied cast, each with their own prejudices and beliefs. If you think that I'm every one of my characters, then apparently I also believe in making stews out of human beings, which happened in a recent issue. In most of my work, I'm dealing in fantasy, magic and the fantastic... all that kind of stuff, but I personally believe in none of it. As a matter of fact, I specifically believe that magic doesn't exist. I think it makes for wonderful stories, but I have no personal beliefs here. Someone who tells you that they're a practising witch may well be a fine person, but they're also delusional.

Do you have a favourite issue or story-arc that you've written?

I hate to sound glib, but to a certain degree, if you're looking fondly back at some story from a long time ago and saying, 'Boy, I wish I could write like that again,' then there's something wrong with what you're doing now. I'm happy enough to report that currently my enthusiasm is boundless for the stuff that I'm doing now or is just on the horizon. It always seems that the scene I'm most desperate to write is one or two scenes away from the one I have to do now, and I hope that continues.

One of the things I love most is being able to slowly set the groundwork for future stories. In *Fables*, I've made a lot of long-range plans. There's this evil villain part of me that's just rubbing my paws and cackling because two or three years from now you're going to see the results of things that I'm starting to plant now. I think that's the best part of this. I can't do that with *Robin*, unfortunately, because it's not my book. I'm only guaranteed twelve issues, and if at the end of this run we decide to do another twelve, then I'm only guaranteed those. And this is part of the Batman family, so there's lots and lots of input from various other sources, and unfortunately I can't make long-term plans the way I can with *Fables* or the way I did with *Elementals*. But again, that's not necessarily a drawback, it's just another one of those things that differentiates *Robin* from *Fables*.

Do you have any tips for up-and-coming writers?

There's really two categories of tips. Those you'll most often get concern the mechanics of actually how to break in to the comics industry. There's a lot of that out there already, and I'm not sure I've got much to add. The tips I would offer fall into the category of what to write and how to do it well... and that's the hardest part of this job, it really is. In any literary or artistic form you can do a crappy job fairly easily and maybe get away with it, but to do it well is tough. And since it is so tough don't waste your time with anything you're not dying to do. If the first thing you stick under some editor's nose is a labour of love you've worked hard at and put your heart and soul into, it shows and maybe that's why you'll get the job. Don't waste your time doing a story that you're not into or just some Wolverine knockoff because you think that's what's hot now.

Regardless of the medium, writers are — first and foremost — in the business of telling stories. We're in the business of jumping up on a stage, saying, 'Hold on, I've got a story to tell you and I deserve your attention for as long as it takes me to tell it.' Which, okay, is a vastly egotistical thing to do. It really is. And yet, that's what makes Hollywood actors stars and all that stuff. We vastly appreciate those who can do it, but we have nothing but contempt for those who jump up on the stage and waste our time. So the one thing you don't want to do is jump up on the stage and

---

Fables

Snow White's a piece of ass. Prince Charming's a dick. And the Big Bad Wolf? Turns out he's not such a bad guy after all. No, we haven't been eating any strange mushrooms; we're just talking about Bill Willingham's Vertigo series *Fables*. Run out of their various lands by the mysterious Adversary, famous characters from all sorts of fables and folklore have made their way to a secret magical hideaway in Manhattan. Transformed somewhat (the Big Bad Wolf is a scruffy detective who goes by the name of Bigby), these 'Fables' live in the 'real world', with average humans completely unaware of their legendary backgrounds. And just because fairytales are involved, don't think it's all good, light-hearted fun. Sure, there's plenty of wit, humour and barbs to go around, but there are also very dark moments, including murder, deception and an all-out revolution for starters. But the real charm of *Fables* is seeing how your favourite fairytale characters interact in the real world — like Prince Charming, who seduces women in order to scrounge food and a place to crash off them. Featuring everyone from the three little pigs to Bluebeard, the only certainty in this wonderfully fantastic world is that 'happily ever after' doesn't necessarily mean forever.

say, 'You know, I've got this great story to tell you… So, what kind of things are hot right now? What kind of stories do you like now? Just tell me what you want me to tell ya.' That'll get you booed off right away. All I'm saying is if you're truly ready to write, that means you're in the act right now of jumping up on the stage and saying, 'I've got a story to tell you.' And you damn well better have a good one by the time your feet land and you turn around to face that audience.

Where would you like to see your career go?

[*Laughs*] Actually, you know, it's kind of heading where I want it to go right now. Maybe I shouldn't jinx it. I'm doing comic books and we've got the *Fables* movie thing going. Maybe something will happen there, maybe it won't. I'm meeting some nice people in Hollywood, which busts all of the old clichés. No one has given me the, 'You'll never work in this town again,' speech that I've heard many times in comics. So I'm kind of rethinking the Hollywood they've been selling us in the past: there may actually be some nice people out there after all. How horrible would that be? So I'm doing some stuff there, and I'm writing some prose. Overall, I'm pretty happy with things.

A *Fables* movie would be great. How similar is writing a comics script to writing a screenplay?

Everyone assumes comics scriptwriting is like screenplay writing and it's not. You have to be almost schizophrenic to do comics well because it's almost like there's two different people at the keyboard. You have to do scene description, and for that you have to write with clarity, like a technical writer, and keep the passion out of it. Just specifics and clarity, that's all you need for the artist; tell them what it is you need them to show in this panel and the next. So in that sense, you have to be this dry, technical writer kind of guy. But then you have to switch gears every single panel and be that guy who comes up with that gripping or funny dialogue or that captivating caption. You have to keep switching gears back and forth, constantly, and if you can't do that, you can't be a successful comics writer. I suppose you could try and do pages worth of dialogue and then go back and do pages worth of panel description, but it's hard to carry that over from one scene to the next. That's why this is a specific skill set that no other medium requires.

*   *   *

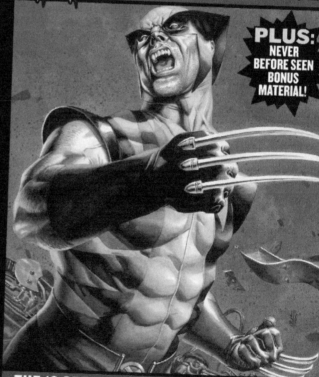

Coming Soon from TITAN BOOKS

COMICS CREATORS ON FANTASTIC FOUR

Edited by TOM DeFALCO

One of comics' most popular teams is dissected, discussed and deconstructed by the creators who propelled them to greatness. From their creation by comics genius Stan Lee to their current incarnations, the rise and rise of Reed Richards and company is mapped by this fascinating selection of interviews, many illustrated by sketches, artwork and original script pages, from some of the biggest and brightest names in the comics pantheon.

Featuring

John Byrne	Keith Pollard
Warren Ellis	Paul Ryan
Jim Lee	Bill Sienkiewicz
Stan Lee	Walter Simonson
Scott Lobdell	Joe Sinnott
Ralph Macchio	Roy Thomas
Doug Moench	Mark Waid
Carlos Pacheco	Mike Wieringo

Also available from TITAN BOOKS

WRITERS ON COMICS SCRIPTWRITING

Edited by MARK SALISBURY

In the bestselling forerunner to *Artists on Comics Art,* the biggest names in comics scriptwriting talk candidly to writer/journalist Mark Salisbury about their profession, their approach to writing and the comics industry as a whole. Packed with how-to advice, views and anecdotes, this is both an exploration of the writer's craft and a who's who of the hottest comics' talent around today. Features extracts from the writers' original scripts (provided exclusively for the book), reproduced exactly as they were written.

Featuring

Kurt Busiek
Astro City

Dan Jurgens
Superman

Peter David
The Incredible Hulk

Joe Kelly
Deadpool

Chuck Dixon
Batman

Jeph Loeb
Batman: The Long Halloween

Warren Ellis
Transmetropolitan

Todd McFarlane
Spawn

Garth Ennis
Preacher

Frank Miller
Sin City

Neil Gaiman
The Sandman

Grant Morrison
JLA

Devin Grayson
Catwoman

Mark Waid
Kingdom Come

www.titanbooks.com

ARTISTS ON COMICS ART
Edited by MARK SALISBURY

In a series of revealing, in-depth interviews with the hottest artists in the business, journalist Mark Salisbury uncovers the secrets of translating comics script to graphic storytelling.

Technique, style, layouts, approach, pencilling, inking... no facet of the artist's craft is left unexplored. Salisbury gets to grips with the lively creative personalities behind the pencil and ink, presenting an unparalleled insight into the widescreen mind of the comic book artist. Revealing, instructional, shocking, humorous, not to mention fully illustrated throughout with scores of previously unpublished designs, sketches and layouts, *Artists on Comics Art* has something for everyone, from comics fans to budding artists to hardened professionals.

Featuring

Brian Bolland
Batman: The Killing Joke

Dave McKean
Sandman

J. Scott Campbell
Danger Girl

Frank Miller
Sin City

Steve Dillon
Preacher

Joe Quesada
Daredevil

Dave Gibbons
Watchmen

John Romita Jr
Spider-Man

Bryan Hitch
The Authority

Alex Ross
Kingdom Come

Jim Lee
WildC.A.T.S